Information Management

Electronic Data Interchange Implementation Guide

Ray Harris
Martin Silman

London: HMSO

© Crown Copyright 1996

Applications for reproduction should be made to HMSO's Copyright Unit.

First published 1996

ISBN 0 11 330 842 6

For further information regarding this publication and other CCTA products, please contact:

Customer Services
CCTA
Information Interchange Branch
Rosebery Court
St Andrews Business Park
Norwich
NR7 0HS

Contents

Chapter			Page
	Foreword		11
	Acknowledgements		13
1	**Introduction**		15
	1.1	Purpose	15
	1.2	Who should read this Guide	15
	1.3	Structure of the Guide	15
2	**Basic Concepts**		21
	2.1	Why Electronic Data Interchange?	21
	2.2	What is EDI?	26
	2.3	The logical components of EDI	36
	2.4	Selection of hardware, software and network	45
	2.5	Setting up EDI projects	50
3	**Preparing for EDI**		55
	3.1	Initiating an EDI strategy	55
	3.2	Feasibility (Scoping) study	61
4	**UN/EDIFACT**		69
	4.1	Historical background	69
	4.2	Structure of the UN/EDIFACT organisation	70
	4.3	Western European EDIFACT Board	71
	4.4	Message development groups	71
	4.5	UN/EDIFACT building blocks	73
	4.6	The next steps	92
	4.7	Business application/EDI interface	101
5	**Communications Options**		103
	5.1	Communications for EDI	103
	5.2	Computer and communications hardware	103

	5.3	Type of connection	104
	5.4	Telecommunications access line	111
	5.5	Line protocol	115
	5.6	Application transfer protocol	119
6	**Software**		**123**
	6.1	Components of an EDI system	123
	6.2	Data extraction and conversion	123
	6.3	Message security	132
	6.4	Application transfer	132
	6.5	EDI gateways	136
7	**Legal Issues**		**139**
	7.1	Business contracts	139
	7.2	Special projects	141
	7.3	UK legislation	142
8	**Security**		**147**
	8.1	EDI security	147
	8.2	What are the threats?	148
	8.3	The countermeasures	149
	8.4	Choice of security technique	154
	8.5	UN/EDIFACT security recommendations	160
	8.6	Security hardware and software	162
	8.7	Audit	164
	8.8	X.400 security implementation	164
9	**EDI in Finance**		**167**
	9.1	What is Financial EDI?	167
	9.2	Benefits of Financial EDI	168
	9.3	Financial EDI in the private sector	173
	9.4	Examples of Financial EDI	175
	9.5	Financial EDI payment strategies	179
	9.6	Financial EDI in the public sector	181
	9.7	Message frameworks for Financial EDI	183

10	**Managing the Implementation**		185
	10.1	Overall organisation	185
	10.2	Use of PRINCE project management methodology	186
	10.3	First EDI implementation for government department or Agency	188
	10.4	Roll-out of EDI implementation with business process partners	194
	10.5	Follow-on EDI implementations in government department or Agency	195
11	**Operational Management**		197
	11.1	Operating in an EDI environment	197
	11.2	Role of an operational attachment	206
	11.3	User benefits	206
	11.4	Fundamental points	206
12	**Trading Partner Management**		207
	12.1	Common practice in the private sector	207
	12.2	The importance of an ongoing, overall management system	208
	12.3	Role of a central focal point (or responsibilities to be performed in its absence)	210
13	**EDI in Europe**		213
	13.1	European Commission programmes	214
	13.2	Country profiles	221
14	**Future Directions**		229
	14.1	Usage today	230
	14.2	Overcoming the current difficulties of EDI	232
	14.3	Encouraging developments	236
	14.4	Diverse and hybrid EDI solutions	238
	14.5	Summary	245

EDI Implementation Guide

Annexes   **247**

    Annex A Case Studies   **249**

        A.1   EDI status in the United Kingdom   249
        A.2   Selection of the case studies   249
        A.3   Introduction to case studies   250
        A.4   NHS   252
        A.5   Recent developments (March 1996)   271
        A.6   CCCJS   273
        A.7   INCA   282
        A.8   MOD   314

    Annex B Preparing an EDI Business Case   **319**

        B.1   Aim and scope of this annex   319
        B.2   Important considerations   320
        B.3   Financial EDI peculiarities   330
        B.4   Process change revisited   331
        B.5   Checklists and worksheets   332
        B.6   Example of the financial business case   334
        B.7   Stage 2 savings and costs   337
        B.8   Stage 3   340

    Annex C Format of the Business Case   **341**

        C.1   Introduction   341
        C.2   Strategic issues   342
        C.3   Business requirement   343
        C.4   Existing working practices   344
        C.5   User requirement   345
        C.6   Identifying options   345
        C.7   Business options   346
        C.8   Technical options   346
        C.9   Identifying variations   346
        C.10 Delivery options   347
        C.11 Analysing options   347
        C.12 Financial analysis of options   348
        C.13 Costing period   348

C.14	Whose costs should be included?	349
C.15	Implementation	349
C.16	Risk	351
C.17	Sensitivity	353
C.18	Post implementation review	355
C.19	Recommendation	355

Annex D Other EDI Data Standards — **357**

D.1	UNTDI	357
D.2	ANSI X12	358
D.3	UCS	359
D.4	AECMA	360
D.5	VDA	361

Annex E IS Notice 31: Electronic Data Interchange — **363**

E.1	Introduction	363
E.2	Background and purpose	363
E.3	EDI in action	363
E.4	What is EDI?	364
E.5	EDI Action Plan	364
E.6	Candidate business processes	365
E.7	Costs and benefits	365
E.8	EDI standards	366
E.9	The network options	368
E.10	Action	369
E.11	Enquiries	370

Annex F Standard Interchange Agreement — **371**

Annex G Sample Operational Attachment — **387**

Annex H HM Customs & Excise Guidance on EDI Usage — **393**

Annex I Useful Contacts and Addresses   401

Annex J Bibliography   403

Annex K Glossary of Terms and Acronyms   407

Figures

1	EDI concepts	26
2	Types of communication	27
3	EDI logical model	37
4	Physical implementation of EDI	46
5	Styles of physical connection	49
6	Business relationships	52
7	EDI and the planning process	56
8	Planning an EDI project	57
9	An example of a 'closed-loop' EDI implementation	60
10	An EDI implementation with many partners	64
11	United Nations EDIFACT structure	70
12	Western European EDIFACT Board structure	72
13	MDG areas of responsibility	72
14	Sample UN/EDIFACT message	75
15	Sample UN/EDIFACT Message Directory entries	76
16	Sample UN/EDIFACT Segment Directory entries	78
17	Relationship of interchange components	79
18	UN/EDIFACT UNB segment	80
19	UNA segment usage	81
20	Sample UN/EDIFACT Code Lists (EDCL) entry (partial extract)	82
21	Sample UN/EDIFACT Data Element Directory (EDED) entries	84
22	Sample UN/EDIFACT Composite Data Element Directory (EDCD) entries	85
23	Sample UN/EDIFACT Composite Data Element Directory (EDCD) entry	86
24	Point-to-point EDI	106
25	Communications with a Value Added Network	108
26	Store-and-forward services	109
27	EDI Translator components	126
28	X.400 Message Handling System	135
29	Authentication and integrity checking	151
30	Certification Authority mechanisms	159
31	UN/EDIFACT security segments	162
32	Financial EDI in context	168
33	An example of private sector Financial EDI	173
34	Financial EDI using a banking service	175
35	Financial EDI using simple funds transfer	176
36	Financial EDI using a hybrid approach	177
37	System test steps	192
38	Parallel processing	194

39	The computing environment BEFORE and AFTER EDI	198
40	Hybrid EDI options	240
41	Example of an Interactive EDI application	244
42	Sample TRADACOMS message	358
43	Sample ANSI X12 message	359
44	Sample UCS message	360
45	Sample AECMA message	361
46	Sample VDA message	362

Foreword

This volume is part of CCTA's Information Management Library. The library covers Information Management, Data Management, Geographic Information Systems and Information Interchange. The volumes in this library address the effective production, coordination, storage, retrieval, dissemination and management of information from internal and external sources in order to improve the performance of an organisation. Information is a valuable resource and its use overall should be effectively managed.

Information Management is not concerned simply with Information Technology. Nor is it the exclusive business of the traditional experts – librarians, records managers, information scientists, data base administrators, traders and so on. Information Management is both a policy matter for senior managers and a practical management task for information service professionals and practitioners who have responsibility for its implementation.

The Information Management Library provides guidance on the management of organisations' business-related information. The Library coverage includes Information Management, Data Management, Geographic Information Systems and Information Interchange.

CCTA welcomes customer views on the Information Management Library publications. Please send your comments to:

CCTA
Electronic Commerce Branch
Rosebery Court
St Andrews Business Park
Norwich
NR7 0HS

Acknowledgements

CCTA acknowledges the assistance given in the production of this Guide by the following organisations:

CCCJS
Central Unit on Procurement
Centre for Commercial Law Studies, University of London
Electronic Commerce Association
HM Customs & Excise
HMSO
NHS IMC
Paymaster (formerly Paymaster General's Office)
PFA Limited

1 Introduction

This chapter explains the purpose of the Guide, who should read it and where it sits in the Information Interchange set in the Information Management Library, and describes the structure of the Guide.

1.1 Purpose

The purpose of this Guide is to provide practical information which will enable readers to implement EDI successfully. It is assumed that they have a level of understanding of EDI such as that provided by the CCTA Information Management Library publication titled *Electronic Data Interchange in Government: The Business Opportunities*.

1.2 Who should read this Guide

This Guide is aimed primarily at those who will be responsible for implementing EDI in government departments and Agencies:

- IS professionals
- managers.

The Guide may also be of use to:

- business managers affected by EDI, particularly those who need to understand how best to achieve maximum benefits
- EDI partners outside government who need to understand the approach taken by departments and Agencies.

It is hoped that the lessons contained in this Guide will be found to be equally relevant by those undertaking EDI with no government connection.

1.3 Structure of the Guide

This Guide starts where *Electronic Data Interchange in Government: The Business Opportunities* ends. The boundary between the two publications is at the point where the business managers ask the IS professionals to examine the feasibility of introducing EDI into their business processes. The Guide highlights the stages IS professionals should consider during the introduction of EDI processes.

The Guide should be viewed in three sections:

- Chapters 2 to 9 discuss the theory of all of the aspects of EDI, initially overall (Chapter 2, 'Basic concepts') and then subject by subject, from overall planning and approach to the various technical considerations

- Chapters 10 to 13 provide practical guidance on how to implement EDI and Chapter 14, 'Future directions', concludes the main body of the Guide by putting various future developments and related technologies into context

- The final and perhaps most important part of the Guide contains the annexes, which give detailed examples of EDI implementations, information on, and an example of, how to build the business case for EDI, and suggestions on where to find out more and who to contact.

The individual chapters cover the following topics :

- Chapter 2, 'Basic concepts', sets the scene for the whole Guide by discussing the concepts of EDI and then pointing to where individual topics are covered in the Guide. IS professionals and managers should read the entire chapter; business managers and EDI partners outside government should read the parts which deal with business matters. Subsequent chapters should be read by those who will be specialising in their subject matter.

- Chapter 3, 'Preparing for EDI', describes the actions which will need to be undertaken in preparation for EDI. It should be read by the business managers that own the processes, as well as by technical specialists.

- Because EDI necessarily goes beyond the confines of a single organisation, it is imperative that a common standard is adopted. There is one international standard which should be adopted by all users of EDI: Chapter 4, 'UN/EDIFACT', addresses it and discusses its various elements. All readers should read the first four sections of the chapter; technicians should read the rest of the chapter as well.

Chapter 1
Introduction

- Chapter 5, 'Communications options', discusses the various communication options available in sufficient detail to enable non-technical managers to make a reasoned choice of the most appropriate communications options for their needs.

- Chapter 6, 'Software', describes the software needed to implement EDI and to maintain it. It should be read by technicians and operations specialists.

- The legal implications of EDI can be complex and uncertain: Chapter 7, 'Legal issues', introduces existing legislation in plain language and discusses its implications for EDI implementations. It should be read by legal professionals and technicians.

- In a government environment, security of information can be of paramount importance. Chapter 8, 'Security', discusses the concepts involved and the way in which UN/EDIFACT approaches the problem at a technical level. It should be read by all who are concerned with the security of information.

- Finance brings some unique features to EDI, particularly when the trading partners come from either side of the public/private divide. These are described in Chapter 9, 'EDI in Finance'. This chapter should be read by anyone who deals with Finance and the private sector.

- Chapter 10, 'Managing the implementation', picks up the topics discussed in Chapter 3, 'Preparing for EDI', and discusses how they should be implemented. This chapter should be read by managers who are responsible for implementing or managing the implementation of EDI.

- Chapter 11, 'Operational management', introduces some areas for consideration in system operation and service delivery in an EDI environment, compared to non-EDI. It should be read by those responsible for system management.

- Chapter 12, 'Trading partner management', explains some of the problems that arise when dealing with multiple trading partners (whether in business or administration), particularly when those trading partners may be conducting EDI with multiple government departments or Agencies. Topics covered include the ownership and management of relationships, change management and guidance on the implementation of projects in this area. The topic is of general interest but is specifically aimed at those who will manage or roll out EDI implementations.

- Chapter 13, 'EDI in Europe', addresses the use of EDI for trans-European information interchange. It serves as a pointer to current developments and as an indication of what the future may hold in store. It should be read by anyone who deals with organisations in mainland Europe.

- Chapter 14, 'Future directions', completes the main body of the Guide by putting EDI into the context of some of the new developments and technologies which are being widely spoken of and implemented and details some of the specific developments which will change the way in which EDI is and can be used. This chapter should be read by planners and strategists and browsed by those with specific queries or interest in one of the topics covered.

Several annexes are provided:

- In Annex A, 'Case studies', detailed examples of four EDI implementations in the United Kingdom and Europe are described. They will prove of interest to most readers, especially business managers, as they give a broad view of quite different implementations.

- Then, in Annex B, 'Preparing an EDI business case', advice is given to business managers on preparing the business case for EDI. This annex is not intended as a reference guide on the preparation of business cases – there are many better sources for that. Its aim is to highlight those aspects of an EDI implementation which are significantly different from a normal application development or business investment and to give guidance on the areas where costs and benefits are most likely to lie, and on estimating their magnitude. A worked example is included to

Chapter 1
Introduction

highlight the likely areas of benefit in a typical 'business' EDI implementation.

- Annex C, 'Format of the business case', describes the structure and content of a typical business case, with advice on how the information should be presented.

- Annex D, 'Other EDI data standards', describes some standards other than UN/EDIFACT, which are in current use.

- Annex E, 'IS notice 31: Electronic Data Interchange', examines a number of major issues concerning EDI and offers outline guidance on the use of EDI within government departments and Agencies.

- In Annex F, 'Standard interchange agreement', a sample interchange agreement is provided for those who will be involved in drawing one up for specific requirements.

- Annex G, 'Sample operational attachment', provides a sample operational attachment, which may serve as a supplement to the interchange agreement, covering at a business level items which may change over time.

- In Annex H, 'HM Customs & Excise guidance on EDI usage', potential users of EDI for invoicing can read the current HM Customs & Excise guidance on the subject.

- Annex I, 'Useful contacts and addresses', lists various organisations which specialise in aspects of EDI and which can, therefore, be used as a source of information and support on details beyond the scope of this Guide.

- References to further reading material are given in Annex J, 'Bibliography'.

- Acronyms used in this Guide are deciphered in Annex K, 'Glossary of terms and acronyms'.

EDI Implementation Guide

2 Basic concepts

This chapter describes the purpose and the technical components in an EDI solution. It also provides an introduction to the following chapters and puts them into perspective.

2.1 Why Electronic Data Interchange?

Traditionally, businesses have communicated using paper. These communications can be categorised in two forms: unstructured (eg messages, memos and letters) and structured (eg purchase orders, dispatch advices, customs clearance forms, licence requests). The unstructured communications tend to be person-to-person and also tend to be 'one-off' occurrences rather than 'business as usual' activities. Conversely, the structured forms are usually part of a process within the organisation and will typically be sent to the organisation as a whole rather than to a specific person. Thus these communications can be classed as process-to-process or person-to-process. When organisations decide to improve efficiency or effectiveness, there are several aims they usually try to fulfil. They want their processes to be cheaper to operate, they want them to operate more quickly and they want them to achieve the task with fewer problems and exceptions than at present.

There are many ways in which these aims can be achieved – from full Business Process Re-engineering to minor changes in existing practices. However, the most common tool or technique is to use computers more widely, to automate those tasks currently undertaken by people and, as a result, to take some of the paper out of the system (which itself helps achieve many of the aims).

This is fine when a process is wholly contained within an organisation but most processes start or end with one of the paper-based business communications already mentioned. Thus a technique is needed to automate these activities and to allow computers to communicate with each other between organisations, if real improvements and process changes are to be achieved. There are a number of ways in which this can be achieved but, simplistically, we can say that Electronic mail (E-mail) deals with the handling of unstructured data by computer and Electronic Data Interchange (EDI) covers the exchange of structured data between computers. And it is this structured data which needs to be automated if we are to improve processes.

2.1.1 Why not fax or E-mail?   The transmission of facsimile (fax) is being used increasingly as a mechanism to send unstructured documents. It is possible for a document to be written using a word processor and sent straight out in fax format without ever being printed. The fax can be viewed by the recipient on paper, if using a normal fax machine, or it can be received directly into a computer and the document can be viewed on a screen as a digitised image. However, it is impossible for a recipient to take the fax image directly into a word processor and modify it before sending it on to someone else. (Unless, of course, it is a structured document with a format both parties have agreed in advance – in this case, this is a form of EDI but it lacks many of the benefits of EDI as the recipient will have to use fax interpretation software set up specifically for that trading partner.) Generally, the received fax is not in a format which can be re-processed directly by a word processor. In contrast, an E-mail document can be received and viewed but it can also be directly re-processed by the recipient's word processor.

The important point here is that, while both fax and E-mail give speed advantages through using electronic transmission, only E-mail allows the document to be accurately received and edited by the recipient without the need to re-key. This, then, differentiates the suitability of E-mail and fax for use in computer applications. However, in both examples, someone is required to import or enter the information. This is fine for person-to-person communications, but when two organisations have processes which need to communicate, then full automation is required and EDI is a more appropriate tool.

EDI is a technique for exchanging structured data between computers in a way which enables it to be automatically processed by the receiving computer application without re-keying or other form of manual intervention. This factor **singles out EDI as an important tool for increasing the effectiveness of business and administrative processes**. When used to automate existing business processes, the data contained in each of the current documents is formatted into an electronic

Chapter 2
Basic Concepts

version, using a structure which is understood by both the sender's and receiver's business applications software. This structured document is automatically created by the sender business application and can also be processed automatically by the recipient business application. (In this context, 'business application' refers to any computer application used within an organisation to operate or automate its internal processes.) If unstructured electronic documents are sent between computers, there may be benefits in speed of transmission but not generally in the avoidance of re-keying and manual intervention.

EDI is particularly effective when the same kind of data is to be exchanged with more than one organisation – for example, a retailer who buys goods from many different suppliers and a supplier who sells his goods to many different retailers. In each case, there will be a range of business documents, from orders through to invoices and payments, which need to be sent to many different organisations, each of which will operate predominantly similar activities in response to the arrival of one of these documents. The documents being sent will all have the same structure and, more importantly, the received data from each organisation will also have an agreed structure. This means that automating the processing of received documents will be of benefit to all existing EDI partners and any new EDI relationships which are established, without the need for any changes on the part of the existing community of EDI users – this is another key differentiator for EDI over alternative technologies or tools.

EDI is most cost-effective if the data exchanged is of high volume and repetitive, with a defined set of processing actions which will allow complete automation. Since the accuracy of the data on the receiving computer will be as good as that on the sending machine, the whole mechanism can be implemented with a high level of confidence. However, there are some classic exceptions to this rule – for example, large corporations using EDI to receive telephone billing via EDI. It is large volume but not repetitive, occurring only once a month or quarter. Yet there are examples where implementations of this nature have saved many thousands of pounds.

To summarise the preceding points, EDI benefits can be achieved with alternative solutions (E-mail, fax), but not with the same ease of automation **and** generic usability between multiple partners, and this is particularly beneficial when there are a large number of partners with a high volume of 'standard' format transactions between them.

Automating existing processes could be called Electronic *Document* Interchange instead of Electronic *Data* Interchange and there are real benefits to be obtained simply from treating it in this way. However, EDI can be the trigger which allows the existing processes to be re-evaluated and it may be much more efficient to design new exchanges of data, which are not necessarily based strictly on the existing document flow. For instance, a number of organisations are now of the opinion that invoices (manual or electronic) do not add value to a purchasing system; the information found in a dispatch advice is virtually the same as in the invoice (indeed many organisations use the same multi-part documents for both with some areas blanked out). By adding extra data into a dispatch advice there is no need for an invoice. The dispatch document can initiate the payment cycle and can even be used to generate the electronic payment advice to the bank, based on the concept of paying for goods received rather than waiting for an invoice to be sent and then responding to it. This is based on the fact that if the customer and supplier have used EDI to exchange a 'request for quote' and a 'response to quote' which have subsequently been updated by an order, a delivery request or call-off, advance notification of delivery, goods received etc, then there is little value in issuing an invoice when both parties know exactly what has been ordered and received and therefore what is due. Indeed, an American motor car manufacturer has gone one stage further than removing the invoicing step from its process; it has shortened the standard payment terms for those suppliers using EDI in order to share the benefits obtained and thus give encouragement to the suppliers to make the necessary investments which allow the manufacturer to benefit in this way.

This example has been taken from commerce to show that EDI is not some bright idea from a small government office somewhere. Do not be misled, though; the benefits in government are often even more appealing than they are in the commercial sector, simply because the volumes

Chapter 2
Basic Concepts

of transactions are so much higher. Read through any of the case studies in Annex A, 'Case studies', for current examples from the UK and European government sector.

When looking at how or where to use EDI, it should never be assumed that the data which is to be exchanged is a direct replacement for paper documents. It may be more efficient to build redundancy into the data structures in order to allow for future streamlining of the business processes. This kind of re-evaluation of administrative or business procedures is known as Business Process Re-engineering (BPR) and, while EDI and BPR are not synonymous, EDI can have an important role to play in supporting the new systems. CCTA has produced guidance on re-engineering in *BPR in the Public Sector* (see Annex J, 'Bibliography') and, additionally, five case studies in BPR, including one which is an EDI project, are available from the same source.

Figure 1 shows four organisations exchanging data using EDI. The circle shows the conceptual boundaries of an EDI implementation which extend right into the computer applications (and thus the business processes) of the organisations and do not stop at the telecommunications interfaces (the gateways as shown in the diagram). EDI uses network services to transmit the structured data but, since the network or transmission functions used can vary from one implementation to another, the Network Services are shown within the boundaries of EDI as a separate layer. EDI is concerned with how the data is structured and processed and not with how it is transmitted.

This diagram shows that the EDI layer joins the multiple organisations and allows them to trade together. The EDI boundary extends into the organisations' internal processes and defines the way in which they will exchange information; indeed, it shows that processes extend across organisational boundaries and this is made possible by EDI. The diagram also shows that the computer systems and applications in each of the organisations may be completely different but EDI defines the way in which they communicate. What the diagram does not show is that new organisations can be added to this 'EDI community' without affecting the implementations of the existing organisations, provided

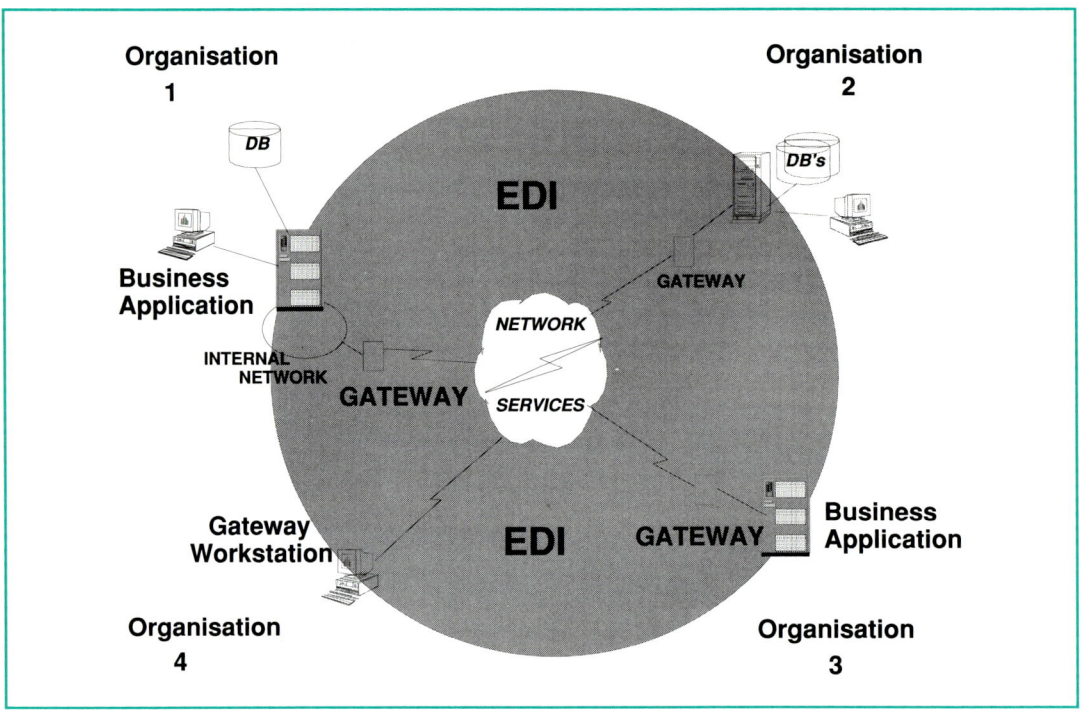

Figure 1: EDI concepts

they adopt the same EDI standards. This is one of the great strengths of EDI. Once it has been implemented for one process or partner, the infrastructure is in place for use with other partners or processes with minimal, if any, additional investment.

It is for this reason that EDI has significant potential for government in the UK and Europe.

2.2 What is EDI?

EDI is normally defined as:

the electronic exchange of structured business information between two or more computer systems using agreed message standards.

It can be seen that nearly all exchanges of data between computers fall within this very broad definition of EDI. It is necessary to look at several parts of the definition in more detail in order to understand what is behind it. The following pages look at parts of this definition in order to provide a framework for understanding EDI and how it can be implemented and used.

Chapter 2
Basic Concepts

2.2.1 Electronic exchange

The electronic exchange *of structured business information between two or more computer systems using agreed message standards.*

The definition simply states that the data should be exchanged between computer systems. It would be more explicit if the definition said that the exchange of data should be between *computer business applications*, where a business application is considered as the part of the IT system which supports a business function, eg customs clearance, social security payments or driver licence administration.

Figure 2 shows the essential difference between three main types of computer communication. In order to make the distinctions more clearly, the terminal and keyboard functions are shown separated from the computer application processing function. This way of representing the functions is more like the physical implementation of a mainframe system or a client-server application; however, the diagram applies equally well to personal computers (PCs) if the separation is seen as logical and not physical. All of these mechanisms enable data to be exchanged between computers and are used to enable communication between organisations as well as within the same organisation. However, they do not all provide good mechanisms to implement the transfer of data between business applications or processes.

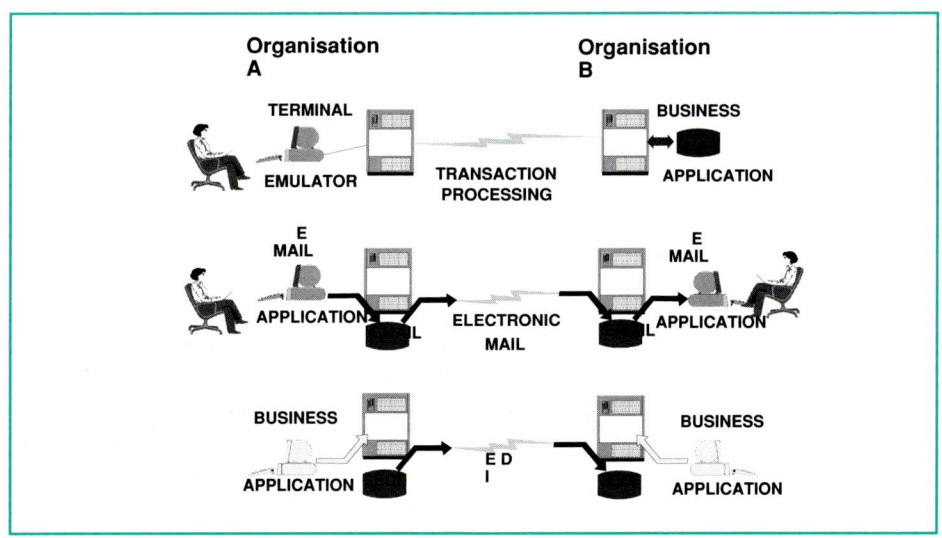

Figure 2:   Types of communication

2.2.1.1 Transaction processing

Transaction processing (TP) is characterised by someone communicating directly from a terminal to an application; the data being created by the person at the terminal exists only on the remote computer and is 'owned' by the application. This should be seen as person-to-process communication and, as such, it is a particular hybrid of person-to-person and process-to-process business communications discussed at the start of this chapter. The way in which the data is entered and presented to the terminal user is controlled by the remote application. Sometimes, the terminal is connected via a terminal emulation program in the local computer, which emulates the characteristics of a terminal on the remote computer. In Figure 2, if the data being sent and received from organisation B's computer is 'captured' by the emulation program on organisation A's computer, then it could be argued that the data now resides on both machines and has been exchanged. This mechanism has three major disadvantages for exchanging data between applications (business processes):

- the data is embedded in screen layouts and must be stripped out before it can be processed by another application. If any changes, even minor, are made to the screen layouts of an application on organisation B's computer, then the data stripping will not work

- this mechanism becomes increasingly cumbersome if it is used to communicate with many different, remote applications. There will either be one terminal connected to each remote computer or there will need to be one emulation program for each remote application

- error conditions are difficult to handle since the error messages from the application on organisation B's computer are designed to be read by people and not interpreted by another application.

Despite these limitations, this kind of mechanism is used by many organisations to automate their connections to remote applications. For example, many organisations used this method to automate their connections to the old HM Customs & Excise clearance application before it was replaced by the current version, which has EDI interfaces.

Also, the travel agents booking services, such as SABRE (developed in the 1970s by American Airlines), follow this approach, which is ideal as travel agents historically do not have their own business applications, so simply require an interface to that of the service provider or airline. However, even in this example, a travel agent will not want a screen for each airline or hotel chain with which they deal and as travel agents are becoming more sophisticated (see example in Chapter 14, 'Future directions') they need solutions which interface with their own process rather than having to fit into somebody else's.

Several factors determine whether TP or EDI is the preferable solution:

- Are people involved or is it possible to work directly computer-to-computer?

- Do all of the transactions go to or from a single organisation (hub), as opposed to a number of hubs or central partners within the community?

In the last case, TP becomes unrealistic.

2.2.1.2 Electronic mail

E-mail is primarily used to communicate information in readable formats between people. As such, it is a person-to-person form of communication and is of no interest to anyone wishing to implement process improvement or automation. However, because of its ease of use, some organisations have implemented a structured form of E-mail with the aim of achieving the same benefits as with EDI, at lower cost. The risk is the lack of operational tracking and manageability (a topic more fully discussed in Chapter 11, 'Operational management') and the high cost of extending such a solution to each new trading partner, compared to EDI.

With E-mail, a message is constructed by using either a terminal signed on to a mainframe E-mail application, or a word processor on a PC. The message is then put into a data base ready for transmission. From here, it is transmitted to the E-mail application of the recipient. When the recipient goes into the E-mail application on organisation B's computer, the message sent by A can be selected from a list of received mail.

EDI Implementation Guide

This process uses similar transfer mechanisms to EDI but there are three important characteristics which differentiate it:

- E-mail is a specialised application for communication of information primarily designed to be read and is not a business application by our definition (Business Application in this context simply means an application for the transmission or use of business-to-business as opposed to person-to-business transactions in the widest sense of the term 'business')

- the E-mail application has no understanding of the text and does not attempt to take any automated action based on its content

- in order to view the information the user normally looks at a list of the messages which have been received and decides in what order, and how they will be processed; the processing of the data is not automatic.

E-mail systems are sometimes used to transfer data files, such as spreadsheets, but this kind of a transfer is still handled in an 'E-mail' way. It is a person-to-person transfer and the recipient decides, by looking at the incoming mail, that it is a spreadsheet and imports the data into the correct application. The processing is not normally handled automatically.

2.2.1.3 Electronic Data Interchange

In EDI, the data is generated by the sending business application and should be processed automatically by the receiving application. For example, data could be typed into a purchase order application which was destined to go out to several different suppliers. The EDI gateway functions would put the data into the agreed EDI structure for each supplier and send it electronically. The EDI gateway on the receiving machine would recognise the incoming EDI data as a purchase order and pass it directly to the order-processing application. The order-processing application would extract each of the pieces of data from the EDI message and process the order as if it had been typed into the application after being received in the normal way on paper or by telephone. The application could then verify the credit status of the customer, check the stock records and generate a picking list, before automatically creating an EDI confirmation of order to go back to the customer's application. The involvement of people in this process would be determined by the business requirement – for example, if the item was out of stock or the credit check failed.

The original preparation of an order could be performed manually, but it could also be done by an order re-stocking application detecting that the minimum level of an item in a stock data base had been reached and automatically generating an EDI order. This would require no human involvement at all.

It is always more difficult to process EDI data at the receiving application than to generate it at the sending application. An application which is designed to print documents can usually be fairly easily modified to generate the same print data in a way in which it can be used to construct an EDI message. At the receiving organisation, most business applications have interactive data entry front ends which prompt the user to enter data in an exact sequence. Each piece of data is verified by the application as it is entered and often requires manual confirmation – eg if a customer number is entered, the full name and address will be displayed for confirmation. This kind of visual prompting and validation is not well suited to EDI where the complete set of data is delivered to the application at one time. The older type of batch validation systems are often easier to modify for EDI than on-line data entry systems. It is for this reason that many EDI projects have achieved very successful automatic generation of outgoing data but have resorted to printing incoming data before it is manually entered into the application systems.

However, one aspect of the automation of business processes which is often overlooked is that current manual business controls also need to be automated or alternative and adequate controls need to be developed as part of the new system. Chapter 11, 'Operational management', includes discussion of potential changes to existing systems.

2.2.2 Structured business information

*The electronic exchange of **structured business information** between two or more computer systems using agreed message standards.*

Structured business information covers any type of information which can be put into a fixed format so that the receiver can uniquely identify each data item. Many organisations receiving information from a large number of senders try to achieve this objective by using forms which specify what information should be put into the boxes, eg tax forms, customs declaration forms, import/export statistical information, driver licence and vehicle registration forms. This approach makes it easier to type the information into a computer application. Specifying the structure of the information on paper forms is a good starting point for moving towards EDI and by making the 'form' electronic it could be directly processed by the receiving application. The advantage to the sender is that the information could be directly generated from computer instead of having to be written on the form.

Most of what has been described so far has concerned the exchange of business data; replacing paper documents with electronic versions containing similar data. In many cases, it would be useful if other forms of information, such as technical drawings and related information generated from Computer Aided Design/Computer Assisted Manufacturing (CAD/CAM) systems, could be sent using the same sort of mechanism. This would allow an order for a part to be accompanied by a CAD/CAM drawing and the data to drive an automated machine tool. This type of exchange is usually called *technical* EDI.

Two factors limit the growth of this type of exchange. Firstly, current EDI standards do not make any provision for carrying this type of data (although some proposals have been made, they are not yet incorporated in any of the standards) and there is not yet any totally reliable standard for exchanging data between different CAD/CAM systems.

The second factor which will affect the rate at which this type of exchange will grow is the cost of telecommunications. The amount of data required to send a CAD/CAM drawing is very large and therefore the data transfer rate of the communication line would need to be very high to send the data in any reasonable time. The cost of a high-speed line could only be justified if it were used on a regular basis to exchange drawings.

For these reasons, technical EDI exchange is still in its infancy, and the use of EDI for business data is far more common. However, it is to be expected that the uptake of technical EDI will proceed rapidly as these factors become resolved or less of an inhibitor.

Chapter 2
Basic Concepts

2.2.3 Two or more computer systems

*The electronic exchange of structured business information **between two or more computer systems** using agreed message standards.*

It is not always easy to determine whether an accepted standard should be adopted over a proprietary or in-house standard, when only two parties are involved in an exchange. The overriding factor should probably be whether the exchange will always remain one-to-one or whether there is a possibility that other users could also take part.

EDI is obviously equally applicable to exchanges of data between computers within the same organisation or department (intra-organisation) and with the outside world (inter-organisation). However, EDI using an accepted data standard is normally most applicable where one or more of the following criteria applies:

- European legislation on the use of applications and IT standards and procurement is applicable

- more than two machines are, or could be, involved in the exchange and an accepted standard makes it easier to reach agreement between all the parties involved

- the exchanges are inter-organisation and some of the parties are already part of a community where the use of agreed standards is essential

- the exchanges are between machines of dissimilar types and an existing standard for exchanges is not in place.

2.2.4 Agreed message standards

*The electronic exchange of structured business information between two or more computer systems using **agreed message standards**.*

The definition of EDI refers to the use of *agreed message standards* and it is obvious that any exchanges of data between computer applications must use them, otherwise the exchange could not take place. In the context of EDI, what is normally meant by this phrase is the use of international, national or business sector agreed standards for formatting the EDI data.

EDI standards consist of four distinct types:

- syntax
- messages
- data dictionary
- codes.

The *EDI syntax* defines the character set used to carry the data and specifies the way data fields should be formatted and organised into meaningful groups. The syntax also defines how the data fields will be separated and how the start and end of groups of data can be identified. The syntax could be compared to the grammar of a language; it specifies how the words and sentences are put together but it does not specify how the words can be used to convey meaning.

An *EDI message* defines which data fields are grouped together to convey a business function to the receiving party. Many different messages can be constructed using the same data dictionary and the same syntax to convey different business functions.

The *data dictionary* defines the meaning of the data fields which are used in the messages. The definition of the *codes* which may be used in the message is part of the data dictionary but they are so important in EDI that they are identified here separately. Codes are used to give specific meaning to an item of data; for example, an item could be a date but the receiver needs to know how it is formatted (*dd/mm/yy* or *yyyy/mm/dd*) and also what kind of date it is (start date, end date, or availability date). These qualifications to the meaning of a data item are carried by codes.

The way in which the messages will be used and any specific ways of working between EDI partners is formalised in a document which is drawn up between the parties, called the *Interchange Agreement*. This document becomes an extension to the terms and conditions of the EDI partnership and specifies the legal and technical framework when parties agree to use EDI. A sample agreement is given in Annex F, 'Standard interchange agreement'. Items of a variable nature may be specified in an operational attachment. An example is given in Annex G, 'Sample operational attachment'.

The most commonly used international EDI standard is UN/EDIFACT, which is the only International Organization for Standardization (ISO) standard for EDI and covers syntax and messages; for a detailed description of the standard, see Chapter 4, 'UN/EDIFACT'. The data dictionary is addressed by ISO 7372 standard. Most new initiatives now use UN/EDIFACT and the subsequent chapters of this Guide, therefore, focus upon it; however, it should be remembered that in the US the use of the ANSI X12 standard is pervasive and with the emergence of Electronic Commerce and the openness of the Internet, it is unlikely that any one standard will ever have the clear position that it may once have had.

Although UN/EDIFACT is being used for new initiatives, many of the messages still in common use in the UK were defined using the older United Nations Guidelines for Trade Data Interchange (UNTDI) syntax. Most notable among these are the TRADACOMS messages that were designed by the Article Numbering Association for the retail industry. There is now a defined set of compatible messages which conform to UN/EDIFACT syntax but some organisations have not yet changed to the new messages.

Other message and syntax standards exist and some of these, including UNTDI, are listed in Annex D, 'Other EDI data standards', for completeness. It is fair to say that the choice of standard should be based on what is most appropriate for the community in which an organisation operates – but with the CCTA Guidance on the use of UN/EDIFACT (see Annex E, 'IS notice 31: Electronic Data Interchange') and even large communities such as the US EDI community, which has a long history of using the ANSI X12 message standards, now showing greater compatibility with UN/EDIFACT, there is considerable merit in the choice of UN/EDIFACT as the preferred standard. However, new moves in the US Electronic Commerce initiative have focused once again on ANSI X12 and the increasing use of the Internet suggests that other alternatives may need to be considered. Indeed, it is often simpler and wiser to adopt a standard that is already widely used in a sector than to try and implement something which is new.

Thus a sensible policy would be to assume:

- EDI is useful

- EDI uses agreed standard messages

- There are many choices for messages. If there is an UN/EDIFACT message ready or emerging and it suits 'trading' partners, then it should be selected. If not, then the next most widely used in the domain should be chosen

- Co-existence should be planned into gateway product and network service interfaces for the foreseeable future.

Other standards used in EDI: Any organisations wishing to exchange EDI data must also reach agreements on aspects of EDI and telecommunications not covered by UN/EDIFACT. These include:

- application processing options

- data content to be carried in the messages

- security

- telecommunications data transfer protocols

- telecommunications line protocols.

There are relevant standards which relate to security and telecommunications, but in order to implement EDI there will also need to be agreements between organisations which are not covered by any standards. The following section provides an overview of which standards are applicable to each of the logical layers of an EDI implementation and where agreements must be reached which are not covered by standards.

2.3 The logical components of EDI

Figure 3 shows two organisations, A and B, using EDI to integrate two business applications. The flow of data and information between the applications is represented by

Chapter 2
Basic Concepts

the large shaded arrow which goes down the vertical stack of functions in organisation A's computer and up the equivalent stack in organisation B's computer. The layers marked 1 to 6 (in each of the vertical boxes below the organisation) show the functions which will be involved in the exchange. The group of boxes shown in the centre and marked 'Network Services' gives an indication of the functions a private, or public, network service could play in the exchange. The two upper boxes of the network service functions are optional and may not always be used or provided.

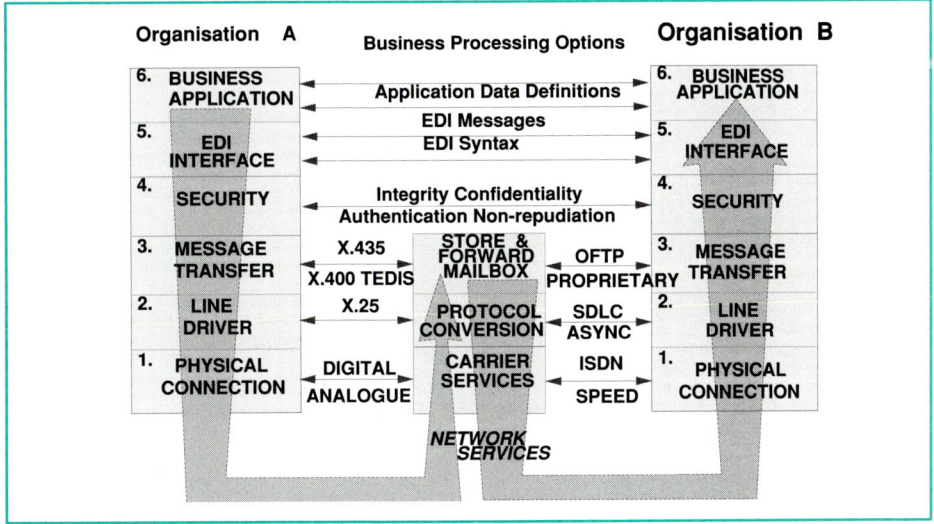

Figure 3: EDI logical model

In order to achieve application-to-application communication there must be agreements between the two organisations covering what implementations and standards will be used in each of the functional layers of the process. The arrows joining each of the boxes show what kinds of agreement must be reached for each functional layer and give some examples of the types of standard which are applicable to each of the layers; these are only indications and are not intended to be complete or show the only choices. The following section provides an overview of each of the functional layers in an implementation and the implications for standards and agreements. Each of the functional layers will be dealt with in detail in subsequent chapters of this Guide.

Broadly speaking, layers 1, 2 and 3 are concerned with the transmission of the data from one computer to the other

EDI Implementation Guide

(telecommunications) and layers 4, 5 and 6 are concerned with agreements over data content, structure and processing. To implement EDI, all six functional layers require some agreement over standards but very often only the standards and agreements applicable to functional layer 5 are referred to as EDI standards.

2.3.1 Business application

The two organisations, or departments, must agree at a business level the *processing options* and what functions will be allowed. The agreement will cover the flow of information which will be supported, eg will every business request result in a confirmation of action, will changes be allowed to an initial request or will the flow only support cancellation and re-submission? Each part of this business information flow will result in an EDI message being transferred between the parties. No standards are applicable to the agreements about business flow but they are normally embodied in the interchange agreement.

The level of function which will be supported will have an effect on which standard EDI messages are chosen and what processing function codes will be allowed in the messages. If an organisation is joining an existing community of EDI users then an interchange agreement may already have been drawn up for the community and new members may have only a limited choice in what they must support.

There must also be an agreement over the *application data definitions* for each of the data fields involved in the exchange. This agreement must cover not only the structure of the data, eg length of field and number of decimal places, but also its meaning, eg part numbers, licence numbers, social security number, offences on a driving licence, category of vehicle. Some of these pieces of information will need to be coded in an agreed way which may not match the way they are represented on either of the existing application data bases. The other important part of this agreement will cover how numeric values are to be interpreted, eg the number of items or number of boxes of items, weight in kilograms or tonnes, number of points on a driving licence and the format of dates. The UN/EDIFACT Trade Data Element Dictionary will already contain specified codes for many of these pieces of data but codes may not have been defined for all the necessary data and new ones may have to be developed.

Chapter 2
Basic Concepts

2.3.2 EDI Interface

Organisations must make two agreements at the EDI interface level. They must decide on the EDI syntax standard and what EDI message standard to use. The choice of UN/EDIFACT for the syntax standard will be assumed but there will still be choices to make about which of the United Nations Standard Messages (UNSM) most correctly suits the business requirement. There will also need to be agreement about which subset of this message is to be used. If there is no suitable UNSM already available then a new message will have to be defined. See Chapter 4, 'UN/EDIFACT', for further information on why and how subsets are used, the structure and development of messages, and the overall need to use them. It is not uncommon for an EDI user to use more than one message standard, as dealings will be with multiple communities and it may be that different subsets are used within the same message standard. While this complicates the role of the multi-community partner, it simplifies the task of the majority, who deal in a single community and take the benefit of a simple, clearly defined and appropriate subset.

The job of the EDI Interface Layer is to put outgoing data into the agreed UN/EDIFACT message and syntax structure ready for sending, and to convert received data from the agreed UN/EDIFACT structure into an internal file and record format which can be processed by the business application. The process of conversion is normally referred to as *translation*.

2.3.3 Security

Several aspects of security will need to be agreed between the exchanging parties: the first, and most important, is what level of security is appropriate to the transfer. It should be borne in mind that one of the advantages of using EDI to communicate between organisations is that it is inherently more secure than transaction processing, which allows terminals or computers from other organisations to have direct access to in-house applications. EDI messages are received into the in-house computer and only the data from the message is passed to the business application for processing. The message must have a strictly agreed function and will not be processed unless it conforms to the agreed structure; there is no concept of being able to gain access to either data or functions which are not specified in the message format. To achieve this level of protection in a transaction-

EDI Implementation Guide

processing system, a lot more care has to be put into protecting parts of the system and data base from unauthorised access by a terminal which is allowed to perform only certain functions. This adds a significant overhead in terms of cost, implementation time and computing power required. This is one of the reasons why most existing users of EDI have no additional security over that inherent in the Value Added Network (VAN) and software they use. Generally most organisations find this level of security and control perfectly adequate.

The purpose of any additional security in EDI systems, therefore, is to protect the messages while they are in transit between the two computers. Security functions can be set up which will provide differing levels of protection, depending upon what is required. Protection can be set up to ensure that:

- the data has not been changed while in transit – *data integrity*

- the message has come from an authorised partner – *authentication*

- a partner who has sent data cannot later deny it – *non-repudiation*

- the data cannot be viewed by any third party while in transit – *confidentiality*

- the data cannot be received out of sequence and missing items will be recognised – *message sequencing*.

Each of these levels of security comes at a cost in terms of the computer processing for each message and the overhead of administering and controlling the security procedures between the organisations. All of these mechanisms use some form of secret key, either to generate digital signatures or to fully encrypt the data. The most expensive level of protection to achieve is confidentiality, so this should be used only if absolutely necessary. In this context, 'expensive' need not only signify financial cost but can also reflect the higher level of justification required in terms of risk analysis and management.

Chapter 2
Basic Concepts

Whatever level of security is deemed appropriate, there must be agreement between the parties as to the standards and implementations which will be used. A more detailed explanation of the mechanisms and implementation options is given in Chapter 8, 'Security'.

2.3.4 Telecommunications layers 1, 2 and 3

Layers 1, 2 and 3 of the EDI logical model (Figure 3 on page 39) are all concerned with how to provide for the electronic transfer of the formatted and secured EDI messages from one computer to another. The transport mechanisms are largely separate from any decisions and agreements related to the messages and their contents and in some of the early implementations of EDI the transfer of data was performed using magnetic tape and diskette. Nowadays, EDI is always assumed to use telecommunications to transfer the messages but there are many different ways this can be achieved and agreement must be reached between the parties as to which choices will be made.

Figure 3 shows a group of network service functions which may be used to support the communication between the computers of the two organisations. Which of these services to use presents the first choice for agreement.

It is possible to implement EDI without all of these services, each of which could be provided by third parties or in-house on a private network. Figure 3 shows that, by using network services (usually referred to generically as Value Added Network Services or VANS), there can be a lot more flexibility in the choice of telecommunications standards because there is no longer a need to have direct agreement between the organisations. The network services can act as a buffer between the organisations. This is a lot more significant when more than two organisations are involved, since the telecommunications choice for one organisation may not suit all the others.

Regardless of whether network services are used or agreements are reached directly between the organisations, each functional layer in the model must be implemented using standards. An overview of each of the layers is given in the following subsections and a more detailed explanation of telecommunications is given in Chapter 5, 'Communications options'.

EDI Implementation Guide

2.3.4.1 Physical connection

The choices here are concerned with the type of communications connection to be used. If the two computers are sited close together, this could be a Local Area Network but, for EDI, it is more likely that the connection will be to an outside organisation and will be supplied by a telecommunications operator (eg BT or Mercury). This could be a leased line or a dial-up connection over the public switched network. If no VAN (public or private) is being used then both organisations must make the same choice of analogue, digital or Integrated Services Digital Network (ISDN) circuits to work at the same speed. If a VAN is used then each organisation may choose the type of connection and speed which is best suited to the expected usage and their computer. The necessary conversion of speed and connection type will be done by the VAN.

Increasingly today, the Internet is used in place of direct links or links through a VAN service. While the Internet has the appeal of wide accessibility and low cost, great care should be taken to ensure connected environments are adequately protected (for example, using firewall software which controls and monitors access) and messages transmitted are also protected (for example, by the use of encryption – see Chapter 8, 'Security', for further detail). It is likely that the Internet will alter the scope and reach of VANs in the future, once security and control limitations are overcome, and allow new entrants into the market place, offering additional services.

2.3.4.2 Line driver

The line driver protocol determines the way in which raw data is sent down a communications line and the way in which the connection is controlled. The protocol determines how each character, or block of characters, is sent and how the start and end of each block of characters is signalled to the receiving end. The protocol also determines how bad data, which has been corrupted during the transfer, is detected and how it is corrected.

In order to achieve data transfer both ends of a connection must use the same protocol. There are many protocols in common use, some of which were originally developed by individual computer manufacturers but are now so widely adopted that they have become *de facto* standards, and some which have been developed by standards bodies. The most commonly found protocols in use for EDI are:

- asynchronous (often shortened to 'async'), which is a very simple protocol and used widely for dial connections from PCs because of the low cost of the hardware required

- synchronous protocols in various forms, such as HDLC, SDLC or BSC, which are used mainly on leased lines

- X.25, which is an ISO standard packet protocol used mainly in packet switched networks (both private and public) but also on leased lines.

2.3.4.3 Message transfer

This layer has been left until last because it is the bridging point between the EDI standards layers and the telecommunications layers of the model and is the subject of most discussions in any EDI implementation. The function of the layer is to provide the addressing for the EDI messages and then to ensure that each message is sent to the correct receiving party.

Using an analogy, the job of the message transfer layer is similar to that of the postal service; it controls the flow and routing of messages but it also addresses the envelope and puts the message inside. The format of the electronic address must conform to the rules specified by the message transfer protocol which is being used.

If we continue the analogy, the message transfer layer will give the envelope to the post van (the line driver), which will carry it either directly to the address on the envelope (point-to-point transfer), or to a sorting office (store-and-forward mailbox service) from where it will be forwarded either directly to the recipient or another store-and-forward service. Exactly as with postal services, the delivery mechanism to get to the sorting office (a postal van) may be different from the one used to get from the sorting office to the recipient (a bicycle). The analogy breaks down, however, when it comes to the addressing structures and the format of the envelopes. Different message transfer protocols use different addressing structures and lay out the electronic envelopes in different ways. In our analogy the postal sorting office would have to put the message in a different envelope and change the address.

There are many message transfer protocols which are in common use for EDI and they fall into four categories:

- proprietary protocols
- community standards
- OSI protocols.
- Internet protocols

Proprietary protocols have been developed by the Value Added Network providers for use with their own EDI mailbox services.

Community standards have been developed for use by a particular EDI user group. The most common of these, which has become a *de facto* standard, is the ODETTE File Transfer Protocol (OFTP), which was developed by the automobile user community.

OSI protocols for E-mail have been developed by the international standards bodies and are generically known as the X.400 protocols. The most recent of this family of data transfer protocols to be finalised was X.435 for use in EDI. Many EDI communities were well established, based on public network mailbox services, or were using industry standards, such as OFTP, long before X.435 was finalised, and they continue to use these standards. The use of X.435 is still uncommon. However, many of the VAN mailbox services are now offering X.435 connections, as well as proprietary protocols, and will provide conversion services between the two. This will ease the growth of X.435 for new users and allow existing users to migrate as and when they find it worthwhile. See Chapter 5, 'Communications options', for a more detailed explanation

Internet protocols: The use of Transaction Control Program/Internet Protocol (TCP/IP) is becoming widespread as the *de facto* protocol in the UNIX and Internet environments. As such, it is to be expected that EDI-aware protocols based on IP will develop ('EDI-aware' is used to signify protocols that are cognizant of the EDI transactions that they carry and therefore provide

Chapter 2
Basic Concepts

functions that are useful to the EDI user, in much the same way as X.400 mail components and VAN EDI Services have developed functions to simplify the overall operation). Today, however, all that exist are TCP/IP versions of the more common proprietary protocols.

2.4 Selection of hardware, software and network

2.4.1 Hardware

The whole point about using EDI is that it is independent of architecture and hardware. Each organisation can choose an implementation to suit itself. It may choose to put its EDI software on a separate machine (PCs or UNIX machines are the usual choices for this approach) or it may put the software on the same machine that runs the business applications. The choice of hardware is dictated by the availability of software and price; PC packages are normally cheaper than mainframe implementations.

Other hardware considerations relate to the network connection. To connect to a telecommunications line will require a piece of hardware of some sort. This may be provided by the telecommunications operator in the case of digital circuits or in the case of analogue connections a suitable modem will have to be purchased by the organisation. Hardware may also be required on the machine which runs the communication software to provide the correct physical connection and line driver protocol.

See Chapter 5, 'Communications options', for a fuller description of these aspects.

2.4.2 Software

EDI is also largely independent of the operating system on the hardware. The only consideration here is the character set encoding used by the operating system. UN/EDIFACT specifies a character set which is basically American National Standard Code for Information Interchange (ASCII). If the machine which runs the EDI software uses another encoding set (eg EBCDIC) then it will have to be converted somewhere. There are some choices about where this can be done:

- as part of the line protocol driver functions, if the EDI software is on a mainframe

- between the mainframe and the gateway machine as part of the in-house file transfer

- in the network service mailbox. Some VANS provide a conversion from EBCDIC to ASCII as part of the service.

EDI Implementation Guide

Most organisations buy EDI-enabling packages, sometimes called gateway software, which will perform all the functions of EDI message-handling and telecommunications – layers 5, 3, 2 and 1 of our model. Some packages can also offer security functions but these are normally add-on components and will need to be customised to handle whatever security is required.

EDI-enabling software can be installed in two ways:

- on the same machine as the business application (as a separate set of applications functions)

- on a separate machine, a PC for example, which is connected to the business application machine. This is the method shown in Figure 4.

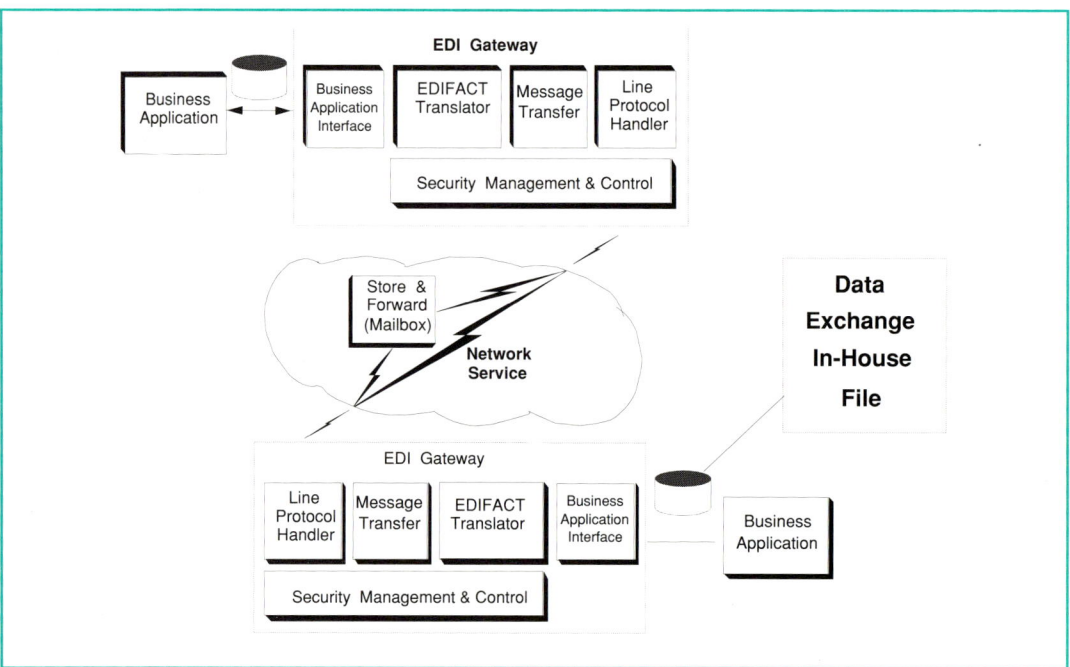

Figure 4: Physical implementation of EDI

EDI data is passed to and from the gateway and the business application in files. The coupling between the gateway and the applications is normally designed in this way to cause minimum changes to the business applications. The files which are passed to the gateway

Chapter 2
Basic Concepts

contain all the data fields which are required to construct an EDI message, but they are not structured to conform to any EDI syntax at this stage. This file is normally called the 'in-house' file. The job of the translator in the EDI gateway is to convert this file into an EDI message.

Most translators are table-driven and understand the format of the in-house file on one side and the EDI message format on the other. The tables are set up by someone who acts as an EDI administrator. Incoming EDI messages go through the process in reverse and the file which is sent to the application contains all the data from the incoming message in a form which is convenient to the business application.

Most EDI gateway software packages have a range of telecommunications options which will handle addressing and routing of the EDI messages either for point-to-point connections or to VAN mailbox services. The telecommunications options could be replaced by a corporate mail gateway, if that is required, but this would undoubtedly require some individual customisation.

2.4.2.1 EDI workstation software

For many organisations going into EDI for the first time, integrating the EDI functions into their business applications may be too difficult or risky as a first step. The choice here is to build a simple, stand-alone application which sits on top of a PC gateway and allows the input of the data required to create messages and view/print received messages. These applications are usually built using high-level application generators and they are coupled to gateways using in-house files in the same way as business applications. It is possible, therefore, at a later date to couple the gateway into the business application and stop using the stand-alone PC application. This migration can even be done in stages, probably implementing outgoing messages first, which are usually easier to integrate.

2.4.3 Network

Most EDI takes place using store-and-forward (or more often 'store-and-collect') VANS and there are some practical reasons for this. Figure 5 shows some networking scenarios, which will be looked at in turn. These scenarios show only six connections for ease of readability; in practice there could be any number of connections.

EDI Implementation Guide

The discussion on this topic is very closely related to that concerning business relationships between organisations, which is covered in Chapter 3, 'Preparing for EDI'.

Point-to-point: In this scenario each of the organisations makes a direct connection to all of its EDI partners using only a carrier service. (That is, a Public Telephone and Telegraph (PTT) or public telephone service.) Each organisation would have to use the same protocols and must be prepared to receive data at any time from any other. The larger the number of organisations in this type of community the more difficult it becomes to manage.

VAN store-and-forward mailboxes: In this type of connection each organisation puts its messages into the mailbox of each business partner and in turn it receives all the messages from its business partners via its own mailbox. There is one connection to the VAN mailbox and this could be a dial-up connection. Two types of mailbox service are offered by VANS: both are loosely called store-and-forward but one type should probably be called store-and-collect. A store-and-collect service will leave the messages in the mailbox until they are requested by the owner of the mailbox. A store-and-send will deliver the messages as soon as they arrive in the recipient's mailbox. Store-and-collect is well suited to organisations which wish to use a dial-up connection. Organisations with permanent connections could use either mechanism or a combination of both depending on the business requirement.

Connections to multiple VANS: If all of the business partners are connected to the same VANS, then the simple situation above will work but as soon as a new partner joins who is already connected to another VAN mailbox service the situation becomes more complex. The new partner may have to connect to two mailbox services. Many EDI software packages allow for connections to multiple services but it increases costs and raises complexities. The alternative is an *Interconnected VAN Service* which allows the user of one mailbox service to address messages to a user of another service. Interconnections of this type are becoming more common between the major public VAN suppliers. It also provides mechanisms for users of private VAN services to connect to the public suppliers.

Chapter 2
Basic Concepts

2.4.4 Performance

The issue here is how long it takes to get a message from one business application to another. There are four major components which make up the time taken to achieve this:

- the time to cross the network
- the time taken by the VAN service mailbox functions
- the time taken by EDI message-handling software
- the time taken to perform the security processing.

The time to transfer a message across a network can usually be measured in seconds and is dependent on the speed of the slowest network connection. Connections inside a VAN are usually high-speed since they will be shared lines to support the whole of the network traffic. The slowest speed connection is normally the one between the organisation's computer and the nearest node connection of the VAN. An EDI message of 1 to 2 Kb (about average size) can be sent at about 1 Kb per second down a line with a speed of 9.6 Kb/second. The speed of

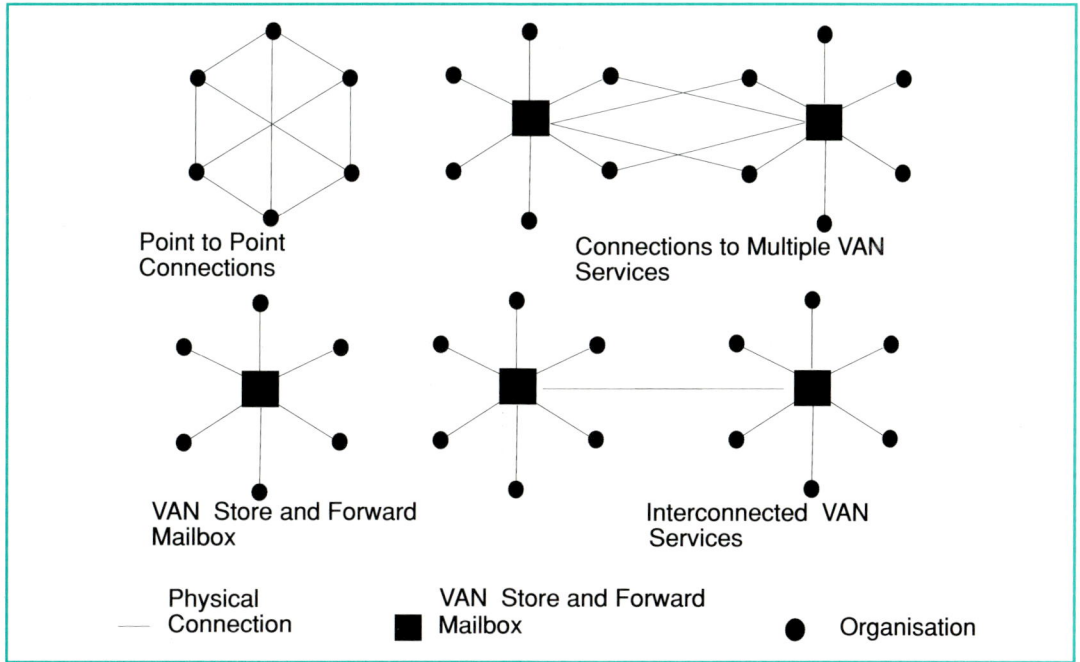

Figure 5:   Styles of physical connection.

EDI Implementation Guide

EDI transfers is not significantly different from the network response times of transaction-processing systems.

If an organisation is using a store-and-collect service then the time is largely dependent on how long the message remains in the mailbox before it is collected. In many cases there is no business requirement for this to be better than a few hours and most EDI communities operate on this basis.

An increasing number of communities would like to reduce this turnaround and have a more immediate response time and for them store-and-collect services are obviously not appropriate. Point-to-point connections would appear to be the obvious choice, since they have no VAN service overheads, but they still have the disadvantages of difficult management and control. In this case, genuine store-and-forward services using leased line connections to the VAN can reduce the network transmission time to only a few seconds longer than point-to-point connections and provide the best of both worlds.

By far the biggest overhead in EDI processing is in message handling, translation and security processing. This time can be measured in tens of seconds and possibly minutes for a PC implementation (depending on the way the software is built).

In summary, the response times of EDI systems are dependent on more factors than for transaction-processing systems but the network speed itself is not normally the decisive factor in determining response time. By far the largest factors are the implementation of the mailbox systems and the EDI processing done by the organisation's own machine.

2.5 Setting up EDI projects

The next chapter looks in detail at the management issues to be addressed in establishing an EDI project or programme within an organisation. However, first it is worth considering how and why an EDI project will be different from any normal technology or process implementation project.

2.5.1 Why are they different?

There are many factors which make EDI projects different from conventional ones, but the overriding one is that they involve outside organisations which work to their own priorities and are subject to their own control. Progress is by agreement unless one of the parties is in a position to dictate the way that choices are made about standards and implementations. There must be mutual benefit from going to EDI but, depending on which business functions are implemented and how much automation can be achieved, sometimes the benefits can be more on one side than the other. This imbalance of benefits can cause difficulties with cost justifications if each function, organisation or process owner looks only at their own piece of the overall process without consideration for the costs of others in allowing them to achieve those benefits. See Annex B, 'Preparing an EDI business case', for a fuller discussion of this aspect.

2.5.1.1 Agreements and documentation

It is essential that the agreements about how messages will be interpreted and processed are carefully documented. The function codes which will trigger a business response by the receiving party must be well understood by both sides. The documentation of the EDI messages will provide most of the system function specifications which will be used by both parties. If this is not clear and the messages are used incorrectly by the organisations when building their own implementation, the result may be costly and time-consuming rework. This is true for any project, but it is too easy, in the case of EDI, for one partner to assume that it has got it right when it is testing its own functions with messages generated according to its own understanding. It is only when it comes to testing with a partner that it will be realised that the two organisations had interpreted the message functions and codes differently.

The documentation of messages which comes from UN/EDIFACT is not normally sufficient to build systems and it will need to be expanded upon in order to build an implementation. This extra documentation forms part of the Interchange Agreement and its associated Operational Attachment.

2.5.1.2 Business relationships in inter-organisation communities

Figure 6 shows the business relationship between parties involved in EDI. The business relationship is expressed by layers 4, 5 and 6 of the logical model (Figure 3 on page 39) and is embodied in the Interchange Agreement between the parties. It covers the style and way in which the parties conduct their EDI business.

EDI Implementation Guide

One growth pattern for EDI communities is based on a group of users who have a mutual need to trade. The driving force behind these communities can sometimes be an industry or government body which acts as a catalyst. This mechanism results in a star or mesh topology with each of the members having an equal say in the choice and use of standards. Several examples of this approach can be found in Annex A, 'Case studies'. Mesh communities can expand very easily into expanded mesh communities without disruption because they grow by mutual consent. They tend to take much longer to establish but are normally very stable and allow the member organisations to reap good, long-term benefits.

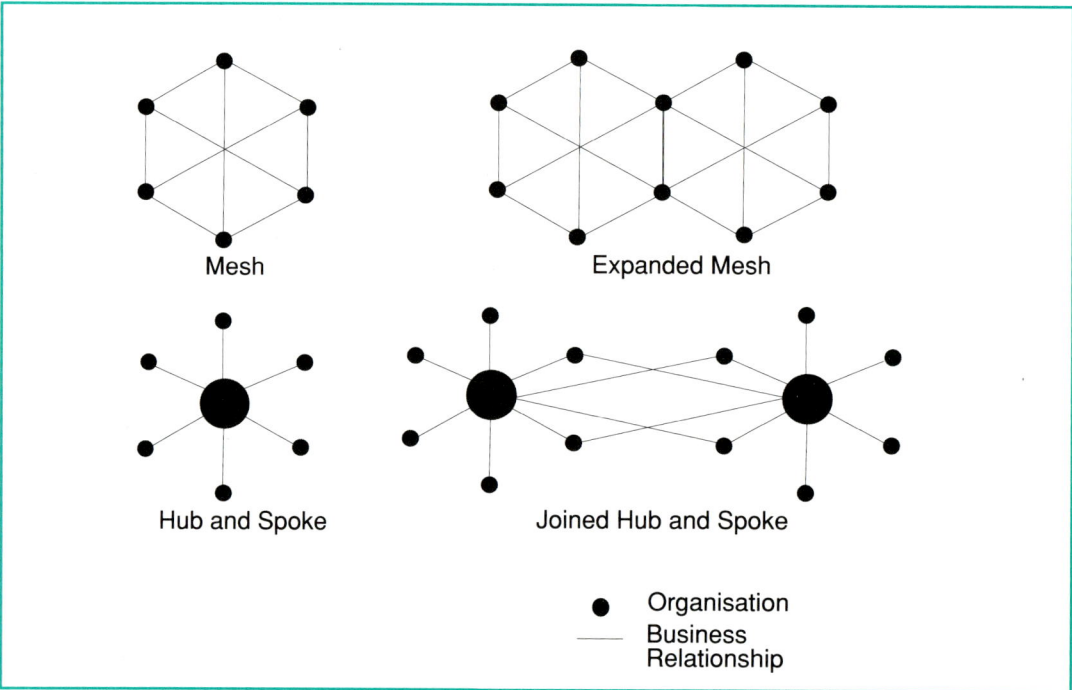

Figure 6: Business relationships

Other communities of EDI users start with one organisation persuading its business partners to use EDI. This approach has been common in the UK retail community, where each big retailer has acted as a hub and has defined the way EDI will operate in that particular relationship. This growth mechanism results in a community of users centred on a single organisation. This

Chapter 2
Basic Concepts

'hub-and-spoke' topology gives the central hub a lot of control over the EDI message structures and how they are used. The hub organisations will set up the EDI environment to suit their own requirements within the bounds of flexibility offered by the standards being proposed to the spokes.

Instability is created within hub-and-spoke communities when one of the spokes finds a need to trade with another hub-and-spoke community. This can result in the spoke finding that the two organisations they are dealing with have chosen different messages to perform similar business functions or, almost as bad, they are using different subsets of the same messages and different codes to specify similar data items. This can result in the EDI implementation of the spoke organisation requiring costly reworking especially if they have automated the receiving of data into their applications.

For these reasons many smaller organisations, which are typically spokes, will choose to keep the level of integration to a minimum and will use PC workstations to receive data and print it out. This gives them minimum benefit from EDI but it does keep down the level of disruption which can be thrust upon them by larger EDI partners.

Change of EDI syntax and messages has a similar effect of disruption on an existing community and, for this reason, once a community has adopted a standard there is a reluctance to change, even for newer versions of the same messages. It is for these reasons that many older EDI standards are still in use and the speed of change is slow. Managing change in an EDI community is an ongoing problem for which there are no simple solutions. There are ways to alleviate the problem but they require careful planning and the choice of the right software at the start. This is further discussed later in Chapter 12, 'Trading partner management'. Indeed, most of the rest of the Guide is focused, in various ways, on overcoming this particular group of problems.

The diagrams in Figure 6 have a deliberate similarity to those in Figure 5. The physical connection type and business relationship are related but one is not dictated by the other. A Hub-and-spoke business relationship could

EDI Implementation Guide

be implemented using point-to-point connections and conversely a Mesh community might well use a single VAN or Interconnected VAN type of physical connection. Even if all the partners in a Joined Hub-and-spoke business relationship were to use a single VAN mailbox it would not change the nature of the incompatibility of the messages. The most painless growth of EDI communities should be achieved by Expanded Mesh business relationships and Interconnected VAN connections.

3 Preparing for EDI

This chapter describes all the key actions and activities which will be needed in order to prepare for EDI implementation in a government department or Agency. (The use of PRINCE project management methodology for this implementation is assumed and explained in Chapter 10, 'Managing the implementation'.)

It should be read by everyone who will be involved in preparing for EDI, including, for example, key management, business process owners, IS and IT specialists, operations personnel and users.

3.1 Initiating an EDI strategy

The decision to implement EDI is usually made for strategic reasons. Of course, the decision must be supported by a sound business case, but the original initiative will often come from an executive or senior manager as part of an overall business vision and strategy for the organisation.

There is no generic master plan which can be used to implement EDI. Every organisation is different and the reason for implementing EDI will depend on the expected benefits, perceived significance, personnel involved and many other factors. This chapter seeks to outline the ideal approach to managing an EDI implementation, such that any problems will be easily identified and an appropriate management system will be in place to resolve them.

It is unlikely that any organisation will be involved in a programme or project that follows this guidance completely – what must be achieved is an understanding of the reason for and logic behind each piece of guidance and an attempt should be made to ensure that if an organisation cannot address the need in the same way, the approach taken has alternative solutions to address the same potential needs.

Thus, the usual starting point is an executive decision based on the assumption that great benefits will ensue. Whether this is the case in a particular situation or not, a sound business case should be developed as soon as possible to support (or correct) the decision. However, before the business case can be built, it is necessary to

EDI Implementation Guide

decide the scope of the overall programme. This is covered in detail in 3.2, 'Feasibility (Scoping) study', but first, we should return to the overall management of the initiative and then the definition of its scope.

Once the decision has been made it is essential to put in place an overall management infrastructure to drive the implementation. The first steps are to establish an EDI champion and an EDI Steering Committee.

3.1.1 Establish an EDI champion

Ideally, the executive or senior manager who initiated the EDI implementation strategy should take on the role of the EDI champion. The creation of this role is vital for ensuring the success of the strategy. If, for any reason, it is not practical or appropriate for this person to carry out this role, then another executive or senior manager should be appointed as EDI champion. Whoever undertakes the role, it is important that the person is an EDI 'believer' and has sufficient seniority and responsibility for (or influence over) all (or most) parts of the organisation that will eventually be involved in the preparation and installation work.

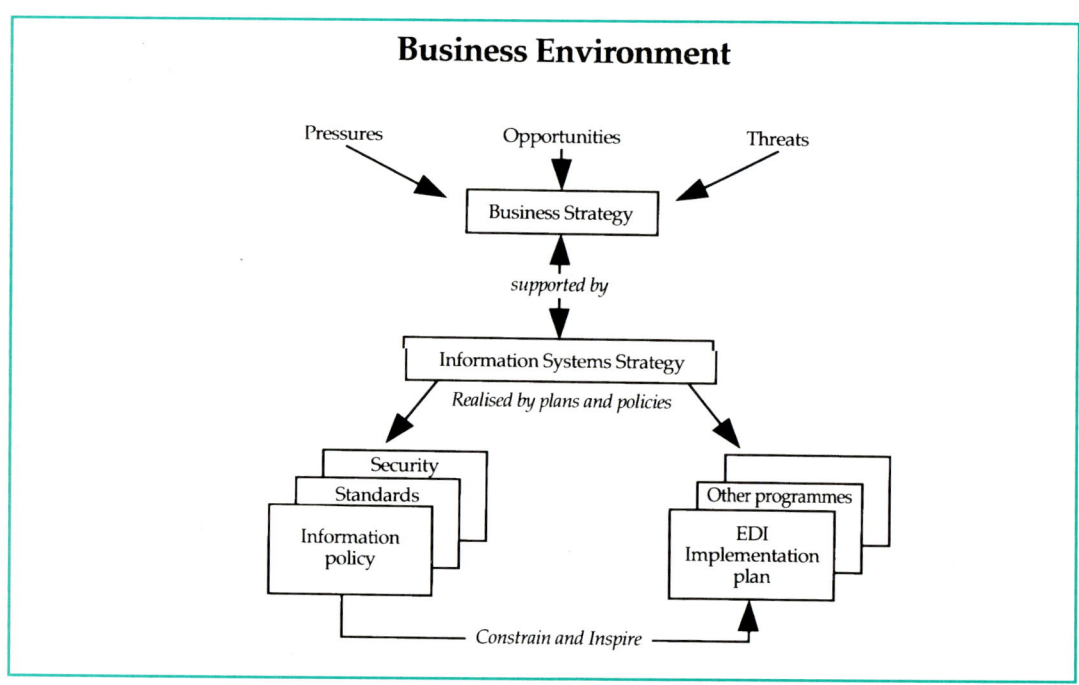

Figure 7: EDI and the planning process

Chapter 3
Preparing for EDI

The decision to implement EDI within an organisation is very fundamental and is likely to have a significant impact on many parts of the organisation. It will cause change to business and IS application processes and to the way many people in the organisation will work. Some parts of the organisation may incur more of the implementation costs but fewer of the benefits than others. There will be a re-deployment of resources and the need to manage change. For these reasons, there will almost certainly be some opposition to the EDI implementation and many problems and potential inhibitors will arise, some technical and some cultural.

All of these factors demand that the role of the EDI champion be established. The opposition and problems must be overcome and this will require strong leadership as well as delicate arbitration. Some of the problems will be caused by conflicts over task priorities within the organisation and possible resource constraints. The EDI champion with cross-functional responsibility will be able to see the overall benefits of the EDI implementation to the whole organisation and will have the authority within

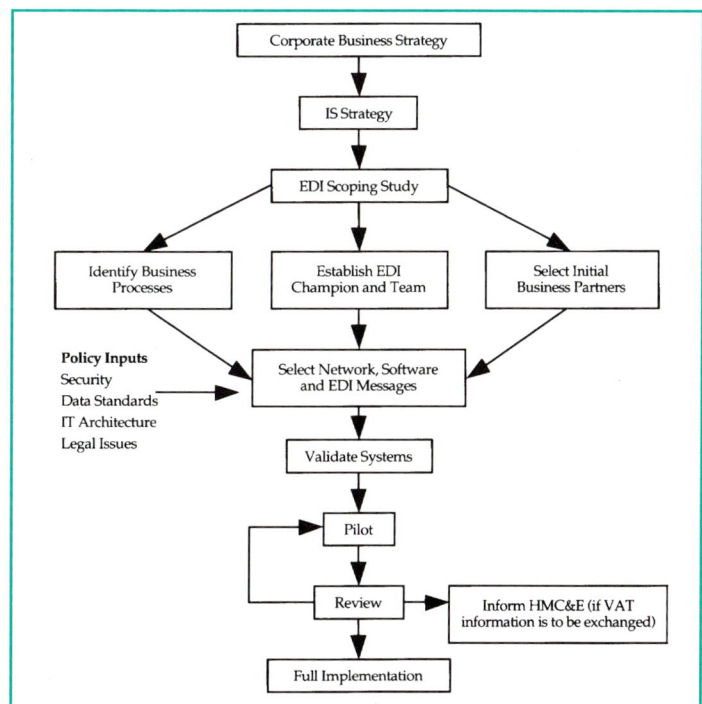

Figure 8: Planning an EDI project

57

EDI Implementation Guide

the organisation to address and resolve any conflicts, while ensuring the EDI momentum is maintained.

The establishment of an EDI champion is perhaps the ideal solution. It may be that an organisation actually needs a broader focus because E-mail or other technologies are also viable options. What is important is that the responsibility exists in a position with sufficient authority to resolve problems. This role may not also have the project responsibilities, the technical skills or the responsibility for achieving or measuring the planned (and any unplanned) benefits but if it does not, appropriate supporting roles that do have these skills and responsibilities need to be defined.

3.1.2 Establish an EDI steering committee

As well as the establishment of an EDI champion, an EDI Steering Committee should be formed to oversee the EDI implementation. This should consist of at least one key manager from each part of the organisation that will eventually be involved in the preparation and installation work and may include a member of the Information Systems Steering Committee (ISSC). Many organisations are subsuming ISSCs in Change Management Divisions or change committees, responsible for all projects. Because of the fundamental change EDI can bring to an organisation, such bodies might well be considered as important enablers for the introduction of EDI projects.

Where should the steering committee sit? Its role should be to oversee and co-ordinate activities and to encourage the introduction of Electronic Trading or EDI, as has been done at HMSO. When the committee gets involved with project responsibilities it is very easy for it to lose the power it brings, in the form of a clear vision. A simple analogy is that of the steering committee driving a car – immediately it gets out of the car and lifts the bonnet, it loses sight of where it is going and the ability to control its direction.

The EDI Steering Committee should meet regularly (ideally every month) to review progress and costs to date, current and future plans and resolution of outstanding problems. Decisions to proceed (or not) at key checkpoints and milestones during the implementation should be the responsibility of this Committee. The Committee should report to the EDI Champion, who may even be the chairperson of the Committee.

Chapter 3
Preparing for EDI

The EDI Steering Committee must ensure that the EDI implementation strategy is 'sold' to the organisation. The benefits must be fully explained and the likely dangers of not implementing must be highlighted. The Committee must also ensure that implementation progress is continually publicised within the organisation.

Responsibility for ensuring that the whole organisation receives appropriate and adequate EDI education, before, during and after implementation, also lies with the EDI Steering Committee.

It should never be forgotten that, however focused upon EDI the management of an organisation is, it can only succeed if its chosen trading partners also succeed. It is, therefore, necessary to extend these focus groups so that they at least communicate with their counterparts in other organisations, where they exist.

3.1.3 EDI as a programme

Having discussed the overall management of the initiative, it is necessary to consider its scope. An EDI implementation strategy will almost certainly affect several business and IS application processes within an organisation. To achieve the full benefits of EDI (reducing or eliminating paper, manual processes and errors caused by human intervention, as well as improving business process speed and efficiency), a 'closed-loop' implementation strategy should be adopted, where possible. For example, if it is decided to implement EDI in a purchasing function by sending purchase orders electronically, then purchase order changes and supplier acknowledgements should also be sent and received electronically. In addition, the EDI implementation can be extended to the finance function by receiving supplier invoices and sending remittance advices and payment orders electronically, and extended again to the distribution function by receiving electronic dispatch advices (see Figure 9).

The wider the coverage of the EDI implementation, the greater the benefits that will be obtained. Most of the initial EDI hardware and software can invariably be utilised by several functions within the organisation, thus minimising overall implementation costs.

EDI Implementation Guide

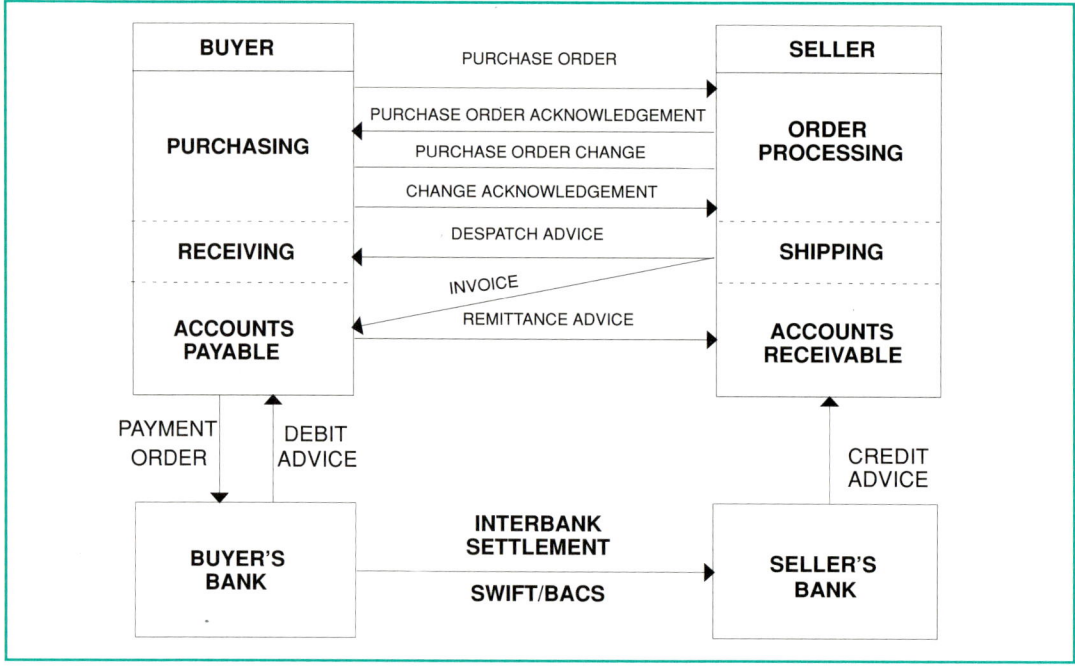

Figure 9:   An example of a 'closed-loop' EDI implementation

Because of the complexity of a total 'closed-loop' EDI implementation, the EDI strategy should be managed as an implementation programme, consisting of a number of independent implementation projects. Each project should be self-contained and separately controlled and managed, with clear objectives and deliverables for completion. Each project should be as small as possible to aid control and to ensure that implementation (and tangible benefits) can be achieved as quickly as possible.

There is no reason why later projects cannot be implemented in parallel, where practical, but it is strongly recommended that the very first EDI implementation project should be 'stand-alone' and should be allowed to stabilise before further implementations commence. This also provides a good opportunity to understand and absorb any lessons to be learned from the initial implementation as well as enabling staff, who have (by now) acquired key EDI skills, to be free to transfer to subsequent EDI projects. Further information on managing a programme is given in *A Guide to Programme Management* and *Management of Programme Risk*, published by CCTA (see Annex J, 'Bibliography').

Chapter 3
Preparing for EDI

3.2 Feasibility (Scoping) study

Once the decision has been taken, for strategic reasons, to implement EDI, the prime preparation activity is to undertake an organisation-wide EDI Feasibility (Scoping) Study. A small team should be established within the organisation to carry out this study. The team should contain key people from a representative cross-section of the organisation and should have access to all parts of the organisation to obtain information and requirements. The team must include people with knowledge of existing business and IS application processes as well as technical IS development and operational specialists (including telecommunications), plus, of course, somebody with a good understanding of EDI and how it should be implemented.

It is recommended that the team be led by somebody from the business process part of the organisation, rather than from IS, in order for it to be seen that EDI implementation is business-driven and is not just the latest IS 'toy'. The team should, of course, report to the EDI Steering Committee.

The Feasibility (Scoping) Study should cover the following areas of the EDI implementation:

- business processes to be included and excluded
- technical solutions to be implemented
- implementation options
- resources and schedules
- business case
- standards selection.

3.2.1 Business processes to be included and excluded

It is, of course, essential to understand and agree which business processes can benefit by the implementation of EDI and which cannot. Any business process which involves the regular mailing out or receiving in of a large number of system-generated business documents is an ideal candidate for EDI. A process which is very time-critical can also benefit significantly from EDI, even though it may involve mailing out or receiving in only a small number of system-generated business documents.

EDI Implementation Guide

However, there are also many new, innovative uses to which EDI can be put and these should not be ignored. For example, if a business process needs the frequent exchange and re-working of technical drawings (for buildings or engineering parts), an electronic exchange, combined with appropriate industry workstation hardware and software at each end, can produce excellent cost-savings in improved speed and efficiency.

The implementation of EDI is also an ideal catalyst for Business Process Re-engineering (BPR), since it gives the opportunity to have a completely fresh look at existing business processes in order to see where and how maximum benefits from EDI can be obtained. An existing business process can be completely removed by the implementation of EDI. However, it should be remembered that BPR is not a prerequisite for EDI, nor is the implementation of EDI a prerequisite for BPR, but they can complement each other perfectly. Another factor to consider is that BPR can be very time-consuming and could delay considerably the early implementation of EDI (and early receipt of benefits). There is nothing wrong with an initial tactical EDI implementation to obtain early benefits, while at the same time carrying out an extensive BPR exercise which could realise even more benefits from EDI in the future.

The importance of the 'closed-loop' EDI implementation, mentioned in 3.1.3, 'EDI as a programme', must also be re-emphasised and taken into account during this part of the study.

3.2.2 Technical solutions to be implemented

The nature and type of technical solutions to be implemented for EDI will depend to a large extent on the business processes to be included in the EDI implementation.

The technical solutions should include:

- all changes required to existing IS application systems used by the organisation, as a result of the EDI implementation; for example, a new interface file may be needed or additional data may be required

- the telecommunications solutions to be implemented (see Chapter 5, 'Communications options')

Chapter 3
Preparing for EDI

- the EDI hardware and software solutions to be implemented (see Chapter 6, 'Software')

- the security and business controls required (see Chapter 8, 'Security').

3.2.3 Implementation options

The method of implementing EDI may vary for each business process for which EDI is to be implemented. Factors to be considered are:

- is there only one EDI partner for the business process (peer-to-peer)? Is this EDI partner already EDI-enabled or new to EDI?

- will there be many EDI partners for the business process (for example, a number of suppliers to a purchasing function)? How many of them are already EDI-enabled?

- how many EDI partners should be involved in the initial testing and operational cut-over? How quickly should remaining partners be cut over?

The simplest implementation option is likely to be when there is only one business process partner and this partner is already EDI-enabled. In this situation, following a period of EDI integration (interconnection) testing (to verify network connectivity) and parallel running (new EDI process running alongside existing non-EDI process), an operational cut-over date can be planned from when only the EDI process will be used and the non-EDI process will cease. (Although, it may remain in fall-back mode for a limited period of time in the event of any significant failure of the EDI process.)

The most complex implementation option will be when many business process partners become EDI partners, some already EDI-enabled and some not. In this situation an initial EDI pilot test should be carried out with a few partners (at least one partner should already be EDI-enabled and at least one partner should not). The purpose of the pilot test is to fully test the system as if it were in operation, but with the tests being carefully monitored and the results being verified, by all parties, for correctness and completion. The old non-EDI process should be run in parallel and should still be used as the

EDI Implementation Guide

operational business process. It may be possible to verify the EDI process results against the non-EDI process results, if identical business data can be used. When the pilot test has been successfully completed, operational EDI cut-over can occur with those business process partners that have participated in the pilot test. The existing non-EDI process will remain in place with other partners until EDI has been implemented with all partners (see Figure 10, for a pictorial example of this type of situation).

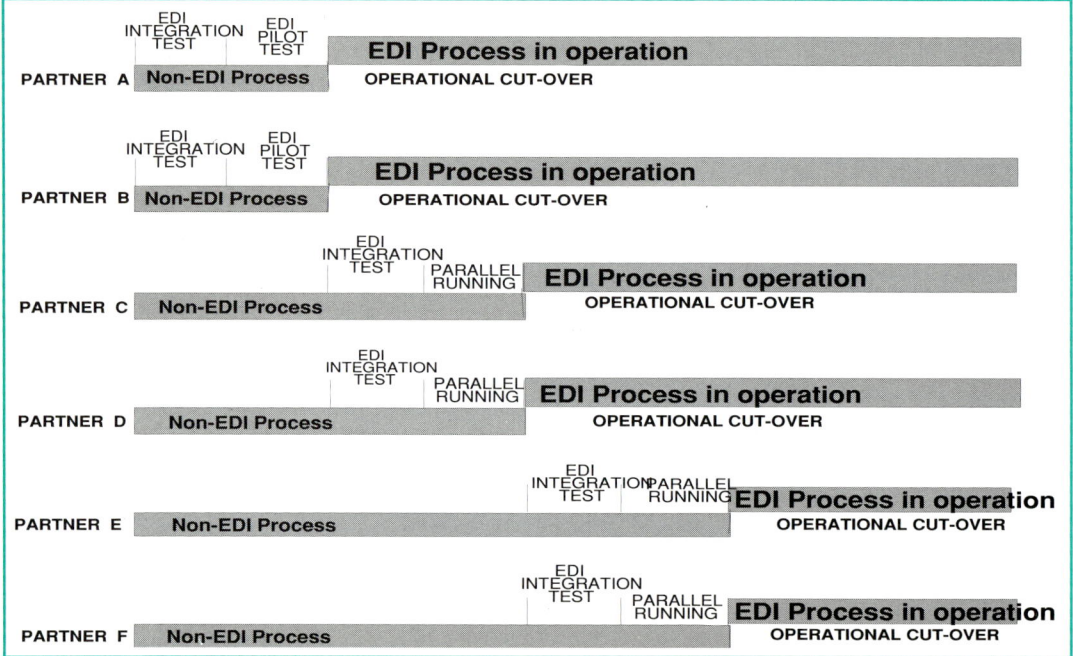

Figure 10:   An EDI implementation with many partners

When implementing EDI with many business process partners, it will be necessary to decide how quickly EDI can be implemented with the remaining partners, following the initial implementation with the pilot test partners. A period of EDI integration testing and parallel running is likely to be needed with every partner, prior to operational cut-over. Remember that each business process partner implementing EDI (especially for the first time) is, effectively, carrying out its own pilot test and sufficient time must be allowed to test and verify that everything is working correctly at both ends before

Chapter 3
Preparing for EDI

operational cut-over. The quicker EDI can be implemented with all business process partners, the better. However, the correct balance will have to be made between the desire to discontinue the existing, non-EDI process as soon as possible and the manageability of EDI testing and operational cut-over with many partners in a short space of time. Ideally, the period of initial integration testing and pilot testing with the pilot test partners should not exceed three months and EDI implementation with all business process partners should be completed within one year.

For more details about EDI implementation test phases and roll-out with many business process partners, see Chapter 10, 'Managing the implementation'.

Where a 'closed-loop' EDI strategy is being implemented, it is also necessary to consider when and in which sequence other business processes will be converted to EDI. Ideally, EDI will have been implemented with all partners for one business process before a start is made on implementing EDI for the next business process, but there may be very good reasons why this is not possible. If the same partners are to be involved in the EDI implementation for more than one business process then it may make sense to use the same partners for any pilot testing (if they are willing and if the previous pilot test was a success). Certainly the pilot test partners chosen should have reasonable experience of operational use of the previous EDI process implemented.

Where many business processes are to be converted to EDI, it is advisable to treat each one as a separate project and to plan the EDI implementation of each one separately. It should be assumed that the EDI implementation for every business process, with every partner, will require a period of EDI integration testing as well as pilot testing or parallel running, prior to operational cut-over. Obviously the first EDI implementation with any partner is likely to be the most difficult and to cause the most problems.

It is recommended that, as an early step in the first EDI implementation with any partner, an electronic mail link be established (if not already in existence). This will not only greatly assist in communications with the partner during the implementation activities, but will also give

EDI Implementation Guide

some early, simple experience of using electronic communication and may help to remove any fear which exists.

3.2.4 Resources and schedules

With any implementation it is necessary to plan the resources and organisation which will be needed and the overall schedules. Since EDI will be new to many people in the organisation it will be necessary to ensure sufficient time is allowed for education and for the acquiring and practising of new skills. This Guide identifies many of the issues to be addressed which will need resources, and endeavours to define when and where they will need to be carried out (see Chapter 10, 'Managing the implementation', for details of parallel running and integration test recommendations).

However, another factor which will have a very big impact on EDI implementation resources and schedules is the need to involve and work with partners. These partners may be another government department or Agency, a local authority, or an organisation in the private sector, and may even be situated in another country. They may have considerable knowledge of, and experience in, EDI implementation or they may have none. They may be very eager and willing EDI partners, having an excellent understanding (and perhaps experience) of the benefits to be obtained, or they may be very reluctant EDI partners and may not, themselves, benefit very much from the use of EDI. If they are in the private sector or in another country they will almost certainly have a completely different set of management practices and disciplines and may have a completely different management culture.

All of this must be taken into account when planning the EDI implementation resources and schedules. Sufficient time and resource must be allowed for discussions and agreements with these partners. The benefits of EDI may need to be extensively 'sold' to them and they may need significant 'hand-holding' during the whole implementation period. The speed with which they are able to carry out their implementation activities may be much slower than hoped for and their lack of specific skills and experience may mean the planning of additional testing time.

Chapter 3
Preparing for EDI

3.2.5 Business case

The business case is perhaps the most important single deliverable within the overall project or programme. It is the business case which will convince the EDI Champion that he is right, that will guide the EDI Steering Committee toward the correct goals and which will highlight the order of priority within the overall implementation. For this reason, the method for preparing a business case for EDI implementation and the factors to be taken into account are fully described in Annex B, 'Preparing an EDI business case'.

The scope of the business case will be defined as part of the feasibility study and at this stage as it is important to ensure that all of the costs and benefits to *all* of the parties involved are evaluated and also that the whole is viewed as more than simply the savings that can be achieved by automating a current process. Rather, it should be considered as an opportunity to gain many new benefits from the implementation.

3.2.6 Standards selection

While a variety of EDI standards have been employed in the past (see Annex D, 'Other EDI data standards', for descriptions), UN/EDIFACT has now become the world-wide standard for the exchange of business data. Indeed, its use is advised for government departments and Agencies in Annex E, 'IS notice 31: Electronic Data Interchange'.

Once it is understood which business processes are to be included in the EDI implementation, it will be necessary to decide which UN/EDIFACT messages are to be used (where business data is being exchanged). Many UN/EDIFACT messages already exist, but if the implementation of EDI within the organisation requires the use of a business message which does not exist as a UN/EDIFACT message, then it will be necessary to decide whether to invest the time and effort to create one. Where a UN/EDIFACT message does already exist it will be necessary to map this message against the business message to be used in the EDI implementation.

An introduction to UN/EDIFACT standards and messages, plus the processes for creating, mapping and using them, is given in the next and following chapters.

This chapter has sought to define the approach to and management of a large EDI implementation. There will be

EDI Implementation Guide

an ongoing responsibility on the part of the key players to ensure that appropriate investment and finance is defined and available at the relevant times and that suitable measurements are in place to ensure expected benefits are achieved.

4 UN/EDIFACT

This chapter starts with a general introduction to International Organization for Standardization (ISO) standard 9735, and related standards, including a discussion of the various components that make up this standard. Following this introduction, there is a discussion of how to make efficient and effective use of this standard.

UN/EDIFACT represents the first determined effort to introduce a true world-wide EDI standard. Until now different parts of the world and different industry sectors have seen a need for local EDI standards but with increasing international trading, everybody needs to speak the same language – at least as far as computerised systems are concerned. UN/EDIFACT goes a long way towards allowing us to achieve this end.

UN/EDIFACT has already described more than 175 business documents in electronic form. These are for a large range of business transactions: from invoices to financial payment orders; from a worker's insurance history to dangerous goods notification.

Unless there are very good business reasons for using some other EDI standard (see Annex D, 'Other EDI data standards', for some examples) the *only* standard to be used should be UN/EDIFACT.

In the unlikely event that a trading partner is using a standard other than UN/EDIFACT, then a clearly defined migration path from this standard to UN/EDIFACT should have been defined by them.

4.1 Historical background

In 1986 the United Nations Economic Commission for Europe (UN/ECE) and American National Standards Institute (ANSI) X12 set up a joint study group called the United Nations Joint EDI Group (otherwise known as UN/JEDI). This group was charged with looking at the creation of a new world standard for EDI. As a result of their deliberations, in 1987, United Nations Electronic Data Interchange for Administration, Commerce and Transport – fortunately abbreviated to UN/EDIFACT! – was created.

EDI Implementation Guide

In September of the same year it was accepted as ISO 9735. In the following year, the European Economic Community (as it then was), in conjunction with the European Free Trade Association (EFTA), set up the Trade Electronic Data Interchange Systems (TEDIS) organisation, whose objectives were to promote the use of EDI in trade, in general, and the use of the new UN/EDIFACT standard, in particular.

4.2 Structure of the UN/EDIFACT organisation

The structure of the organisation charged with carrying out the work involved in promoting UN/EDIFACT around the world is shown in Figure 11. It is intended to accept input from all around the globe, although it is inevitable that the most active groups will be those representing the so-called First World industrialised nations. This input is through a series of Rapporteurs, one for each region.

Rapporteur is a term used to describe a person nominated by his or her government and appointed to initiate and co-ordinate UN/EDIFACT development work in his or her geographical area of jurisdiction.

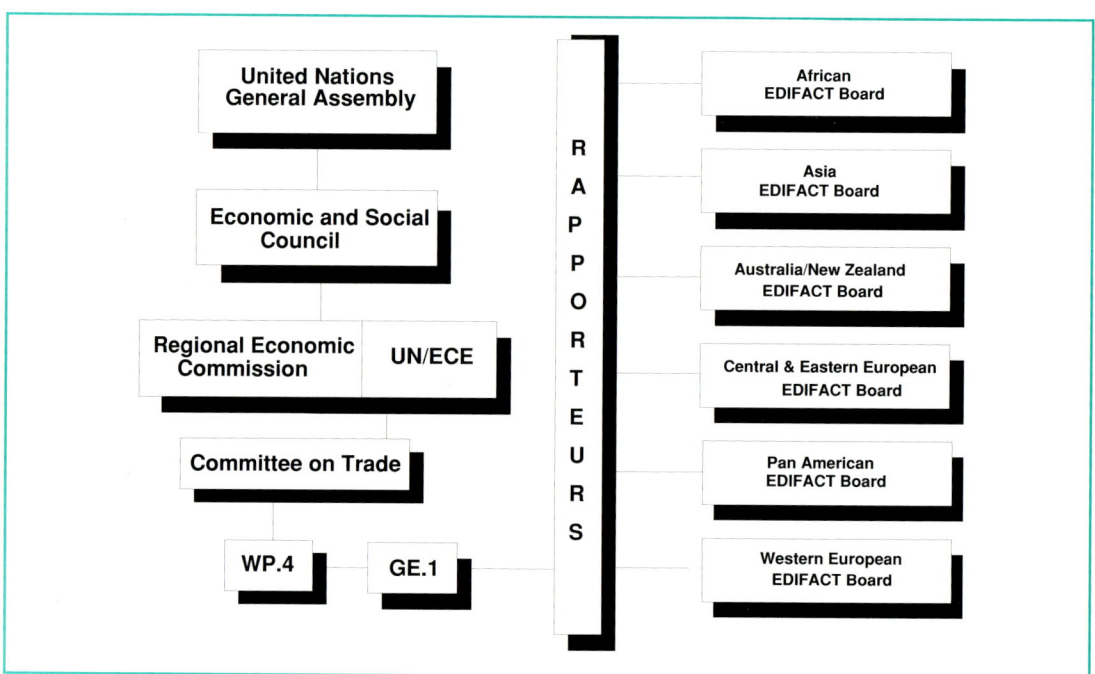

Figure 11:   United Nations EDIFACT structure. WP.4 indicates Working Party 4; GE.1 indicates Group of Experts 1

Each Rapporteur has a support organisation consisting of a regional Board. The Board relevant to the UK is the Western European EDIFACT Board, also referred to as the WE/EB. Its structure is shown in Figure 12. It is an associate body of the Comite Europeen de Normalisation (CEN), the European Committee for Standardisation.

4.3 Western European EDIFACT Board

Three technical groups within the WE/EB report to the Technical Co-ordinating Committee:

- Support Groups

- Special Interest Groups

- Message Development Groups (MDGs).

The Support Groups are responsible for awareness, codes, procedures and documentation and technical assessment.

The Special Interest Groups are responsible for information modelling, the emerging area of interactive EDI, security and user implementation guidelines.

The main groups of interest, as far as this document is concerned, are the MDGs.

4.4 Message development groups

As the name suggests, these groups are responsible for both development of new EDI messages and for modifications or revisions to existing messages. They take input from all of the individual country members.

In addition to the development work for their individual areas of interest, the MDGs are also responsible for ensuring that there is minimal duplication of effort. This is a joint effort between the MDGs, the Support Groups and the Special Interest Groups.

EDI Implementation Guide

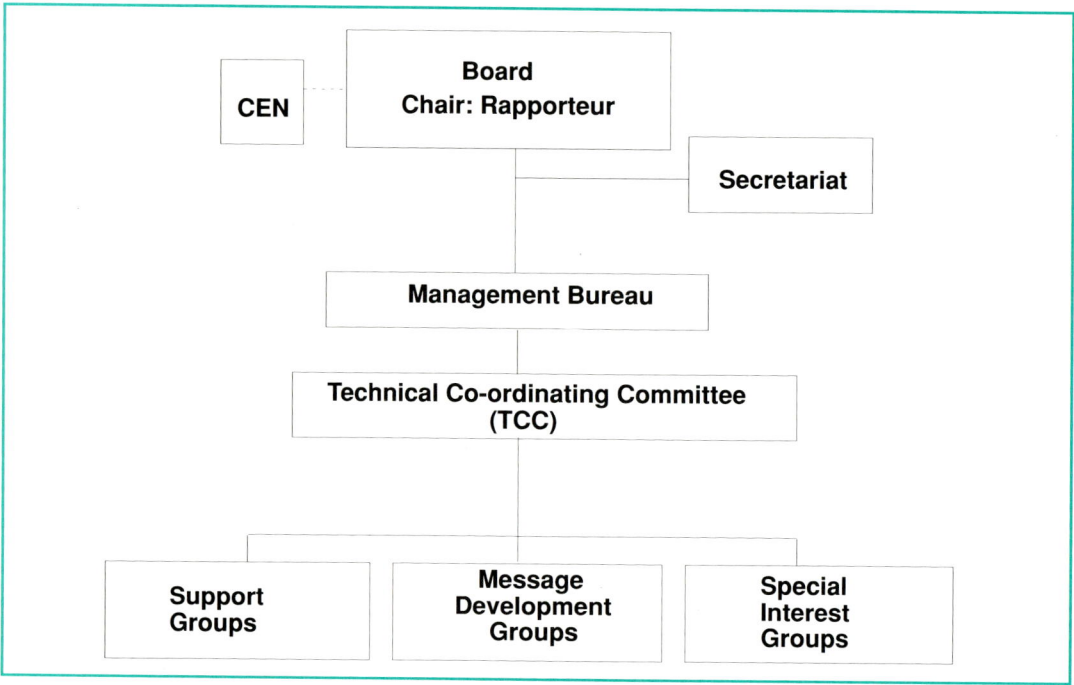

Figure 12:   Western European EDIFACT Board structure

The area of responsibility for each group is shown in Figure 13.

MDG	Area of responsibility
MD1	Trade
MD2	Transport
MD3	Customs and Indirect Taxation
MD4	Finance
MD5	Construction
MD6	Statistics
MD7	Insurance
MD8	Travel, Tourism and Leisure
MD9	Health Care
MD10	Social Administration
MD11	Legal and Accountancy
MD12	Public Procurement
MD13	Network Administration

Figure 13:   MDG areas of responsibility

Chapter 4
UN/EDIFACT

As more sectors become interested in the potential use of EDI there will inevitably be additional MDGs to cater for these specific business areas.

4.5 UN/EDIFACT building blocks

UN/EDIFACT messages are built in an hierarchical structure from the smallest components up to the unit of exchange with a trading partner. In order, from largest to smallest, these components are:

- interchanges
- functional groups
- messages (or transactions)
- segments
- data elements.

They are described in 4.5.7, 'Service segments'.

UN/EDIFACT may be thought of in terms of a form to be filled in:

- *Simple data element*: equivalent to a box on the form
- *Composite data element*: equivalent to a collection of related boxes
- *Segment*: equivalent to a section on a form
- *Message*: equivalent to a complete form
- *Functional group*: a number of forms
- *Interchange*: equivalent to a completed form or forms in an envelope.

The envelope has a return address so that the recipient can see who it has come from. Included is the equivalent of a postmark saying when it was 'posted'.

UN/EDIFACT has a syntax for relating the components of a message:

:   component data element separator

EDI Implementation Guide

+   data element separator

'   segment terminator.

UN/EDIFACT uses a series of *directories* to store all the formal definitions of these components. Before looking at the components themselves, it is worth looking at these directories.

4.5.1 UN/EDIFACT directories   Published by the UN/ECE is a large body of standards, guidelines and directories. Overall this is called the United Nations Trade Data Interchange Directory (UNTDID). This is added to and modified according to agreed procedures to ensure control. It contains the following:

- UN/EDIFACT Application Level Syntax Rules (ISO 9735)

- UN/EDIFACT Message Design Guidelines

- UN/EDIFACT Syntax Implementation Guidelines (SIG)

- UN/EDIFACT Data Element Directory (EDED), a subset of the United Nations Trade Data Elements Directory (ISO 7372)

- UN/EDIFACT Code Lists (EDCL)

- UN/EDIFACT Composite Data Element Directory (EDCD)

- UN/EDIFACT Segment Directory (EDSD)

- UN/EDIFACT United Nations Standard Messages (UNSM) Directory (EDMD)

- UNiform Rules of Conduct for the Interchange of Trade Data by Teletransmission (UNCID).

4.5.2 An example of a UN/EDIFACT message   Figure 14 shows a simple UN/EDIFACT message (actually a single message in an interchange), in this case a *PARTIN* message, which is designed to allow trading partners to exchange location and related administrative and operational details.

Chapter 4
UN/EDIFACT

```
UNB+UNOA:2+SENDER+RECEIVER+941224:2359+12345++PARTIN++++1'
UNH+1+PARTIN:D:93A:UN'
BGM++1+2'
DTM+7+199412242359+202'
FII+BK+12345678:UNIVERSAL EXPORT PLC+:::010203:::BANKEXPORT+MOSKVA'
RFF+VAT+123456789'
DTM+7+19950101+102'
NAD+MS+++UNIVERSAL EXPORT PLC+PO BOX
007:WHITEHALL+LONDON+WC1 0AA'
CTA+AG+JAMES BOND'
COM+01811112222:TE'
UNS+D'
NAD+AG+++UNIVERSAL EXPORT (RUSSIA)+PO BOX 57+MOSKVA++SU'
DTM+7+19950101+102'
CTA+AG+IOSEF DZUGASHVILI'
COM+12345-GO:TX'
UNT+15+1'
UNZ+1+12345'
```

Figure 14: Sample UN/EDIFACT message

4.5.3 Interchanges

Interchanges are a collection of messages, or functional groups, which together are destined for the same trading partner. The interchange is the unit of exchange with the trading partner and contains the addressing details used by the VANs to route it from sender to recipient. Each interchange is bounded, as with the two lower hierarchical levels of functional group and message, by specific service segments to mark the start and end.

4.5.4 Functional groups

Functional groups are a logical collection of the same type of message, which together form a collection of business documents. Each functional group is bounded, as with the messages, by specific service segments to mark the start and end.

All functional groups are identified by the same tag that indicates their constituent messages.

Note: The use of functional groups is not recommended! It is possible that they will be deleted from the standard at some stage.

EDI Implementation Guide

Functional groups are present largely for historical reasons; the ANSI X12 standard, which was a forerunner of UN/EDIFACT, uses functional groups extensively because of the pattern of business in North America. However, business practice *outside* North America tends not to use them.

4.5.5 Messages (or transactions)   Messages are a logical collection of segments which together form a business document. Each message is bounded by specific service segments to mark the start and end. Service segments are discussed below.

All messages are identified by a unique six-character tag. If possible, this tag is the name of the business document in English; for example, INVOIC is the Invoice message. Some, however, are not so obvious – IFTSTA is the International Multimodal Status Report message!

Each message is defined in the *UN/EDIFACT United Nations Standard Messages (UNSM) Directory (EDMD)*. Entries in this directory have a code and a name to identify them uniquely. Figure 15 shows some examples.

The entries in this directory point to complete descriptions of each of the messages, which show the order and status (mandatory or conditional) of segments present within the message. A standard notation is used in each of these descriptions to describe the message.

BAPLIE	Bayplan/Stowage Plan Occupied And Empty Locations Message
CONDPV	Direct Payment Valuation Message
CONITT	Invitation To Tender Message
CONQVA	Quantity Valuation Message
CREADV	Credit Advice Message
CUSCAR	Customs Cargo Report Message
CUSREP	Customs Conveyance Report Message
DEBADV	Debit Advice Message
DELJIT	Just In Time Message
IFCSUM	Forwarding and Consolidation Summary Message
IFTMBC	Booking Confirmation Message
IFTMBP	Provisional Booking Message
IFTMIN	Instruction Message
IFTSTA	International Multimodal Status Report Message
INVOIC	Invoice Message
INVRPT	Inventory Report Message

Figure 15:   Sample UN/EDIFACT Message Directory entries

ORDERS	Purchase Order Message
PARTIN	Party Information Message
PAYDUC	Payroll Deductions Advice Message
PAYORD	Payment Order Message
QUOTES	Quote Message
REQOTE	Request For Quote Message
SUPCOT	Superannuation Contributions Advice Message

Figure 15: Sample UN/EDIFACT Message Directory entries contd.

4.5.6 Segments

Segments are a logical collection of data elements, both simple and composite. There are two types of segment:

- service segments

- user data segments.

All segments start with a three-character segment tag and end with a segment terminator.

Each segment is defined in the *UN/EDIFACT Segment Directory* (*EDSD*). Entries in this directory have a code and a name to identify them uniquely. Figure 16 shows some examples. The EDSD also shows the order and status (mandatory or conditional) of data elements present within a segment. A standard notation is used to describe the components of each segment:

Ref.	the unique id of the data element as in EDED or EDCD
Repr.	the data type, length and status (M/C)
Name	the name of the data element as in EDED or EDCD

Remarks   free format text.

EDI Implementation Guide

Ref. Name	
Function: Remarks	
List of data elements	Repr.
DTM DATE/TIME/PERIOD	
Function: To specify date, and/or time, or period.	
C507 DATE/TIME/PERIOD	M
2005 Date/time/period qualifier	M an..3
2380 Date/time/period	C an..35
2379 Date/time/period format qualifier	C an..3
FII FINANCIAL INSTITUTION INFORMATION	
Function: To identify an account and a related financial institution.	
3035 PARTY QUALIFIER	M an..3
C078 ACCOUNT IDENTIFICATION	C
3194 Account holder number C an..17	
3192 Account holder name	C an..35
3192 Account holder name	C an..35
6345 Currency, coded	C an..3
C088 INSTITUTION IDENTIFICATION	C
3433 Institution name identification	C an..11
1131 Code list qualifier	C an..3
3055 Code list responsible agency, coded	C an..3
3434 Institution branch number	C an..17
1131 Code list qualifier	C an..3
3055 Code list responsible agency, coded	C an..3
3432 Institution name	C an..70
3436 Institution branch place	C an..70
3207 COUNTRY, CODED C an..3	
MOA MONETARY AMOUNT	
Function: To specify a monetary amount.	
C516 MONETARY AMOUNT	M
5025 Monetary amount type qualifier	M an..3
5004 Monetary amount	C n..18
6345 Currency, coded	C an..3
6343 Currency qualifier	C an..3
4405 Status, coded	C an..3

Figure 16: Sample UN/EDIFACT Segment Directory entries

Chapter 4
UN/EDIFACT

It is possible to have a logical grouping of segments to form a SEGMENT GROUP. In many ways a segment group is similar to a composite data element. For example, it is logical to put name and address details (which would appear in an 'NAD' segment), alongside telephone details (which would appear in a 'COM' segment), perhaps along with reference information (which would appear in an 'RFF' segment).

4.5.7 Service segments

UN/EDIFACT defines a special class of segments, all of which have a tag of the form 'Uxx'. These are generally used to mark the start and end of messages, functional groups and interchanges. The relationship of these segments is depicted in Figure 17.

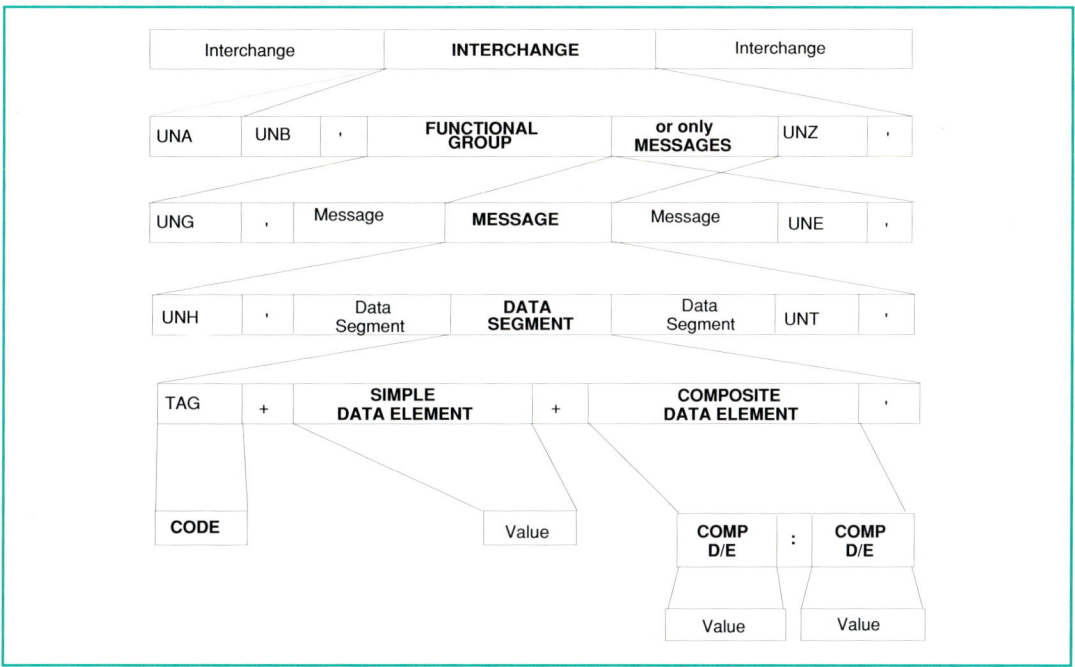

Figure 17: Relationship of interchange components. Header and trailer segments are described in 4.5.7, 'Service segments'.

UNA   Service String Advice
UNB   Interchange Header

Figure 18 shows the layout of this segment.

UNG   Functional Group Header

79

EDI Implementation Guide

UNH Message Header

UNS Section Control

This is used to separate sections within a message, eg header, detail and trailer sections. Figure 14 shows a message that uses one of these segments.

UNT Message Trailer

UNE Functional Group Trailer

UNZ Interchange Trailer.

Segment: UNB INTERCHANGE HEADER
Function: To start, identify and specify an interchange

REF.	REPR.		NAME	REMARKS
S001		M	SYNTAX IDENTIFIER	
0001	a4	M	Syntax identifier	a3 upper case controlling agency and a1 stating level
0002	n1	M	Syntax version number	Increments 1 for each new version
S002		M	INTERCHANGE SENDER	
0004	an..35	M	Sender identification	Code or name as specified in Interchange Agreement
0007	an..4	C	Partner identification code qualifier	Used with sender identification code
0008	an..14	C	Address for reverse routing	
S003		M	INTERCHANGE RECIPIENT	
0010	an..35	M	Recipient identification	Code or name as specified in Interchange Agreement
0007	an..4	C	Partner identification code qualifier	Used with recipient identification code
0014	an..14	C	Routing address	If used, normally coded sub-address for onward routing
S004		M	DATE/TIME OR PREPARATION	
0017	n6	M	Date	YYMMDD
0019	n4	M	Time	HHMMSS
0020	an..14	M	INTERCHANGE CONTROL REFERENCE	Unique reference assigned by sender
S005		C	RECIPIENTS REFERENCE/PASSWORD	
0022	an..14	M	Recipient's reference/password	As specified in interchange agreement
0025	an2	C	Recipient's reference/qualifier	If specified in interchange agreement
0026	an..14	C	APPLICATION REFERENCE	Optionally message identification if the interchange contains only one type of message
0029	a1	C	PROCESSING PRIORITY CODE	Used if specified in interchange agreement
0031	n1	C	ACKNOWLEDGEMENT CODE	Set = 1 if sender requests acknowledgement
0032	an..35	C	COMMUNICATIONS AGREEMENT ID	ID If used, to identify type of communication agreement controlling the interchange
0035	n1	C	TEST INDICATOR	Set = 1 if the interchange is a test

Figure 18: UN/EDIFACT UNB segment

Chapter 4
UN/EDIFACT

By default, UN/EDIFACT uses the punctuation characters discussed earlier. However, if necessary, these can be modified by the use of the 'UNA' Service String Advice segment. User data should not routinely include any of these characters. Their presence should be avoided if at all possible. Otherwise trading partners will need to be alerted to their presence. Most EDI translation software will happily cope but a processing overhead will be incurred to handle the marking of these characters with the 'release' character (by default '?'). For each occurrence in user data of the punctuation character, two characters will be generated. If it is really not possible to avoid including punctuation characters in user data and, as a result, multiple release characters are being included, then consideration should be given to the use of the 'UNA' segment. This segment precedes the 'UNB' of the interchange to which it refers (see Figure 19).

```
UNA:*,? #UNB*UNOA:1*SENDER*RECEIVER*19941224:2359*12345**PARTIN****1#
```

Figure 19:   UNA segment usage

This example shows a redefinition of the following separators:

- component data element – default ':' is unchanged
- data element – default '+' is changed to '*'
- decimal notation – default '.' is changed to ','
- release character – default '?' is unchanged
- segment terminator – default ',' is changed to '#'.

4.5.8 Data elements

Data elements occur in three types:

- simple

- component

- composite.

Simple data elements are single items of data, eg a date, and each is identified by a unique, numeric four-character number.

Component data elements are simple data elements which have been grouped. Logically, the group in turn is known as a *Composite data element*. For example, a complete

EDI Implementation Guide

address might form a composite data element with each address line being a component data element.

All data elements are defined in two of the UN/EDIFACT directories, *UN/EDIFACT Data Element Directory (EDED)* and *UN/EDIFACT Composite Data Element Directory (EDCD)*, discussed above.

Since the philosophy of EDI is the processing of data without manual intervention, it is important that every piece of data be interpreted unambiguously. One way to achieve this is to reduce as much of the data to codes, which then have one, and only one, interpretation. This is the idea behind the use of *code lists*.

Odd-numbered data elements are used to hold these unambiguous values. They are used as *qualifiers* for user data, which is held in even-numbered data elements. These qualifiers are either values taken directly from UN/EDIFACT Board maintained lists (the *UN/EDIFACT Code Lists (EDCL)* mentioned above) or from independently maintained code lists pointed to by the EDCL. The advantage of this latter method is that it relieves the UN/EDIFACT Board of responsibility for maintaining *every* list of *every* code throughout the world! In addition, some of these odd-numbered data elements are used to indicate *how* user data is to be interpreted. A sample EDCL entry is shown in Figure 20.

2379 Date/time/period format qualifier			
Desc:	Specification of the representation of a date, a date and a time or of a period.		
Repr:	an..3		
Code	Format		
2	DDMMYY	Calendar date: D = Day; M = Month; Y = Year	
3	MMDDYY	Calendar date: M = Month; D = Day; Y = Year	
101	YYMMDD	Calendar date: Y = Year; M = Month; D = Day	
102	CCYYMMDD	Calendar date: C = Century; Y = Year; M = Month; D = Day	
103	YYWWD	Calendar week day: Y = Year; W = Week; D = Day	
105	YYDDD	Calendar day: Y = Year; D = Day	

Figure 20: Sample UN/EDIFACT Code Lists (EDCL) entry (partial extract)

Chapter 4
UN/EDIFACT

Even-numbered data elements are used to hold user data, the meaning of which are determined by their qualifiers. For example, data element '2380' is defined as 'date/time/period' in the EDED. What sort of date/time/period? This is determined by a qualifying data element '2005' ('Date/time/period qualifier') which might have a value of '7' defined in the EDCL as 'Effective date/time'. This is still not entirely unambiguous since UN/EDIFACT allows a multitude of date/time/period formats. The format is determined by another qualifying data element, '2379' ('Date/time/period format qualifier'). This allows the business application, finally, to interpret the date unambiguously. The value in '2379' might be '202', indicating a date/time format of 'CCYYMMDDHHMM'.

Figure 14 includes a couple of examples of these data elements, in particular, line 4 ('DTM+7+199412242359+202'').

This may seem a rather complicated system but it gives the user a high degree of freedom to define data as needed for a particular purpose – it is not for a standard to impose artificial limitations on how a business will conduct itself.

4.5.8.1 Simple data elements

Simple data elements have a formal definition within the EDED with the following characteristics:

- a tag

- a name

- a description

- a data type

- a length.

Usage notes may also be included.

The *tag* consists of four numeric characters. Figure 21

shows some examples. The *data type* and *length*, generally known as the *representation*, are described using a standard notation:

a	alphabetic characters
n	numeric characters
an	alphanumeric characters
a3	3 alphabetic characters, fixed length
n3	3 numeric characters, fixed length
an3	3 alphanumeric characters, fixed length
a..3	3 alphabetic characters, variable length
n..3	3 numeric characters, variable length
an..3	3 alphanumeric characters, variable length.

Likewise, there is a standard way of formatting the description of a data element, when used in entries in the EDCD and EDSD. A 'COMPOSITE DATA ELEMENT' always has its description in upper case. A 'DATA ELEMENT' has its description in upper case, except where it is a 'component data element', when it is in lower case.

tag	name
Desc:	description
Repr:	representation
Note:	usage notes
1000	Document/message name
Desc:	Plain language identifier specifying the function of a document/message.
Repr:	an..35
1001	Document/message name, coded
Desc:	Document/message identifier expressed in code.
Repr:	an..3
Note:	See also TDED 5.1. If national code needed, use 1131 and 3055.
3207	Country, coded
Desc:	Identification of the name of a country or other geographical entity as specified in ISO 3166.
Repr:	an..3
Note:	Use ISO 3166 two alpha country code.
3222	Related place/location one
Desc:	Specification of the first related place/location by name.
Repr:	an..70

Figure 21: Sample UN/EDIFACT Data Element Directory (EDED) entries

4.5.8.2 Composite data elements   Composite data elements differ from simple data elements in that they are effectively a 'label' used to identify a logical grouping. They have a formal definition within the EDCD with the following characteristics:

- a tag
- a name
- a description
- a list of component data elements with the representation of each, including the status.

The *tag* consists of the character 'C' followed by three numeric characters. Figure 22 shows some examples.

The *status* (Mandatory or Conditional) of data elements present within the composite is used to tie components together so that, for example, a date alone is meaningless without a proper indication of its meaning.

```
tag      name
Desc:    description
list of data elements

C002 DOCUMENT/MESSAGE NAME
Desc:  Identification of a type of document/message by code or name. Code preferred.
1001   Document/message name, coded              C an..3
1131   Code list qualifier                       C an..3
3055   Code list responsible agency, coded       C an..3
1000   Document/message name                     C an..35

C080   PARTY NAME
Desc:  Identification of a transaction party by name, one to five lines. Party name may be formatted.
3036   Party name                                M an..35
3036   Party name                                C an..35
3036   Party name                                C an..35
3036   Party name                                C an..35
3036   Party name                                C an..35
3045   Party name format, coded                  C an..3

C507   DATE/TIME/PERIOD
Desc:  Date and/or time, or period relevant to the specified date/time/period type.
2005   Date/time/period qualifier                M an..3
2380   Date/time/period                          C an..35
2379   Date/time/period format qualifier         C an..3
```

Figure 22:   Sample UN/EDIFACT Composite Data Element Directory (EDCD) entries

EDI Implementation Guide

A sub-class of composite data elements, which are used exclusively in service segments (see 4.5.7, 'Service segments'), starts with the character 'S' rather than 'C'.

S004	DATE/TIME OF PREPARATION	
Desc:	To indicate the date and time of preparation.	
0017	Date	M n6
0019	Time	M n4

Figure 23: Sample UN/EDIFACT Composite Data Element Directory (EDCD) entry. This composite data element is used in a service segment.

4.5.8.3 Putting this together

Putting together the ideas of simple and composite data elements and using the example earlier in this section of dates, we get what is shown below. A date only makes sense with an indication of what date it is and how it is formatted. This gives rise to a composite data element containing three simple data elements:

Tag	Name	Value
C507	DATE/TIME/PERIOD	no value
2005	Date/time/period qualifier	7
2380	Date/time/period	199412242359
2379	Date/time/period format qualifier	202

This would appear in a fragment of a message as:

...+7:199412242359:202+...

which can be unambiguously interpreted to mean that the effective date and time was one minute to midnight on Christmas Eve 1994.

Composite data element 'C507' cannot contain a value; it just acts as a label to group the following simple data elements.

Chapter 4
UN/EDIFACT

4.5.9 Message status

In recognition of the fact that messages cannot spring into life fully formed, meeting all the requirements of all users, the UN/EDIFACT Board has a process of releasing messages at different levels reflecting their belief in the stability of the message. There are three such levels, referred to as Message Status. These are:

Status 0   Draft document

A message at this level is still undergoing development but is available for trial use. Users who find problems or deficiencies are asked to notify the relevant issuing MDG through their country contacts. Changes to all components will be considered.

Status 1   Draft recommendation

A message at this level, having gone through Status 0, is likely to meet the commercial requirements of many users. However, changes will still be considered, although it is unlikely that they will need to be of a radical nature.

Status 2   Recommendation

A message at this level is available for full commercial use. It will usually remain unchanged for a period of not less than three years. It should meet the commercial requirements of the vast majority of its users.

4.5.10 Message subsets

Since UN/EDIFACT takes input from as many interested parties as possible, it is inevitable that any given message is going to be a combination of all the needs of these parties. As a result, the message is going to contain more than any one party requires. Having built the large structure, various groups have set about reducing it to manageable proportions. This gives rise to the concept of a 'subset', defined by UN/EDIFACT as:

An extract of a message type for use within an industry or application. The extract shall follow the rules for omission of data units and the subset usually indicates only those units needed by the industry or application.

EDI Implementation Guide

The key phrase in this definition is 'within an industry or application'. This is used to formulate a partial implementation within countries, or wider geographical areas, as well as communities. At a country level, business practice, and sometimes legislation, may allow a 'standard' way of presenting information within an EDI message. Generally, subsets are controlled by these industry and country groups and they will issue specific guidelines for the use of 'their' subsets. Examples of such groups include:

UK EDIFACT   Trade Message Convention

This is a joint initiative between the ANA, SITPRO and HMC&E, which currently defines a common usage for various UN/EDIFACT messages. Messages so far developed include:

INVOIC	Invoice Message
ORDERS	Purchase Order Message
TAXCON	Tax Control Message: this is a non-standard message, which is recommended by HMC&E for VAT reconciliation when using the *INVOIC* message.

EDIFICE

EDIFICE (EDI For companies with Interests in Computing and Electronics) has defined specific usages for the same *INVOIC* and *ORDERS* messages, this time for use throughout Europe but restricted to trading between members. So far, it includes:

DESADV	Dispatch Advice Message
DELFOR	Delivery Forecast Message
DELJIT	Delivery Just-In-Time Message
INVOIC	Invoice Message
INVRPT	Inventory Report Message
ORDCHG	Purchase Order Change Request Message
ORDERS	Purchase Order Message
ORDRSP	Purchase Order Response Message
PRICAT	Price/Sales Catalogue Message
QUOTES	Quote Message
REQOTE	Request for Quote Message
RESRPT	Resale Report Message (not yet a standard message).

Chapter 4
UN/EDIFACT

EANCOM

A European initiative by the International (originally European) Article Numbering Association (EAN) for a common European subset. Where appropriate, the UK initiative is compatible with this. This convention already includes:

DESADV	Dispatch Advice Message
GENRAL	General Message
INVOIC	Invoice Message
ORDCHG	Purchase Order Change Request Message
ORDERS	Purchase Order Message
ORDRSP	Purchase Order Response Message
PARTIN	Party Information Message
PRICAT	Price/Sales Catalogue Message
REMADV	Remittance Advice Message
SLSFCT	Sales Forecast Message
SLSRPT	Sales Report Message.

4.5.11 Message frameworks

Another approach is to design from scratch a set of messages which have a set of common segments and usages for those segments and to extend this 'outline' for specific business purposes. This is the reverse of the subset idea, which starts large and produces a smaller message; it starts with a 'core' and builds up from this.

This skeleton is called a 'framework' and it is defined by UN/EDIFACT as:

a template containing a sequenced set of all groups/segments which relate to a functional business area (or multi-functional business area) and applying to all messages defined for that area.

This is what happened in the area of international freight. Various groups and companies together defined the minimum message for any trading to occur and extended this for types of business. This has given rise to a series of related messages following the pattern *IFTxxx*. For example:

IFTMAN	Arrival Notice Message
IFTMBC	Booking Confirmation Message
IFTMBF	Firm Booking Message
IFTMBP	Provisional Booking Message

IFTMCS   Instruction Contract Status Message
IFTMIN   Instruction Message.

4.5.12 UN/EDIFACT trial and standard directories

Confusingly, there is another layer of directories, which contain all components at a given level. These appear in two varieties: Draft and Standard.

Both types of directory have the same name format 'xyya', where:

x 'D' indicates Draft; 'S' indicates Standard
yy indicates the year of issue
a indicates the issue within the year starting with 'A'.

Thus, the first Draft directory for 1993 was called 'D93A'; the second would be 'D93B'.

This is an area of considerable confusion, it has to be admitted.

Each of these directories contains all of the definitions from all other directories (EDED, EDCD, EDSD and EDMD) which make a consistent set. It becomes important to know which of these directories is being used (when the use of UN/EDIFACT messages starts in earnest) since it is quite possible that the meaning of, for example, a data element in one directory is *not* identical to the meaning of the same data element in another directory.

As a result it is critical that all parties understand exactly which directories are in use at any time. Failure to do so could lead to ill-feeling at best and damage to business at worst.

The composite data element 'S009 MESSAGE IDENTIFIER' is used to indicate to the recipient of a message which directory is being used.

4.5.13 Provision for alternative character sets

When UN/EDIFACT was first created, the characters that could be used within a message were limited to upper case 'A' to 'Z', the numeric characters '0' to '9' and a few special characters, primarily for use as delimiters. This was fine if the language in which business was carried out was English. However, even in Europe there are many languages which use a considerable number of additional letters. French, for example, uses 'ç' and 'ô'. It is possible to 'get by' without these but it rather undermines the principle of unambiguous coding. The question arises of whether this character is meant to be 'c' or 'ç'. Misinterpretation becomes a real possibility. As a result pressure grew to allow support for additional alphabetic characters.

However, being pragmatic, as long as both sides of the trading relationship know what is going to appear in a message then it is perhaps not necessary to adhere absolutely to the letter of the rules, just the spirit. Many long-standing UN/EDIFACT users are quite happy to 'stretch' the meaning of the default character set to include lower case 'a' to 'z'. Since these problems are really only likely to occur when 'free text' is being used, as opposed to codes, then if only codes are used there will be a reduced risk of problems.

Amendment 1 to ISO 9735 (issued in 1992) has defined the following codes for data element 'UNB.S001.0001 Syntax identifier' (see Figure 18 for the layout of the 'UNB' segment):

- UNOA

    Upper case 'A' to 'Z', numerals '0' to '9' and certain special characters.

- UNOB

    Upper case 'A' to 'Z', lower case 'a' to 'z', numerals '0' to '9', some unprintable characters and certain special characters.

- UNOC

    Latin alphabet with support for: Danish, Dutch, English, Faroese, Finnish, French, German, Icelandic, Irish, Italian, Norwegian, Portuguese, Spanish and Swedish. Defined in ISO 8859-1.

- UNOD

    Latin alphabet with support for: Albanian, Czech, English, Hungarian, Polish, Romanian, Serbo-Croatian, Slovak and Slovene. Defined in ISO 8859-2.

EDI Implementation Guide

- UNOE

    Latin/Cyrillic alphabet with support for: Bulgarian, Byelorussian, English, Macedonian, Russian, Serbo-Croatian and Ukrainian. Defined in ISO 8859-5.

- UNOF

    Latin/Greek alphabet with support for Greek. Defined in ISO 8859-7.

4.5.14 Security standards within UN/EDIFACT

One major concern that some existing users of UN/EDIFACT have is that of security. This is *not* a concern at the transmission level – that is beyond the scope of the UN/EDIFACT standard – but at the level of the message and interchange. Until 1994 there was no approved way of addressing security within UN/EDIFACT. Now, however, there are formal UN/EDIFACT message level (as opposed to interchange level) security guidelines. These address some of the concerns of:

- message authentication

- message content integrity

- message non-repudiation (both of origin and receipt)

- message sequence.

Message confidentiality is another cause of major concern for some users of EDI.

For a full discussion of all aspects of security, see Chapter 8, 'Security'. The subject will not be further pursued here.

4.6 The next steps

Having looked at the standard itself, how is it going to be used? Indeed, *is* it going to be used? One approach is to say that EDI is the way everybody else is moving, therefore it should be used. In principle, this is fine; it shows commitment. However, it must be tempered with reality. Certain steps must be taken to ensure that the decision is really going to give a business benefit.

To stand any chance of getting correct answers to any of these prompts, then, the first commandment is 'thou shalt know thy business'!

Chapter 4
UN/EDIFACT

The following steps will be needed:

- analyse the business

    Until the answers to the what, why and where of the business are known then all other effort will be largely wasted. This analysis, for all business processes, may be done as part of a general Business Process Re-engineering (BPR) project or perhaps as part of ISO 9000 series certification or assessment.

    EDI can be implemented in a piecemeal approach, as a tactical solution, but this is unlikely to yield the significant benefits that *are* available with a strategic implementation.

- determine existing trading partners – everything from paper clip suppliers to the contractors for a new headquarters building

    Don't forget those 'if only this could be done' situations.

- having analysed the business, does it look as if there really are clear candidates for EDI and/or E-mail? Are there processes that repeatedly re-key data? Is the same data sent out to large numbers of suppliers? What are other experienced EDI users doing? What areas have other users introduced EDI into? Have there already been approaches to receive EDI data? This might have been the original trigger to look at the business processes.

See Chapter 10, 'Managing the implementation', for further discussion of some of the steps needed next.

4.6.1 Analysis of business processes

This should be considered as an exercise to understand the business and its processes and not just as a means of identifying possible EDI candidates. There are many data modelling methods that can be used, but the use of Structured Systems Analysis and Design Method (SSADM) is strongly recommended. This is the most widely used methodology in national and local government and, if used, it means that business processes can be discussed with other government bodies in the same terms; modelling information can be exchanged and other parties will be able to understand it immediately.

In terms of SSADM, there will be seven stages:

Stage 0   Feasibility
Stage 1   Investigation of Current Requirements
Stage 2   Business System Options
Stage 3   Definition of Requirements
Stage 4   Technical System Options
Stage 5   Logical Design
Stage 6   Physical Design

Stages 1 and 2 should now answer the following sorts of question:

- what?
- why?
- where?
- do existing processes show up glaring, and not so glaring, deficiencies in data received? Remember, a human being is superb at coming to correct conclusions from sparse data; a machine is not so forgiving.

Identifiable business processes, business flows and detailed entity descriptions, including attributes and relationships should now be available.

With this knowledge of the business it should be possible to make informed decisions to take the next step. Are some of the processes now clear candidates for BPR? Are some of them clear candidates for EDI, perhaps as part of a wider BPR project? Are some of them totally unnecessary – the 'it's done this way because that's the way it's done' syndrome?

Thus, SSADM identifies cross-system-boundary data flows and interprocess data flows. These are used to build data models. They are also used to identify the input–output structures driven by the required system functions. This should give all of the necessary information to allow EDI message mapping or design to take place. This type of activity will occur at Stage 3, 'Definition of Requirements', after the earlier stages have evaluated the need for BPR (Stage 0) and the options for various technologies and solutions such as EDI, E-mail, CAD/CAM, etc (Stage 2 in the SSADM model).

4.6.2 External or internal exchange?

Some observers maintain that EDI is only appropriate between different organisations (inter-organisational exchange). This may frequently be the case but potential candidates for EDI exchange include different parts of the same organisation (intra-organisational), especially if these parts use disparate computer equipment – EDI is designed to remove dependence on any particular hardware platform. Realistically, if the exchange of data between particular applications IS internal then the overheads of translation to the EDI standard and back again are probably too great.

Similarly, if the exchange, albeit external, is with one and only one trading partner then the investment in EDI translation is also probably too great. It may be appropriate in these circumstances simply to agree a fixed format for the data file to be exchanged.

4.6.3 EDI or E-mail?

There is a great temptation to drive all processes down the EDI route. Avoid it until all the implications have been considered carefully. It cannot be stressed too strongly that EDI is a tool to be used to benefit the way an organisation works, not a panacea. It is not, and never will be, the answer to all problems.

Analysis of the processes may show that there are relatively simple changes to existing processes which allow improvements in efficiency and effectiveness without ever using EDI or indeed E-mail. This should not be a cause for disappointment. The investigative phase was to identify improvements to the business; if this is achieved without EDI so be it.

At the same time, it is almost guaranteed that areas will appear that are immediate candidates for both EDI and E-mail.

Do not be rail-roaded into EDI; do not rail-road others. EDI relies on trust and co-operation. Hitting somebody with a big stick does not encourage co-operation. If this is necessary, at least try and disguise the stick!

While pondering the question of EDI or E-mail, or both, it is worth considering that if full EDI links are developed, then an E-mail link to the trading partners should be considered very carefully. There will always be occasions,

EDI Implementation Guide

hopefully rare, when something in an EDI exchange needs manual intervention and discussion. E-mail gives an opportunity for fast and auditable exchange of ideas. Probably the best approach is to install and use both – E-mail provides a gentle introduction to electronic communication and complements EDI.

Chapter 2, 'Basic concepts', discusses these ideas and concepts in greater detail.

4.6.4 Existing EDI messages

As a result of the analysis and related work, there appear to be some genuine candidates for EDI. The next decision is, which messages? Try not to work in isolation on this decision – ask around, talk to others. If potential trading partners are already involved in other EDI projects, seek advice from them. One aspect of EDI, and the trust and spirit of co-operation that is engendered, is that it will become noticeable, very rapidly, that people from apparently rival organisations happily sit down and swap EDI stories, both successes and failures. This should always be used as a source of information for decisions.

4.6.4.1 Sources of information

National and international sources of information for the descriptions of existing UN/EDIFACT messages should always be used. Some organisations that can be approached are listed in Annex I, 'Useful contacts and addresses'.

4.6.4.2 Industry groups

Appropriate industry groups should always be joined if possible. Information on these can be obtained from the Electronic Commerce Association or the ANA. Some will charge a nominal sum but this can easily repay itself since group meetings can be used to sit down with other EDI users and get advice and guidance from other members, and learn from their mistakes.

4.6.4.3 UN/EDIFACT message description

UN/EDIFACT documentation for each standard message always includes a preamble with the headings of 'Functional Definition' and 'Principles'.

These give explicit details on the applicability of the message to particular business processes. For example, the

'Functional Definition' of the QUALITY Quality Data Message reads:

A message to enable the transmission of the results of tests performed to satisfy product or process requirement. The content includes, but is not limited to, test data and measurement, statistical information and the testing methods employed.

Whilst the 'Principles' read:

- A Quality Data Message detail line may refer to either goods items or services,

- The values within a Quality Data Message may refer to:

    – a product/service
    – a product via batch references
    – process type information of a product.

- A Quality Data Message may contain discrete or statistical values as well as product specification values.

From a combination of the definitions of the business processes, a thorough examination and understanding of possible UN/EDIFACT messages, and from talking to others, it should be possible to decide whether there is a suitable existing message, or whether an entirely new message is needed. The data modelling exercise should show that the basic processes are probably not unique, despite the belief to the contrary!

Although it is the needs of the business that should drive the choice of message rather than trying to squeeze the business into an existing message, the development of new messages should not be undertaken lightly!

4.6.5 New message development

The most important, single piece of advice which can be given on designing new messages is: if a new message is not absolutely necessary, then do not create it. The amount of effort and time which will be demanded in its development should not be underestimated.

If the business needs are so special or so different from others out there, then the business of the development of a new message can start. To be successful at this, and to have a new message stand any chance of being submitted successfully to the WE/EB for adoption, a large amount of hard work will be needed. If the new proposal is for something that will *never* be used outside a given community then less work is likely to be involved – 'never' is an awfully long time.

Any group considering the task of new message development *must* be completely familiar with the following documents:

- UN/EDIFACT Application Level Syntax Rules (ISO 9735)
- UN/EDIFACT Message Design Guidelines (MDG)
- UN/EDIFACT Syntax Implementation Guidelines (SIG)
- UN/EDIFACT Data Element Directory (EDED)
- UN/EDIFACT Code Lists (EDCL)
- UN/EDIFACT Composite Data Element Directory (EDCD)
- UN/EDIFACT Segment Directory (EDSD)
- UN/EDIFACT United Nations Standard Messages (UNSM) Directory (EDMD).

Access to the latest versions of these documents, either as paper documents or, ideally, as on-line documentation must be available.

A complete analysis of the business processes is now available; possible opportunities for one or more EDI exchanges have been identified; a complete analysis of all data is available and a list of those items of data that are *not* held should have been started – there will always be some. What about the notes that appear on pre-printed stationery? The terms and conditions of trade? What about that odd little acronym 'E&OE' lurking in the corner of the pre-printed invoices? 'E&OE' usually stands for 'Errors and Omissions Excepted'. It is critically important that this apparently trivial item is either referred to in the standard Terms and Conditions of trade or an Interchange Agreement, or is coded with every INVOIC message.

Chapter 4
UN/EDIFACT

Now to think about some new messages.

When developing new messages, as many existing segments as possible should be used. For this an understanding of the purpose of all of them is vital. If new messages are created, then the names must not clash with existing ones.

When developing new segments, as many existing composite and simple data elements as possible should be used. Again, an understanding of the existing components will be needed to reduce the incidence of unnecessary new definitions and, again, names must not clash.

When developing new data elements, as many existing codes and code lists as possible should be used. The same warnings about duplication and clashes apply here.

Remember to make use of all possible contacts to see if others are involved in something similar.

Remember that supporting novel messages in some EDI translation software may pose problems. Most commercial software will support standard messages, but this may not be the case for new messages, or at least only at additional cost.

Having created a new message, submission through the appropriate country UN/EDIFACT representatives for approval by the UN/EDIFACT Board should be considered. If it is ultimately accepted, a process which can take a number of years, then the responsibility for maintenance of the message (and its segments, its data elements and its code lists) passes to the UN/EDIFACT Board. Until this time, or if it is not submitted to this process, then responsibility for the maintenance stays with the developers. The cost of this responsibility will have to be included as a cost in the total development process and it is a cost that is almost impossible to estimate, other than that it will be expensive. This may well include the training of new people when the original developers move on to other things. As long as everything is well documented in great detail and kept up-to-date then the problems are lessened.

4.6.6 Mapping data to messages

An understanding of the business and its processes is now in place; the extent and meaning of all data is in place; the appropriate UN/EDIFACT messages have been selected; what now?

The 'mapping' of the business data to the message of choice now needs to be started. Two documents will be needed for each message to be used.

As the originator of a message, then, these documents are:

- an 'internal' document, which describes the source of the data for every data element in the message. It must describe which codes, from which code lists, will be used to qualify these data elements. It may be appropriate to share this information with trading partners but it is probable that they will have no specific need for it. Remember, however, that EDI is about trust and partnership so overall processes with the organisation will need to be discussed and described with trading partners. See Chapter 11, 'Operational management', for further discussion of these issues

- an 'external' document, which is for distribution to trading partners. It describes the *precise* meaning of everything that can possibly appear in a message that is sent.

As the recipient of the message, then, these documents are:

- an 'external' document from a trading partner describing the message in detail. It should be read carefully by all concerned, both in the IT department and in the appropriate business area and clarification should always be sought if there are *any* ambiguities

- an 'internal' document which describes where received data will go.

A very important aspect of the preparation and interpretation of these documents is the people who should be involved. It must be those responsible for running the business as well as those in the IT department. It has perhaps been the case too often in the past that IT people have not always co-operated with the business 'users'! This attitude must change – partnership is what is needed.

Under *all* circumstances, the terminology *must* be defined precisely. Within an organisation, acronyms and jargon may be widely understood. It is distinctly possible that a trading partner may use exactly the same acronyms and jargon but with subtly different meanings, maybe radically different. If it is defined in the documentation then there can be no argument – remove all sources of ambiguity and confusion.

4.7 Business application/ EDI interface

This is an area for some major decisions. How closely should business applications, both existing and new, be 'coupled' to EDI? At first sight, it may seem to be an attractive proposition to build the required EDI message directly in the application; the message is then produced directly and passed on to the relevant communications interface. However, what happens when the message changes? What happens if different trading partners want or need slightly different data in the same message? What if different trading partners are using different directories? The nightmare of constant testing and re-testing of a business application arises, not because of any changes to the business but because of the changes to the EDI message.

The best and simplest solution is probably to isolate the real EDI components from the business application. Strictly speaking, the business users neither care, nor need to care, how the business data is being sent or received, just that this is happening. EDI becomes an 'invisible' application. In some instances, this may allow the straight replacement of an existing component with an EDI equivalent. If an existing business application already generates a data file which is passed to a generalised print routine, then it may be possible to pass this same data file directly to an EDI routine.

For detailed discussion of EDI software and issues associated with it, see Chapter 6, 'Software'.

For a discussion of some of the possible impacts on the business and methods of operating, see Chapter 11, 'Operational management'.

EDI Implementation Guide

5 Communications Options

This chapter describes the communications requirements and options for EDI implementation. It discusses how to connect to a trading partner, what types of telecommunications access lines are available and the different line and application protocols that can be used over that line.

5.1 Communications for EDI

There are five areas to be considered when implementing EDI communications:

- computer and communications hardware
- type of connection
- telecommunications access line
- line protocol
- application transfer protocol.

Each of these areas is explained in detail in the following pages. Together with EDI-enabling software described in Chapter 6, 'Software', these communications options combine to form the technical base of an EDI solution for a department or organisation.

5.2 Computer and communications hardware

EDI can be run on almost any available hardware platform, from a mainframe to a personal computer (PC) subject only to the availability of suitable software and connectivity.

To enable one computer to talk to another computer, a modem or equivalent device[1] is required. Throughout this Guide, the term 'gateway' is used to denote an 'EDI Gateway' as defined in 6.5, 'EDI gateways'. Therefore, to avoid confusion, this chapter will use the term 'modem' to cover all of those devices which can be used to provide connectivity from one computer to another by means of a telecommunications access line. The modem (MOdulator-DEModulator) is used to convert the way a computer

---

[1] 'Modem' is used in the very broadest sense, simply because it is the most widely used and understood device for switched or mobile access. Strictly speaking, it is not required for digital links and an alternative device, known as a terminal emulator, is required for an ISDN link.

EDI Implementation Guide

represents data, in binary '0's or '1's, into a format that can be transmitted via a telecommunications line, such as analogue, which is in the form of a sine wave. Modems vary in capability and price depending on the speed at which data is transmitted and the protocol supported. Low-speed, asynchronous modems are a fraction of the cost of high-speed synchronous modems. The choice will be influenced by computer type, preferred communications method, and the volume of data to transmit. Modems can be external to a computer or internal, when a PC is used. This latter option takes its power from the PC, and no external wires are required.

With the advent of sophisticated network technology, linking computers in offices, buildings, cities and countries, network communication adapters may also be required. Depending on computer type and the communications protocol chosen, these typically are processor cards that are inserted in or connected to the computer. Some examples of this are network cards, Token Ring or Ethernet cards, or adapter cards that allow synchronous or X.25 communications.

5.3 Type of connection

To communicate with a trading partner, a connection needs to be made from one computer either directly to the partner's computer, called *Point-to-Point*, or to a *Value Added Network*.

5.3.1 Point-to-point

Point-to-point communication requires two trading partners to communicate directly with each other's computer. This is possible if:

- both trading partners agree

- their computers are compatible

- the same agreed communications protocol is used

- the same or a compatible software program is used.

There are, however, further considerations:

- although the first two trading partners may have a compatible computer system, as the use of EDI increases, it is highly unlikely that others will be in the

Chapter 5
Communications Options

same situation. As the number of trading partners grows, the need to operate and maintain many different connections and protocols may also increase. At some stage this will become unmanageable

- point-to-point means that one trading partner will have direct access to another's computer system, with inevitable consequences on security

- to transfer data to a trading partner's computer requires that their computer is both accessible and available to receive the data. In the global marketplace, with differing time zones, this may not always be the case.

Figure 24 shows the complexity that can arise with point-to-point communication when the number of trading partners grows. Each has to support a range of network connections such as asynchronous, SDLC or X.25.

These problems can be overcome with the use of a common messaging standard, such as the Organisation for Data Exchange by Teletransmission in Europe (ODETTE) EDI standard or X.400, where all trading partners communicate using the same line and application protocol.

The recommended alternative to Point-to-point is the use of a Value Added Network.

5.3.2 Value Added Network

Networks can be small and local or large, wide area networks, covering not only cities but countries. These larger networks can be for public access, where they are termed Value Added Networks (VANs), or for specialist communities with private access only.

Strictly speaking, a VAN is any organisation which has been awarded a VAN-operators licence by the government of the country in which it operates. The award of such a licence allows the VAN-operator to offer services over and above the basic telecommunications connectivity and voice services that are offered by the incumbent telephone companies.

Thus VAN-operators tend to offer EDI and E-mail services, managed connectivity of networks between customer sites and similar services.

EDI Implementation Guide

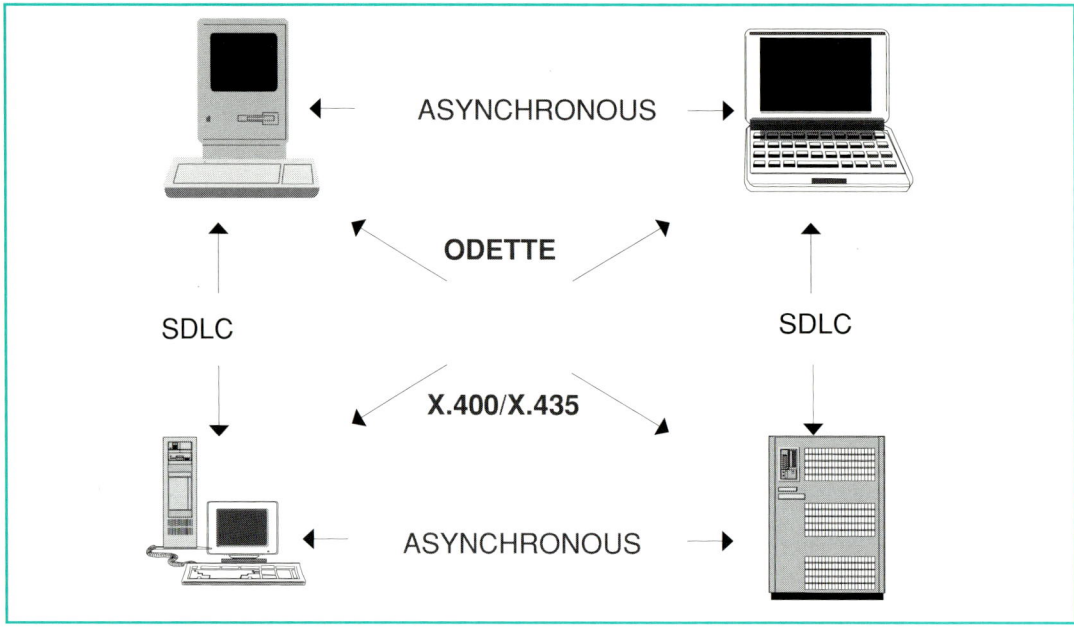

Figure 24: Point-to-point EDI

Their value in an EDI environment is that they allow a user to implement one external connection only, using the communications access and protocols of their choice without the need to worry about the connectivity capabilities or preferences of any of their trading partners, because the VAN acts as a buffer hiding any differences between user implementations.

Private networks typically have a specific use such as exchange of confidential information within a closed community. Examples of a private network are the Government Telecommunications Network (GTN) and the Government Data Network (GDN), which carry voice and data traffic, respectively, for use by government departments only. Some private networks have external connections to VANs, thus allowing the user to connect to the private network and still exchange messages with trading partners connected to the VAN.

The decision to use a VAN is usually based on cost, ease of access to desired trading partners, removal of operational problems, increased security due to buffering and VAN-imposed access controls and the like – all of which are discussed in appropriate sections of this Guide.

Chapter 5
Communications Options

In the UK, the four major Value Added Networks which connect the vast majority of EDI-enabled companies are:

- AT&T Easylink Services

- BT Global Network Services

- GEIS-Information Network Services

- IBM Global Network.

Each offers point-to-point communications and additional services, such as:

- EDI

- E-mail

- bulletin board

- networking

- access to information services.

With the continued growth in EDI, it is probable that many current and future trading partners will already be connected to one of the VANs. In this situation a partner has a choice: to take a connection to the partner's preferred VAN, or to persuade the partner to join the same one as they use. As a result, EDI can become expensive as the subscriptions and charges of VANs mount up.

Interconnection of the major UK VANs is now in place, which can allow automatic routing of EDI messages between the various EDI VAN services, so that it appears to the user as if all other users are using the same VAN service. This means that, for the first time, a user can make a choice of VAN based on cost and quality of service and messages can be sent between trading partners regardless of the VAN to which they are both connected. Therefore, consideration should be given to using an interconnection to access a trading partner, rather than joining two or more VANs. Private Networks are also looking at interconnections to the Value Added Networks. An example of this is the intra-government private network, GDN.

EDI Implementation Guide

VANs are recommended for EDI because they allow the exchange of data with trading partners by means of a single communications link. There is no need to implement a different connection to each trading partner's computer. Instead, a connection is made to the VAN using the preferred communications protocol. When data is ready for sending or receiving, there is no need to consider the availability or accessibility of a trading partner's computer. This is depicted in Figure 25 and is attributable to the way in which the VAN EDI services operate. This approach is called *Store-and-forward*.

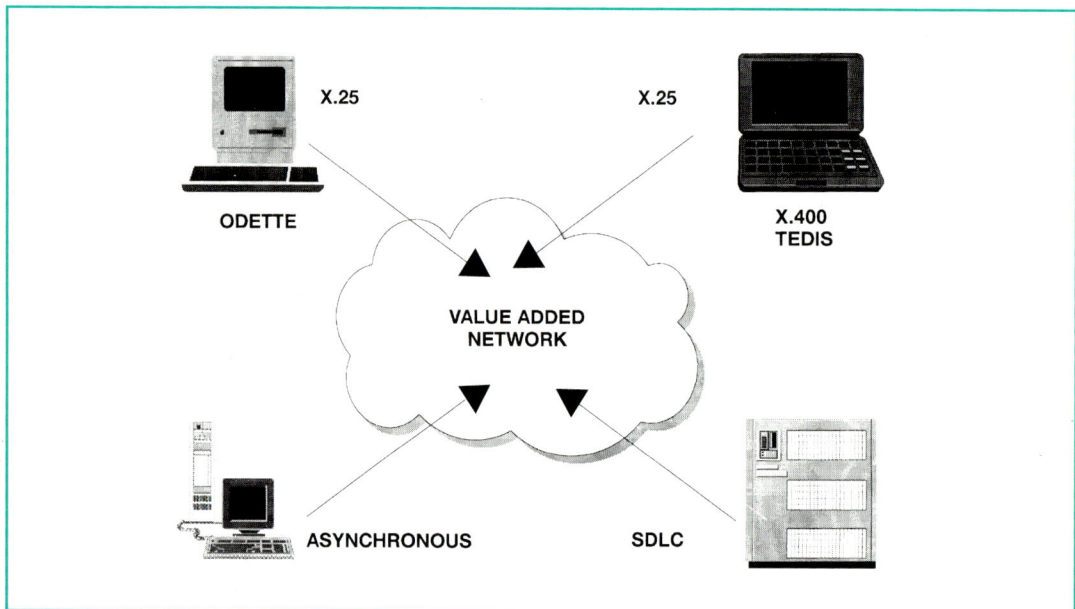

Figure 25: Communications with a Value Added Network

5.3.2.1 Store-and-forward

Store-and-forward is a technique which allows the exchange of data with trading partners, regardless of their geographical position or time zone, and without the need to directly connect each other's computer systems.

Each trading partner has a mailbox allocated on the store-and-forward service. A mailbox is a unique representation of the user within that EDI service. Messages sent between trading partners are addressed to each other's mailbox identity. When a message is sent it is stored by the service and then made available to the recipient. This

Chapter 5
Communications Options

technique is shown in Figure 26. In reality, the messages for all users of the service are stored on the same storage medium, but each partner may see and access messages that are destined only for themselves. At a time to suit the trading partner, and using their preferred communications protocol, they connect and send or retrieve the messages from their own mailbox.

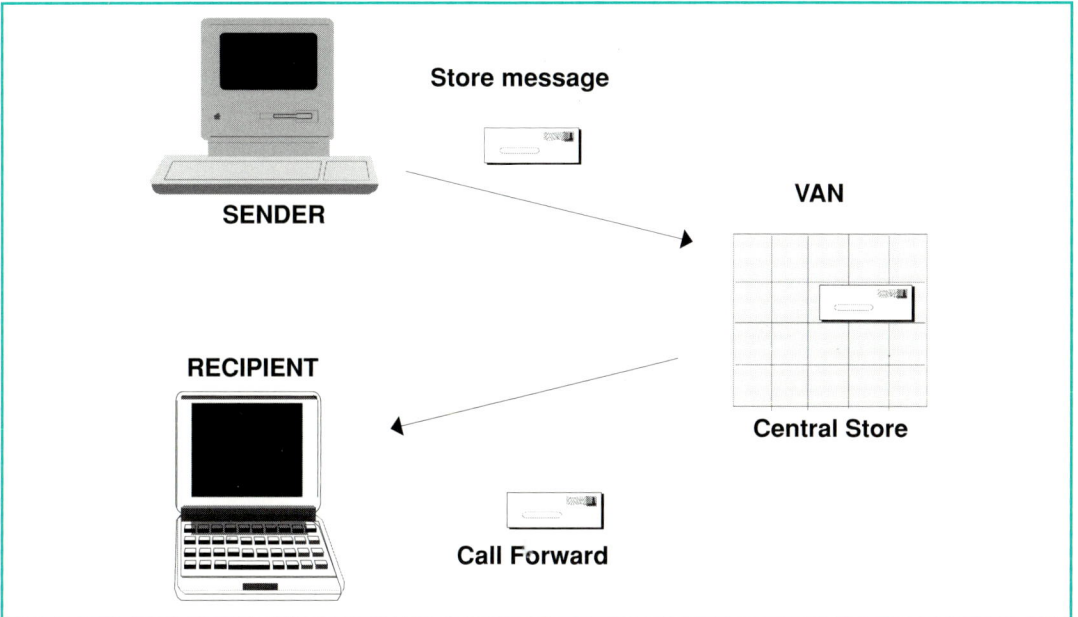

Figure 26: Store-and-forward services

The use of store-and-forward as a method of exchanging EDI messages places a requirement on the VAN to provide the ability to track the progress of a message. This is accomplished by the use of *network acknowledgements* and *audit reports*.

Network acknowledgements inform the sender of a message that:

- the message has been successfully stored in the trading partner's mailbox
- the trading partner has successfully retrieved it to their computer or network
- the message has been deleted or not delivered for some reason.

The acknowledgments are delivered into the sender's own mailbox by the VAN EDI service; they can then be retrieved by the sender for reconciliation and status checking.

Comprehensive audit reports are maintained by the VANs, which can be retrieved and stored on the user's system. These audits are essential when dealing with problems, or compiling statistics on transmissions and receipts. Audit is discussed further in Chapter 8, 'Security'.

The use of a store-and-forward mechanism requires a connection to be made to the VAN for sending or retrieving messages. When there are many messages to be sent over a period of time, this can result in many connections being started. In some circumstances this may not be acceptable. For instance, there may be a requirement for orders to be sent as soon as they are ready and for the trading partner receiving the order to process it immediately and send a response. This could be achieved by a permanent, rather than a dial-up, connection to the VAN, allowing messages to be sent as they are created. For messages awaiting receipt, store-and-forward still requires initiation of the receive operation. An advanced form of store-and-forward is available, called *event-driven EDI*, that removes this problem.

5.3.2.2 Event-driven EDI

Event-driven EDI is the automation of the store-and-forward process, where the VAN service itself automatically forwards any messages to the recipient as and when they arrive in the recipient's mailbox.

There are two methods of achieving event-driven EDI. The first is for the VAN to establish a communications link with the recipient's computer, and start the receive process. This is termed 'call-out'. The second is the use of Advanced Program-to-Program Communication (APPC), which is a feature of the Systems Network Architecture line protocol. Using APPC, both the VAN EDI service and the computer remain in communication, through the use of a leased line. APPC allows the VAN EDI service to start a program on the computer to process the incoming message.

Chapter 5
Communications Options

It should be noted that not all VAN services have real-time EDI capabilities and the APPC example here is just an example; the same solution could be achieved with some other protocols.

Event-driven EDI should only be used where there is a real need for continuous send-and-receive operations, as it does require a more sophisticated communications operation. It should be noted that event-driven EDI is not interactive or real-time, but a simulation of these using current facilities. For the situation where the exchange of an EDI message requires a conversational mode of operation, interactive or real-time EDI should be considered.

5.3.2.3 Interactive or real-time

Interactive or real-time EDI is where two or more trading partners' computers maintain a conversation with each other for the duration of a specific message. An example of this may be the submission of an order, where, prior to submission, a stock check is performed by the order originator on the recipient's stock data base.

Interactive EDI should only be considered when absolutely necessary. At present, it is not offered as a standard VAN service, but can be enabled using a point-to-point link, either direct to the trading partner or via a VAN.

A fuller example of this technique is covered in 14.4.6, 'Interactive – EDI'.

5.4 Telecommunications access line

To communicate electronically, a computer needs an access line either to a VAN or direct to a trading partner's computer.

There are four types of access line to choose from:

- telephone dial

- cellular dial

- leased line

- Integrated Services Digital Network (ISDN).

111

EDI Implementation Guide

The access line type chosen will be dependent on the volume of messages to be exchanged and cost of each type of access line and each of these types is explained below.

5.4.1 Telephone Dial

Telephone dial is where a connection is made, either to a trading partner's computer or a Value Added Network, using a normal dial telephone line.

To establish a communications link, a modem is connected to a telephone socket, and the required number is dialled to connect either to a trading partner's computer or a VAN. The trading partner or the VAN will have a compatible modem installed to receive the call. In the process of connecting, a 'handshake' takes place between the modems to agree on the rules to be used in this communication session. These include the line speed, the communications protocol and such things as error-correction techniques.

Although telephone dial access is widely used, it can be subject to problems, such as noise on the telephone lines. This may result in the loss of communications or data, depending on the communications protocol used. Modern modems have error-correcting techniques that reduce this to a minimum.

Most communications protocols can be used over a telephone connection. The most common is asynchronous communications. All the Value Added Networks offer telephone dial facilities.

When choosing to use telephone dial the following factors need to be considered:

- communication protocol to be used

- volume of messages expected

- hardware configuration.

These three items may determine whether a leased line, or upgrade of existing hardware is a more economic alternative. Dial connections cost less than their equivalent leased line but, if the volume of messages is high and the line speeds are slow, then this may result in large telephone bills or the need to use a higher-speed modem.

Chapter 5
Communications Options

5.4.2 Cellular Dial

Cellular telephones can be used for the exchange of data over radio waves. This method of exchanging information is used by the mobile user where there is a need to send or receive information when away from the normal office or travelling between locations.

A portable PC, built-in modem and a hand-portable cellular phone with data capabilities are all readily available to implement mobile user facilities. Both EDI and E-mail messages can be exchanged using this method.

The sending of data via cellular communications is new. Not many organisations use it yet, although it is growing in popularity. UK coverage is increasing with cellular providers stating that over 90% of the UK is now accessible from a cellular phone. Choice of a provider will be based on careful consideration of their service offerings. Analogue access is now widespread, but the quality of signal and hence data transfer will depend on geographical location within the UK or within a particular building. The new digital access, Global System for Mobile Communications (GSM), offers a better service level and will eventually replace analogue. The use of digital communications, therefore, should be considered wherever possible, provided it is operated in the geographical locations needed.

5.4.3 Leased Line

A leased line is a private line installed between an organisation and a trading partner or a VAN. Private leased lines are of a higher quality and less prone to the problems of dial-up telephone lines, such as background 'noise' causing data to be corrupted in transmission, resulting in communications failure.

Leased lines can be used with much higher speeds, enabling large volumes of data to be transmitted. A leased line can be used for other things at the same time as EDI and hence becomes attractive for the larger organisation.

The cost of a leased line is dependent on the line type, digital or analogue, and the speed or bandwidth with which the line is configured.

Use of a leased line should be considered when the dial telephone costs would be higher or when a high-quality, private connection or a higher data rate is required.

EDI Implementation Guide

5.4.4 ISDN

Integrated Services Digital Network (ISDN) provides 'dial on demand' digital circuits of 64 Kb per second bandwidth.

An ISDN circuit does not consist of two fixed end points but any combination of two ISDN terminations which can communicate when mutually dialled. The 64 Kb ISDN circuits or channels can be aggregated by the user at call set-up to provide greater bandwidth in multiples of 64 Kb. Similarly, again under the user's control at call set-up, a single 64 Kb channel can be 'rate adapted' to provide a narrower bandwidth. Therefore, combining the fact that a single ISDN termination point can dial another ISDN termination point with a different bandwidth, the user has a very flexible medium for dial communications.

ISDN can be used for data, voice, fax and video, as can some other connection types such as leased line. Typical uses for ISDN in the data environment are:

- dial-up application access where a greater transmission speed and quality is needed than that offered by traditional telephone dial. Additionally, call set-up times are much faster than conventional dial where modem initiation can add 20-25 seconds to each call

- data transmission when the frequency or duration of transmissions does not justify the cost of permanent lease circuits. A rough estimation is that ISDN should be considered where data transmission is less than two or three hours per day

- leased circuit back-up. ISDN is installed at strategic business premises for back-up use in the event of a leased circuit failure

- disaster recovery. ISDN is installed at a 'second' site to facilitate ongoing data communications in the event of a main site loss.

ISDN charges are in line with traditional voice call charges. A data dial-up call over a voice circuit at 2400 bits per second will incur exactly the same call charges as a data call over an ISDN circuit at 64000 bits per second.

Chapter 5
Communications Options

Note: Use of ISDN to a VAN has advantages of allowing an organisation to get high-speed access and data transfer without incurring the costs of a leased line connection as long as the overall volume is sufficiently low. It also means that the trading partner can utilise non-ISDN access methods without impacting the ISDN organisation – this would be effective, for example, with a large retailer sending many small orders to multiple small suppliers. The retailer could benefit from ISDN without the need for the suppliers to invest if a VAN were used.

5.5 Line protocol

For computers to communicate, they need to talk a common language. These languages are called communications protocols. The most commonly used protocols are:

- asynchronous

- Systems Network Architecture (SNA)

- X.25 packet switching

- Frame Relay and Asynchronous Transfer Mode (ATM)

- Transmission Control Protocol/Internet Protocol (TCP/IP)

- Local Area Network (LAN).

LANs are not line protocols as such but are placed in this group for completeness as they are commonly associated with the line protocols.

5.5.1 Asynchronous

Asynchronous communication deals with the transmission of American National Standard Code for Information Interchange (ASCII) data. The data is represented as either a 7-bit or 8-bit coded character set, and is transmitted as either a digital or an analogue signal in either a character or block mode.

In character mode, each character is sent down the line as it is keyed. In block mode, the data is stored and then sent as a continuous burst of characters. The receiving device simply captures and stores the data. There is no synchronisation with the sending device to indicate successful receipt of the data. It is up to the application program that will read the data to determine if data has been corrupted, dropped or stored out of sequence.

Most workstations now have asynchronous communication built into the hardware. Therefore the only extra hardware needed to communicate is an asynchronous modem. This makes asynchronous communication the cheapest and easiest option for EDI communications and is recommended where a simple dial-up operation is needed.

It should, however, be noted that asynchronous communication may not be a viable option when large messages are to be transmitted. This is due to the error rate usually associated with dial-up asynchronous access. Modern asynchronous modems contain error correction techniques that have dramatically improved communications. In addition, the adoption of digital networks by the PTT and VANs, replacing the old analogue systems, has also reduced problems with bad telephone lines.

5.5.2 Systems Network Architecture (SNA)

SNA was introduced by IBM in 1974 and is now widely used throughout the telecommunications industry. It provides a layered structure for networking that can evolve as hardware and software advances.

SNA initially addressed the problems associated with connecting remote terminals to a mainframe. Prior to SNA, communications between the terminal and the application required explicit coding by the programmer. SNA provided the means for one terminal to communicate with multiple applications, and share the communications resources along its path.

Today, SNA supports communication over LANs and X.25. New elements have been introduced such as Advanced Peer-to-Peer Networking and Advanced Program-to-Program Communication (APPC). Here application programs on different computers and different networks can hold a conversation and exchange data.

Communication using SNA protocols takes place synchronously. Blocks of characters are packaged for transmission. When sent, the block is accompanied by

Chapter 5
Communications Options

information about the data and is sequenced with a data block number. This allows the receiving device to determine whether the data has been received without corruption and whether the data block is in the right sequence. The receiving device then acknowledges successful capture of the data. This method of transmission is referred to as Synchronous Data Link Control (SDLC). SDLC requires the installation of special drivers, both hardware and software, such as a synchronous modem, SDLC communications cards and emulation software.

SDLC is almost error-free, compared with asynchronous communication, owing to the error-correction techniques contained within the protocol as well as in the modem. Use of SDLC should be considered, either dial-up or via a leased line, when the APPC function is needed, such as for event-driven EDI, or when there is a need for an SNA connection for other applications.

5.5.3 X.25 Packet Switching

X.25 is one of the X-series of recommendations for packet switching systems, which form a set of rules and protocols that govern the transmission of data across Public Data Networks (PDNs). The X-series belongs to the International Telecommunications Union – Telecommunication (ITU-T). The ITU-T consists of national members from the Public Telephone and Telegraph (PTT) administrations.

In packet switching systems messages are split into separate packets, which are then sent to their destination. The success of X.25 lies in its vendor independence, which has engendered its universal acceptance by both hardware manufacturers and service providers. X.25 is the most commonly used communications medium.

X.25 should be considered when an 'open' protocol is required. For dial-up connection to a VAN, subscription will be needed to a Packet Switched Service as well as the VAN. This will add to the cost. Asynchronous communications should be considered as a cheaper alternative.

5.5.4 Frame Relay and ATM

Historically, narrow-band services have been based on fixed-speed channels such as 64 Kb. In the future, more flexible services with much higher data rates will be

EDI Implementation Guide

required. These will utilise digital connections and carry voice, data, video and any other type of transmission. Frame Relay is the first step in this direction but is limited to data and comparatively low-speed transmissions (though considerably higher than the 64 Kb capability currently available). Asynchronous Transfer Mode (ATM) has been designed specifically for the purpose of combining voice, video and data effectively at considerably higher speeds (typically 150+ Mb/sec).

Frame Relay was designed by the Comite Consultatif International de Telephonie et de Telegraphie (now called the ITU-T) and the American National Standards Institute as a packet mode interface for ISDN networks; most Frame Relay usage is not reliant upon ISDN because the primary usage is for point-to-point connectivity using leased lines. The protocol is a high-speed switching technology analogous to X.25. Frame Relay provides improved throughput over X.25 by performing less processing on each frame. It can also transport any higher protocol transparently, such as X.25, SNA and TCP/IP. However, the reader should be aware that Frame Relay has limitations (such as the arbitrary loss of frames (data) when capacity limits are approached).

ATM is the basis of a new standard. The technology is characterised by fixed-length packets, or cells, that contain the source and destination information for transmission.

Both these protocols are designed for use by organisations that require high bandwidth and are not really recommended solely for an EDI installation. They are costly to implement and operate but, if they are justified for other networking needs within an organisation, then to also use the infrastructure as the base transport for EDI becomes a sensible and practical alternative to dedicated links either between partners or to and from a VAN. Typically, a Frame Relay link will perform the same function as a leased line to a VAN and will be transparent to the applications using it. VANs and PTTs are moving to this technology to provide 'super highways', where users will benefit from being able to exchange large volumes of data quickly.

5.5.5 TCP/IP

Transmission Control Protocol/Internet Protocol was originally defined by the Defense Advanced Project

Chapter 5
Communications Options

Research Agency project of the United States Department of Defense.

TCP/IP was designed to build an interconnection of networks that provide universal communication services with inherent stability, such that if some of the network were damaged in a nuclear attack, the remaining components would continue to operate by dynamically finding alternative routes around the damaged area. Each physical network has its own technology-dependent communication interface in the form of a programming interface, which provides basic communications functions. The Internet is a collection of networks interconnected through TCP/IP. Many hardware manufacturers implement TCP/IP protocols in their UNIX-based systems. It has been adopted by academic and military institutions around the world.

Most VANs now support TCP/IP access to their EDI services. Use of TCP/IP should be considered when implementing EDI on a UNIX-based platform.

5.5.6 Local Area Networks

Traditionally, LANs have been used to provide communications between personal computers, allowing the sharing of common resources such as disk storage and printers. They now provide communications backbones for entire buildings, with all devices attaching to the LAN.

LANs have experienced massive growth in size, speed and number. Most of the protocols described previously can be used over a LAN. In a LAN environment it is probable that an EDI gateway will be installed. This is where one suite of communications and EDI software is installed, with one connection to a VAN. Within a department or organisation, many users will send and receive messages to their trading partners, all using the gateway. Gateways are more fully described in 6.5, 'EDI gateways'.

5.6 Application Transfer Protocol

In defining the communications requirements to implement EDI, a choice of hardware platform, modem, communications line and line protocol to be used will already have been made. To manage the exchange of EDI messages an application transfer protocol is needed. The

EDI Implementation Guide

protocol allows instructions to be given to the VAN or a trading partner's computer about the exchange, such as:

- what recovery action to take in event of a problem
- what acknowledgments are required
- cancelling an undelivered message
- reporting on messages awaiting receipt.

All of the major UK VANs have their own proprietary protocols for this and, therefore, are outside the scope of the Guide.

There are, however, two standards that can be considered today, that are not proprietary to the VANs – X.400 and ODETTE. Additionally, as EDI across the Internet becomes a viable option, then Simple Mail Transfer Protocol (SMTP) may also become viable; however, at this time, few EDI services on the Internet offer sufficient audit or security to justify consideration for serious usage. This will change rapidly as we approach the new millennium with initiatives such as the US Government Electronic Commerce initiative, which aims to make the Internet usable for business communications.

5.6.1 X.400

X.400 forms part of the Open System Interconnection architecture, which has been designed to address the interconnection and interoperability of disparate systems.

With the advent of many communication protocols, some proprietary to hardware manufacturers, the CCITT (as the ITU-T was then called) defined the X.400 series of recommendations specifically for the interconnection and operation of message-handling systems. The first version of the standards was published in 1984, and the second in 1988. The standard defines the packaging of the messages that are to be exchanged, and the exchange environment. X.25 is the communications protocol.

Chapter 5
Communications Options

X.400 systems comprise four elements:

- message transfer agent (MTA)

    The X.400 application entity that performs the store-and-forward routing of electronic messages. It is the component that forms the backbone of the X.400 mail transport network.

- user agent (UA)

    The application entity that provides the interface between the local mail-handling package and the X.400 network.

- message transfer system

    A collection of all the MTAs on a system.

- message handling system

    The aggregate of entities that participate in an electronic message exchange system. A collection of all the MTAs and UAs.

The packaging of the messages for X.400 defines a structure for the 'envelope' or addressing details, and the structure for the actual data, referred to as the 'body'. These structures were designed for the exchange of interpersonal mail and not EDI messages. There were performance issues with the speed of delivery when using X.400 for EDI messages. The message size was limited and typical EDI requirements such as full audit and security were lacking.

To overcome these limitations and to allow the implementation of EDI over an X.400 system, the X.435 standard was developed. The X.435 standard defined specific EDI requirements such as:

- security and audit

- acknowledgements

- administration

- interworking.

EDI Implementation Guide

VANS and PTTs either have installed or are installing X.435 systems. X.400 and X.435 are seen by some as the standards of the future for interpersonal mail and EDI and, as such, should be seriously considered when looking for an international open EDI system. However, it should be borne in mind that this approach will increase cost and complexity because of the additional components and software that will be required unless EDI is being added to an existing X.400 environment.

5.6.2 ODETTE

Although not a communications protocol, Organisation for Data Exchange by Teletransmission in Europe (ODETTE) was formed in 1984 by the European motor industry. Its purpose was to develop and promote the use of EDI within the motor industry, for both manufacturers and suppliers.

ODETTE defined a series of EDI messages, which were initially based on the UN/TDI standard; however, the second version of ODETTE messages is based on the syntax of UN/EDIFACT. The ODETTE group also developed an ODETTE File Transfer Protocol (OFTP). OFTP defines a data flow for exchanging messages between two computer systems. The communications protocol chosen by ODETTE is the ITU-T X.25 recommendation.

The ODETTE standard has now been adopted by other industry sectors, including manufacturing, electronics, coal and steel.

6 Software

To use EDI, every trading partner will need access to an EDI system. This chapter describes the software components that support an EDI system and the function that each performs.

6.1 Components of an EDI system

An EDI system normally consists of software that performs the following functions:

- data extraction and conversion

- message security

- application transfer.

Each of these components is described in detail below. An alternative to this approach consists of the use of an *EDI gateway*, where a group of users, instead of each installing their own EDI system, access a single, common EDI system. The additional benefits of this approach are described at the end of this chapter. It should be noted that, in this context, an 'EDI Gateway' is a specific form of EDI system and bears no relation to the bridging or routing technology mentioned in the previous chapter.

6.2 Data extraction and conversion

In order for EDI messages to be exchanged with EDI partners, data needs to be converted into a format which is understood by them. Several options are available to do this:

- creating a file containing the formatted EDI message directly from an existing application

- writing an in-house conversion program

- using a third-party software package called a *Translator*.

It may seem that developing an in-house solution, using either of the first two options, is the best approach, especially if it appears to be an easy modification to an output file or program. However, there are reasons why the wisest choice may be to use a third-party solution:

- cost

    The development cost can be considerable when writing, testing and implementing an in-house solution. See 2.4.2, 'Software', for a fuller discussion of this point.

- maintenance

    To implement one EDI partner and one message may look an easy option but, as the number of EDI partners and messages increases, so do the overheads: standards continue to evolve; changes occur at regular intervals, again requiring modifications to the software. An in-house solution requires a long-term commitment to maintenance. The resource required can significantly increase as EDI relationships grow and more documents are committed to EDI.

For these reasons, use of a third-party translator solution is recommended. Specialist software takes away the above problems and provides a high-performance product. Otherwise, there will be a need not only for the initial programming effort but also for all future maintenance which may be considerable. The key when selecting an EDI system is flexibility – the reason it is preferable to an in-house solution is that it gives the flexibility an in-house system lacks. Throughout this chapter examples of the type of flexibility to look for are given. As would be expected, the overall degree of flexibility is often proportional to cost and, therefore, a compromise often needs to be made.

Translator software is available for most computers, and varies in both price and function. Off-the-shelf packages are available that incorporate the translator, message security and application transfer functions. These represent value for money and should be considered. The costs for EDI translator software differ, depending on the hardware platform to be used and the functionality provided. PC-based translators can be purchased for as little as £200, whereas mainframe translators can cost over £30,000. However, when considering software purchase, the key determinant should always be the level of integration with the business process that is required and the degree of flexibility needed to achieve this. This will also be the major cost element.

Chapter 6
Software

When choosing software to enable EDI, it is recommended that the EDI *Yearbook* or the *Electronic Commerce Association Casebook* is consulted. Both these publications provide comprehensive details on the providers of EDI software and their offerings; publication details are given in Annex J, 'Bibliography'.

The components of an EDI translator are now described.

6.2.1 Translator software

In essence, a translator performs a simple task. It takes data from an in-house application, in-house file or data-entry screen and converts it to an EDI formatted message, such as an UN/EDIFACT message. It also performs the reverse operation, taking an EDI message and converting it to a format acceptable to an in-house application or file. In reality, this task can be complex, and hence the person setting up this process needs both skills in using the translator, and a detailed knowledge of the in-house systems and processes. Also, remember that the role of the translator is not just to reformat but to substitute codes for text, based on complicated qualifications and directory references. Thus the task of a translator very easily becomes complex, and the role of maintaining it as well.

A translator consists of three functions, as depicted in Figure 27:

- data input and extraction

- data conversion

- data management and control.

6.2.1.1 Data input and extraction

Data to be converted to EDI format will originate either from an existing in-house application or from input at a workstation or terminal. Data that is received from an EDI partner has to be processed by an application or presented on a workstation or terminal. To implement this, translators provide an Application Programming Interface (API). The API will enable one or more of the following functions:

- a screen-build and data-entry facility

   The translator provides a facility for a data-entry screen to be built allowing an operator to key data

EDI Implementation Guide

directly into the translator or for a received EDI message to be displayed.

- the use of existing in-house files

    The translator accesses existing in-house application files to extract or create data. Tables instruct the translator which files to use and the layout of the data records to be read or created.

- the use of a translator file

    The translator requires a special file to be created that contains the data to be formatted. A program will have to be written which extracts the data and creates this file. For received messages the translator will create a special file which can be used by existing applications.

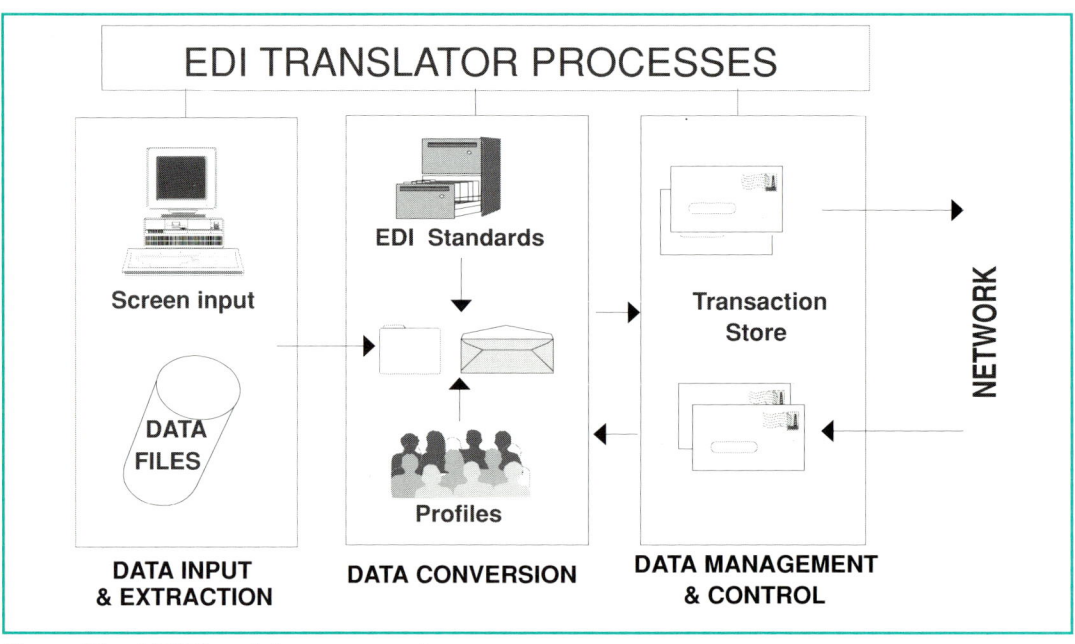

Figure 27: *EDI Translator components*

This whole aspect fits neatly with the SSADM process, the role of the translator being to perform the production mapping of data from the form defined in the SSADM Requirements Specification to that in the EDI message design. This is particularly appropriate to remember when considering maintenance and production processes.

Chapter 6
Software

Data input and extraction is the start and the end of the EDI process and hence is one of the key areas to a successful implementation. As such, care must be taken in the choice and implementation of this part of the EDI translator. When evaluating a translator, an API should be selected that suits the installation needs. It should be flexible, easy to use and require no modifications to existing applications or files. The ability to extract or create directly from existing in-house files is recommended.

All EDI partners have to agree upon the essential data to be incorporated into an EDI message. Not all the data stored in a purchase order system, for instance, may need to be transmitted. It may be that additional information is needed, such as definition of units of currency or measurement. Again, flexibility is important – can the chosen system produce or calculate a data element based on the contents of several fields? Can a field be used in several data elements? Will the system automatically accumulate totals or will this need to be coded separately?

6.2.1.2 Data conversion

This is the part of the EDI translation that performs the *mapping* or *constructing* of the data extracted to UN/EDIFACT. The reverse process, from UN/EDIFACT back to a format suitable for in-house processing, is called *translation*.

Mapping or constructing may produce an EDI formatted message without any addressing information. In this case, there is a further step in the data conversion process, called *enveloping*. This is the point at which one or more mapped messages, destined for the same EDI partner, have the addressing segments attached. Once mapped and enveloped, the EDI message is referred to as an EDI *interchange* or *transaction*.

The translation of received interchanges may also be in two stages. First, the received EDI message is *de-enveloped*, the addressing details are removed, and then the actual EDI message is translated.

Translators can be purchased in a 'ready to use' state, where a selection of messages is pre-configured – but any future changes or additional messages will probably result in a request for assistance to the software vendor and an additional cost. It is, therefore, wise to look for software that includes a set of customisation tools to define mapping and translation routines and standard update processes.

There should be separate mapping, translation and enveloping functions for greater flexibility and control. This allows document creation and processing to be independent of mailing or receipt. It is also recommended that, when the translator is to be used as an EDI gateway, there is support for multiple concurrent users, locations, applications, functions and translations. For example, a large organisation could implement a single translator image to support all the departments in its multiple divisions, thereby reducing costs and centralising control. In essence, a software package should be selected that, like its API, is flexible and easy to use, but has high functionality.

So how is the mapping or translation process defined? For each message standard there are many types of document that are available in electronic form. The segments and elements used by each message are stored by the translator in a *message data base*. As standards evolve, the same message, at a different level, may be kept within the same data base, allowing EDI partners who are not in a position to use the latest version of a standard to use a back-level. Again, it is worth checking the flexibility of the system chosen: will it handle different versions or release levels of the same message in use with different trading partners or will there be a need to spend time or money finding an alternative way to overcome this potential problem? A *data dictionary* also exists within the data base, and defines elements, field names and their characteristics.

When creating the mapping of an EDI message for a particular EDI partner, these data bases are used to select the required EDI message. Mapping then proceeds to tailor the delivered standard for an EDI partner.

The mapping process is in two stages, syntactic and semantic:

- syntactic conversion defines the relationship between in-house data and the construction of the elements and segments within the standard

Chapter 6
Software

- semantic conversion takes care of code conversions and unit conversions, such as kilometres to miles.

Translator software normally can support multiple releases of the leading data standards, should this be required, including:

- UN/EDIFACT

- ANSI X12

- ODETTE

- UN/TDI.

The translator will assist in installing only those releases and standards which are required, with updates that are furnished periodically by the software provider. For increased flexibility, translators should offer the capability to customise data standards, enveloping values and application data formats to suit business needs.

For example:

- re-usable transaction maps allow a single transaction map to be used for multiple EDI partners, conserving system resources and simplifying maintenance. This means that one definition of a business document can be used for many EDI partners

- maps can be copied and edited for EDI partners with varying requirements

- an import and export facility for maps can save valuable time and effort. This means that a group responsible for managing EDI can create a map and then distribute it between divisions, departments or users. These users can then import the map into their translator data bases, thus improving productivity and efficiency.

To complement the API and the mapping facilities, the software should contain a comprehensive data management and control facility.

129

6.2.1.3 Data management and control

As EDI typically runs without an operator, the process requires management tools such as audit reports, recovery files and error reports. The management functions of an EDI translator package can be wide and varying but should include:

- transaction data base
- audit and control
- profile management
- security.

Transaction data base: The transaction data base holds copies of the electronic interchanges after they have been sent or received as an archive. The reasons for an archive operation are:

- back-up

    When a message is sent or received, re-transmission or re-processing of a particular message may be called for. The data base can be used to retrieve an exact image of the original message and re-transmit it.

- fulfil legal requirements

    To meet requirements such as VAT, documents need to be kept in their original format for several years. The use of the transaction data base for this purpose should be thought of as a short-term measure, as it will fill rapidly. For longer-term archiving, other methods such as microfiche or magnetic tape should be considered.

Audit and control: One of the most important features of any software translator is a set of tools that provide for tracking, reporting and management of documents at the EDI rather than the application level.

It should be possible to monitor and control day-to-day operation on a by-exception basis, where only severe errors are brought to attention for immediate action.

Chapter 6
Software

Audit and control should include facilities to:

- check the status of individual transactions

- select transactions for action by such identifiers as EDI partner, transaction type, application, network or status

- resend transactions to EDI partners in a new envelope with a new control number

- view transaction images, status information and event log entries

- receive detail and summary reports of transaction activity on screen, on paper or in a file.

Profile management: Translators communicate with EDI partners either directly, point-to-point or using a VAN. In all cases the translator needs to be told how to address the EDI partner in order to create the addressing details in the EDI envelope. To perform this task the translator has two directories, network and EDI partner.

The network directory contains the information necessary to gain entry to a VAN or to link to an EDI partner's computer on a point-to-point basis. The information held in the network directory is:

- mailbox address

- communication parameters for access to the network

- any special commands for the network service.

The EDI partner directory is used to hold details of all EDI partners. There will be a profile for every message either sent to or received from each EDI partner. Each profile will contain:

- version of standard to be used for translation

- network addressing details

- routing instructions for incoming and outgoing interchanges

- addressing details.

EDI Implementation Guide

Security: As the translator software is both the originator and recipient of EDI messages it is important to establish a secure operating environment. The security facilities should include profile member name (EDI partner), EDI partner transactions (maps), encryption key names and authenticator key names as protectable assets.

6.3 Message Security

Security within a translator can only protect the data and messages while they reside within the translator. Once transmission takes place they are open to many threats. This aspect of security and the methods of protection available are discussed in Chapter 8, 'Security'.

When using any specialist software it is important to ensure that it is compatible with the translator software. It may be necessary to 'exit' to the security software from the mapping or translation process.

Security exits should be available before, during and after the data conversion process to allow for EDI message security processes to be performed. The need for this level of interaction can be seen from the description of the construction and positioning of UN/EDIFACT security segments in 8.5, 'UN/EDIFACT security recommendations'. This is because no translator can be expected to accommodate all possible forms of security implementation. It thus needs to be possible for a partly constructed message to have security elements added. This effectively means that the translator needs to be able to build or create a message step by step. (The need for flexibility again.)

An example of this process is the construction of an EDI interchange which requires security elements to be inserted within the body of the message. The security elements are produced during the construction by taking either a partly or a fully constructed message and computing the security elements to be inserted. This is no small task – therefore, great care needs to be taken to ensure that only the security that is absolutely necessary is implemented.

6.4 Application transfer

To enable communications with an EDI partner, either point-to-point or via a VAN, consideration will need to be given to the mailbox software and the line protocol software or, if X.400 is to be used, the software that packages the EDI messages for X.400 transmission.

Chapter 6
Software

6.4.1 Mailbox

To send and receive EDI messages either point-to-point or via a VAN service, an 'interface' program will be needed that provides:

- navigation of network entry to access the VAN mailbox or EDI partner

    VAN, private networks and point-to-point communications to an EDI partner's computer will require identification to be given before messages are exchanged. The software will provide an identity code or mailbox code, password and other information relevant to establish access.

- exchange of messages between computers

    Once access is gained, the software will direct the exchange of messages.

- reporting of problems

    Problems in the exchange of messages will be reported and recovery action taken where appropriate.

- audit trail of actions performed

    A comprehensive audit report should be produced by the software, listing all messages sent and received.

- integrity of the physical transmission

    In the event of a transmission failure, such as a bad data line, the software should take the appropriate recovery action, depending on the recovery techniques of the network. This may entail taking checkpoints as the data is being transmitted, thus allowing for a restart when a failure occurs.

The type of mailbox control software will depend on choice of VAN or the X.400/X.435 standard. It may be a stand-alone product, requiring operator intervention to start any transmission process, or automated from within the translation software and transparent to the end user.

Most translator products are delivered with a connection to the network of the user's choice. If connection is

EDI Implementation Guide

needed to more than one VAN, then additional, separate communication modules may have to be purchased.

Some VANs publish their EDI service interfaces and allow users to integrate their applications directly to the EDI service. These typically require programming and communications skills, as the underlying data exchange contains proprietary commands and responses to 'drive' the mailbox access and subsequent conversation.

6.4.2 Line Protocol

The mailbox software will connect to an EDI partner or Value Added Network using a particular line protocol, such as X.25 or asynchronous communications. Depending on the line protocol in use, extra software may be required.

Most workstations have the basic asynchronous communications protocol installed at the hardware level, and hence no extra software is required whereas, for synchronous or X.25 communications, emulation software will be required.

6.4.3 EDI over X.400

At the time of writing this Guide, there are not many X.400 EDI implementations. This is probably due to the existence of two versions of X.400, called 1984 and 1988, the high cost of X.400 software and its relative newness. Additionally, the existing forms of X.400 are designed for E-mail and lack the security, audit and control capabilities required when sending business data. This is addressed to some extent by the newer X435 standard. However, all the VANs offer X.400 for inter-personal messages and EDI but not necessarily using the X.435 version, which is specifically designed for EDI. As X.400 and X.435 are adopted as the open international messaging standard, then more implementations will take place. This will have the effect of driving the cost of the software down.

Figure 28 depicts an X.400 message-handling system and its components.

6.4.3.1 Message Transfer Agent

The Message Transfer Agent exchanges the X.400 packaged messages with another X.400 MTA. It is essentially a message server.

It may be that an organisation will install its own MTA to create a Message Handling System, but it is also possible

Chapter 6
Software

to connect a UA to an MTA maintained and run by a third party, such as a VAN.

6.4.3.2 User Agent

The UA takes the data to be transmitted, either an inter-personal message or an EDI formatted message, and makes it X.400-compliant. It then passes it to the MTA for transmission. In reverse, the UA receives X.400 packaged messages, removes the X.400 packaging and presents the end-user with the messages in whatever format is required.

X.400 is able to carry any type of message, from flat files to inter-personal messages, to EDI formatted documents. EDI documents are best handled by the X.435 recommendation which has an EDI-related UA.

The packaging for transmission entails the creation of the X.400 'inner' and 'outer' envelopes. The 'inner' envelope is used to convey information such as what type of data is being exchanged and what actions are to be taken on receipt, eg acknowledgment. Three types of inner envelope are defined by the X.400 standard:

- P0 Identifies an unformatted data content

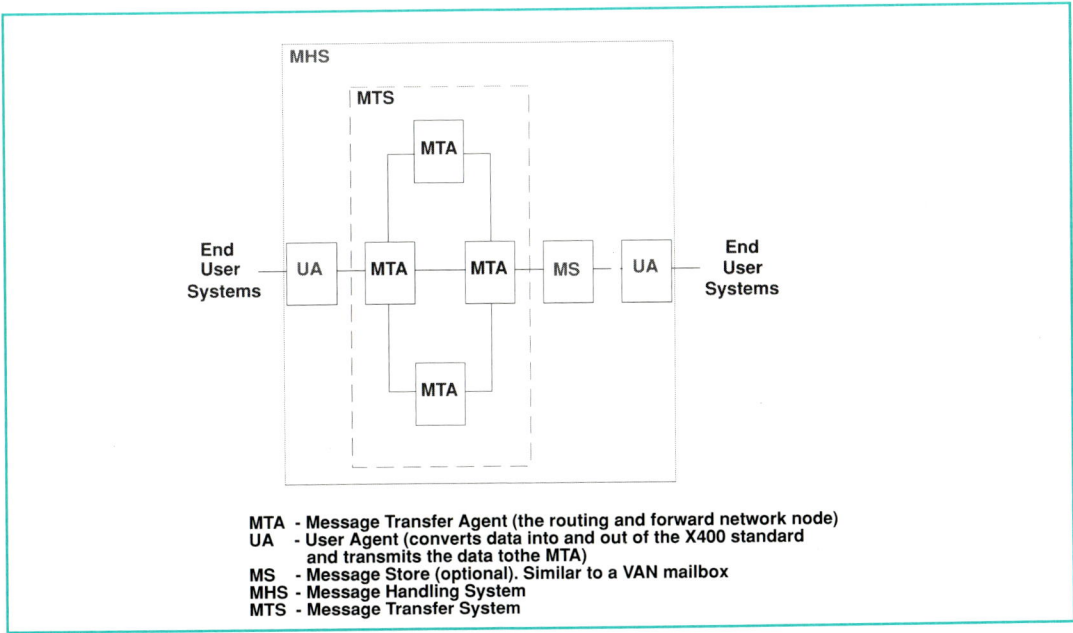

Figure 28: X.400 Message Handling System

- P2 Identifies an interpersonal message

- P-edi Identifies an EDI formatted document.

The 'outer' envelope, defined as 'P1' by the X.400 standard, contains the directional information for the MTA, such as address of the recipient. Many UAs can connect or communicate with one MTA, making X.400 the model for an electronic gateway.

6.4.3.3 User Agent API

To access the User Agent, an Application Programming Interface (API) may be required. The API can be used to link a translator directly to the UA, or to allow applications to interface to X.400 natively.

6.5 EDI gateways

When an organisation adopts EDI or E-mail, it will probably install multiple software packages to cater for what are seen as different systems, locations or business areas.

A gateway, in this context, is an application that supports the routing and interfacing to all in-house operations as well as communications to one or more networks or EDI partners. The transmission of any document, note or file is handled by the gateway. It is nothing to do with the gateways, bridges or routers of OSI networking terminology.

The objectives of a gateway can be:

- to optimise investment through a single approach to Electronic Trading

- to provide one access point for all external EDI partners

- to provide one external access point for all sites within an organisation

- to provide a single administration point with centralised and shared EDI partner information

- to minimise the need for expensive skills by providing centralised technical expertise

- to provide greater control and flexibility to cope with the ever-changing standards and additional messages

Chapter 6
Software

- to remove EDI knowledge, skills and programming from individual applications

- to respond quickly to changing market needs.

Gateways are still in their infancy. Organisations are beginning to centralise operations where there were traditionally multiple computer suites and this is fuelling the move toward gateways.

Unfortunately, many users think of gateways simply as routing devices. This misses the major benefit of such a tool – a gateway provides information at a level of detail and in a form that is essential in any large-scale implementation and the real benefit comes from the usage of this information.

If we consider a translator on its own, not acting as a gateway, then the audit trail within the translator will be able to tell that it processed a particular interchange at a specific time on a specific day. However, when a problem arises, it is often a user department responding to a customer query such as 'What happened to order number 1234?'. The translator audit trail would be of no use for this query. The operator will be able to tell that a file was sent at a particular time on a particular day, but not what was in it. The real benefit of a gateway is that it can hold and track business information and, ideally, will be able to co-relate linked information. For example: it will automatically monitor at a business level. When an order is sent, it will hold details which are accessible via the order reference and also via the EDI interchange, so that problem determination from both ends is possible. Thus, not only will someone from operations be able to tell that a specific interchange was sent at a particular time, but he will also be able to see which orders it contained, for example. Conversely, someone in the procurement group will be able to see on the internal procurement system the current status of an order, whether it be awaiting translation, waiting in the mailbox or received by the trading partner but not yet acknowledged. This, then, gives immense power to the end-user and drastically reduces the potential problem determination overhead and the need for operations support.

If a basic gateway offers this function, then it can be brought in-house into an order system, letting the users

EDI Implementation Guide

answer their own queries or automatically updating the appropriate records with status details, thus increasing the level of automation and integration within the system.

The next logical step is that if a gateway can track orders in and invoices out, say, then it should hold the orders in an open status until such time as the appropriate invoice is received which 'closes' the loop. This automatic reconciliation is a simple progression once gateways start to be used at a business level rather than at an EDI transaction level.

If this stage is reached, then it becomes feasible to monitor status and automatically report out-of-line situations – for example, a business acknowledgement to a request for quote has not been received within the stipulated 48 hours, or no payment has been received against an invoice raised 30 days ago, or simply a transaction has not been retrieved from an EDI partner's mailbox within the stipulated 24 hours.

Some of these concepts may seem a little futuristic to an organisation which is starting out on EDI, but a number of large corporate users have already achieved this level of integration and automation. Their experience has been that, having created the information data base and the means of updating it, it has been a minor task to create 'logical views' of the information. Each group of users only sees what is of interest to them, in a form intelligible to them. It has removed the need for significant operational support and management as these activities can be built into the process and automated within the gateway. (See Chapter 11, 'Operational management', for a full discussion of the types of operational support which need to be implemented and which can be significantly reduced with an appropriate EDI Gateway.)

X.400 and X.435 have the potential to offer gateway routing solutions for the future but do not necessarily give the benefits of audit, control or problem determination. The implementation of an EDI gateway should be considered at an organisational level. Although the initial set-up of the gateway will require more resource and cost than a simple translator installation, the end result will provide a solution which safeguards the future. As new departments or users can take advantage of the gateway, the initial cost of the gateway will be justified by the flexibility and control which it allows.

7 Legal Issues

This chapter introduces the areas of the legal system which affect the use of EDI. Practical guidance on the subject is contained in: Annex A, 'Case studies', Annex E, 'IS notice 31: Electronic Data Interchange', Annex F, 'Standard interchange agreement', Annex G, 'Sampled operational attachment' and Annex H, 'HM Customs & Excise guidance on EDI usage'. For guidance on digital signatures, authentication and the application of other security techniques, see Chapter 8, 'Security'. Further discussions and research will be needed for any particular area of interest.

There are excellent reasons for having a legal structure surrounding business but it should be there as a support mechanism not a straight-jacket. Unfortunately, almost anything that involves the Law is seen by many as immediately complicated and confusing. It can be, but the aim should be to use the legal aspects of business and, by extension, of EDI as a help, not a hindrance. Remember, EDI is just another tool in the business armoury and in just the same way that nobody would consider *not* having some contractual framework for current paper-based business transactions, there should be a similar framework for any electronic systems.

7.1 Business contracts

As stated before, EDI is another tool for use in the business. As with any contract for the supply of goods and services, there will always need to be an underlying trading relationship, which might be written or verbal. EDI is just another mode of communication and, therefore, it will be appropriate to have a contract to cover this. Typically, contractual relationships should be separated into three distinct components:

i. The normal terms and conditions of business

ii. An interchange agreement to define the terms and conditions specific to EDI activities

iii. An operational attachment to the Interchange Agreement for each specific EDI message or business process, defining the attributes and expectations specific to that message or process.

EDI Implementation Guide

Thus the Operational Attachment (or sometimes an EDI User Manual) will describe the messages that will be exchanged and will define the method of exchange – which is likely to involve the use of a VANS EDI service. If a VANS EDI service is being used there will also be a contract with the supplier of this service.

In some business communities the use or existence of an Interchange Agreement is lacking for one of two reasons: EDI started as something of a technical experiment that spread faster and further than expected; there is a 'big stick' approach by some dominant trading partners, which means that the smaller parties are loath to question the absence of such a contract.

7.1.1 The user manual/operational attachment

This may be a single document or it may be two; it may not be called by this name; it may be known as a mapping document. Whatever it is called, it will describe which messages are being sent and received and what each message will contain and what each data item will mean. Some of this information may form an additional document – a Technical Annex or an Operational Attachment – which may become part of the Interchange Agreement. It gives details at a business level of items that may change with time, for example:

- frequency of transmissions

- types of transactions, ie which EDI messages

- networks used

- mailbox ids used

- frequency of checking for mail

- contact names, addresses and telephone numbers, in event of queries or problems

- definitions of the 'business day'

- noting of dates of public holidays.

These last two items, apparently innocuous, become very important if there are trading links outside the UK – public holidays are more frequent in some countries, for example.

Chapter 7
Legal Issues

See Annex G, 'Sample operational attachment', for a sample Operational Attachment. Each government department or Agency needs to build an Operational Attachment of this form for each EDI project implemented.

7.1.2 Network Service Contract

In addition to the Interchange Agreement there is a need, assuming a third-party network is being used, to sign a contract for one or more of the EDI services that are available in the UK. As with any contract for services, the potential user should hold discussions and negotiations with network service providers to ensure that the business requirements are met satisfactorily by the service offered.

When considering network service agreements, business managers should be aware of the provisions of the *Supply of Goods and Services Act 1979*, which ensures that network services providers are required to exercise 'reasonable care and skill' when providing a service.

Business managers should also be aware that the *Unfair Contract Terms Act 1977* limits the ability of network service suppliers, among others, to impose liability exclusions in their contracts.

7.1.3 Interchange agreements

There are a number of model agreements, of which the most widely used in the UK is that published by the Electronic Commerce Association (ECA) (see Annex F, 'Standard interchange agreement', for the text of this agreement). Also relevant in the government sector are the Interchange Agreements which have been developed in the UK by the Ministry of Defence for their EDI initiative and also by TEDIS as part of the overall programme (see Chapter 13, 'EDI in Europe').

The Interchange Agreement will include references to any User Manuals in use and may well include references to the relevant network agreements.

It may be appropriate to include the definition of a formal process for settling any disputes which may arise through the use of EDI. See Chapter 11, 'Operational management', for details of the types of consideration which ought to be covered.

7.2 Special projects

A number of projects have been set up under the auspices of Trade Electronic Data Interchange Systems (usually known as TEDIS) to look at the legal implications of EDI. Two project reports are already available:

- *The legal position of member states with respect to EDI*, published in September 1989

- *The legal position of EFTA member states with respect to EDI*, published in July 1991.

Other projects include:

- SOLON is looking at legislation, administrative procedures and regulations which may hinder the implementation of EDI across national and international government business in both the European Union (EU) and six other countries that were members of the European Free Trade Area (EFTA)

- PORTIA is more specific than SOLON and is looking at the legal implication of a set of some 27 UN/EDIFACT messages, again in the EU and EFTA.

The reports of the conclusions for both projects were due for publication in 1995.

7.3 UK legislation

There is an extraordinary range of legislation which is seen as impinging on, or supporting, the use of EDI and electronic messaging in general. The following list is not intended to be comprehensive, it is just a flavour, indicating the areas of interest for the particular piece of legislation. For further information there are many publications dealing in depth with the legislation. A number are listed in Annex J, 'Bibliography'.

- *Statistics of Trade Act 1947* was drafted in such a way that no medium of submission for statistics was specified and it can, therefore, be used by some government departments to request figures used for compiling details of imports and exports.

- *Statistics of Trade (Customs and Excise) Regulations 1992* specifically covers the submission of VAT statistics using EDI. (See Annex H, 'HM Customs & Excise guidance on EDI usage'.)

Chapter 7
Legal Issues

- *Civil Evidence Act 1968* is believed by most observers to be sufficient to allow the admissibility of computer transactions in court.

  The law specifies certain criteria for admissibility of computer records, among which is the requirements that a computer system is operating correctly and is routinely used for the collection of these records.

  A Law Commission Report (Report 216 or Cmnd 2321) has recommended changing the rules of 'hearsay'. This report was published in October 1993. As of the beginning of 1995, the Government has taken no action on these recommendations.

- *Interpretation Act 1978* governs the 'default' meanings of terms used in legal proceedings. Probably the most important definition in this Act is that of writing:

  . . . typing, printing, lithography, photography and other modes of representing or reproducing words in visible form, and expressions referring to writing are construed accordingly.

  There is still some uncertainty as to whether this definition includes computer records.

- *Sale of Goods Act 1979* embodies many principles of common law relating to goods and services. They are applicable to business in general rather than specifically to EDI.

- *Value Added Tax Act 1983* contains the provisions for the electronic transmission of invoices. It also gives authority to the Commissioners of Customs & Excise to impose the conditions under which this can happen.

- *Data Protection Act 1984* provides for control of the storage and use of personal information held on computer. Any users new to computing and intending to hold almost any personal information *must* be registered with the Data Protection Registrar.

  It should be remembered that, in the public sector, data collected under an Act of Parliament for one purpose may not easily be used for another. This discourages the use of EDI to move data from an existing process to a new process, and could be a serious inhibitor. If this limitation may apply, further guidance should be sought from departmental legal representatives, or from the Data Protection Registrar.

- *Companies Act 1985* requires all incorporated companies to identify themselves in 'legible characters' in all business transactions. These identifiers are to include the registration number, the full name of the legal entity and its address. The question is whether these details as transmitted in an EDI transaction are sufficient. As yet it is still undecided. However, HM Customs & Excise (HMC&E) have addressed themselves to the issue by insisting that these details must appear at least once in any EDI transaction that is to be used for the purpose of claiming Value Added Tax (VAT), with the company registration number replaced by the company VAT registration number. This means that invoices and credit notes (which may be subject to VAT) fall into this category. See 7.3.1, 'HMC&E guidance and requirements', for further discussion of these issues.

- *Finance Act 1985* gives the Inland Revenue authority to inspect any computer system which they believe is relevant to their business. This may include the right of access to the systems operated by a network service supplier.

- *Computer Misuse Act 1990* encourages organisations to ensure adequate security for their computer systems, since without this the Crown Prosecution Service would be unable to take criminal proceedings against anyone attempting to gain unauthorised access to these systems. See Chapter 8, 'Security', for guidance in this area.

- *Finance Act 1992* imposes an obligation on companies to supply certain information to HMC&E. While not referring specifically to EDI, it does at least allow EDI to be used to supply this information.

One potential difficulty is that, as yet, there is no EDI case law. If, or when, this happens it will inevitably lead to amendments in legislation.

7.3.1 HMC&E guidance and requirements

HMC&E has two distinct branches which are heavily involved in EDI. The first is responsible for VAT within the UK and the second is responsible for all customs matters.

7.3.1.1 VAT

There are guidelines published which refer specifically to transactions involving VAT – primarily invoices and credit notes. Unless these requirements are met, companies will be unable to claim any VAT back. See Annex H, 'HM Customs & Excise guidance on EDI usage', for the text of these guidelines. These guidelines are imposed under the Value Added Tax Act 1983.

7.3.1.2 Customs

HMC&E is very active in the use of EDI for the speeding of clearance for imports and exports. Also there is now a service for accepting all statistical information for EU cross-border VAT purposes. This system, run by the Electronic Data Capture Service, usually referred to as EDCS, can accept data from a number of different networks and went 'live' to coincide with the creation of the Single European Market on 31 December 1992.

7.3.2 Encryption and its implications

As discussed in Chapter 4, 'UN/EDIFACT', and later in Chapter 8, 'Security', there are many good reasons for considering the use of encryption, either partial or total. However, it must be borne in mind that there may be legal restrictions on such use. As long as the transactions are within the UK there is no problem but elsewhere, including certain parts of Europe, it may be illegal to transmit encrypted data. This may be both within a country and, more likely, across national boundaries. Clarification of the position with particular trading partners will be needed if there are any plans to make use of any transactions which might involve encryption.

7.3.3 Digital signatures

Following logically from discussion of encryption is the topic of digital, or electronic, signatures. These are used, as with traditional handwritten signatures, as a means of authentication – I am who I claim to be. Suitable, carefully generated digital signatures can give a higher degree of confidence than handwritten signatures since they are far more difficult to forge.

There appear to be no obstacles to the use of digital signatures since English Law nowhere stipulates what precise form a signature should take. Other legal jurisdictions may take a different view, although many with their origins in English Law have a similar view. International acceptance of digital signatures is boosted by the definition found in the United Nations *Convention on International Bills of Exchange and International Promissory Notes* which states:

> 'signature' means a handwritten signature, its facsimile or an equivalent authentication effected by any other means.

For futher discussion of the mechanics involved in generating electronic signatures, see Chapter 8, 'Security'.

8 Security

In paper-based systems, where two trading partners exchange information, there are checks to prevent clerical errors and fraudulent requests. When implementing an EDI system, there is a need to replace those checks with a security system that is at least as effective. This chapter discusses the threats to an EDI message during transmission and the techniques that exist to protect against those threats.

Throughout this Guide, checks such as these are referred to as 'Business Controls', irrespective of their application.

8.1 EDI Security

Security of information is defined in terms of confidentiality, integrity and availability (CIA). One of the first issues in determining the level of security to apply to an EDI message is to identify and evaluate the risks to which it is exposed (based on CIA). A standard method of performing this evaluation is provided by CCTA's Risk Analysis and Management Method (CRAMM). Consult the Departmental Security Officer/Departmental IT Security Officer for advice on EDI security, including the use of Risk Analysis and Management Methods.

To secure an EDI message costs time, effort and money. However, most messages deserve some security. There is a base level of security good practice which must be applied to systems and will protect messages of low value.

For EDI messages that require extra levels of security, two aspects need to be considered:

- the physical and logical environment of each trading partner's site

- the transmission of the EDI messages.

An EDI message is no different from any other information created and stored within a computer system and this Guide does not address the physical or logical environment, ie access control to hardware, software and data storage. These are described in the CCTA IT Infrastructure Library module titled *Computer Installation and Acceptance* and, in greater detail, in the CCTA IS Guide titled *Security and Privacy*.

EDI Implementation Guide

However, it should be remembered that the physical and logical security of trading partners' sites is important. If such controls are inadequate and are not at least mirrored at each site, then the investment will have been wasted.

The exchange of EDI messages between two trading partners has to take place through a public or private network – the EDI message may be processed or altered prior to reaching its intended recipient, ie during transmission. This chapter considers the threats posed during transmission and the countermeasures available to protect the EDI message against loss of CIA during this phase.

8.2 What are the threats?

In paper-driven systems there are many checks to identify errors and fraudulent actions. Experienced clerical staff often identify these errors and actions, providing a secure environment. Many of the threats to paper-driven systems are equally applicable to EDI systems, particularly those related to verification of collected data before processing, along with the countermeasures to protect against them.

For EDI messages a threat is any action that would compromise CIA. Some examples of these threats are:

- loss of confidentiality through:

    - accidental or deliberate misrouting of EDI messages
    - hacking, including browsing
    - oversight of the message, including through passive monitoring or line tapping
    - theft of equipment or media that may contain the EDI message and subsequent access

- loss of integrity through:

    - fraud on the part of sender or recipient
    - message replay (resending an already successfully processed message)
    - system abuse for profit or gain
    - message repudiation by either the message originator or the recipient (the practice of denying having sent or received the message)
    - changing or inserting additional information into the EDI message

- loss of availability through:
  - misrouting
  - deliberate deletion (hacking or viruses)
  - accidental deletion (system or operator error).

To protect against loss of CIA, electronic countermeasures offer equal, if not better, protection than their equivalent paper-based processes. They fall into five categories:

- user authentication

- message content integrity

- confidentiality

- non-repudiation of origin and receipt

- message sequencing.

These countermeasures are 'transmission-oriented' – normal practice will provide protection while data is resident on its host system. Also, these items should be seen in the context of the operational controls in use for a fuller picture (see Chapter 11, 'Operational management').

8.3 The Countermeasures

8.3.1 User Authentication

In a paper-based system the identity of the sender can usually be verified by examination of the sender's signature in conjunction with the physical characteristics of the received document, eg letterhead and water-marks. By using special postal techniques, such as registered letters or person-to-person courier, a sender can be sure that the document was in fact received by the authorised recipient.

It is not possible to mimic these physical characteristics in an electronic document. However, a unique electronic *digital signature* can be generated by the sender and attached to the electronic message, which will perform the same function.

A digital signature is a unique number that may be generated by taking all or part of an electronic message and processing it by using a set of procedures, known as an *encryption algorithm*, and a variable called a *key*. The digital signature is then either sent with the EDI message, or under separate cover, to the recipient. On receipt the digital signature is decrypted using a key held by the recipient. This produces an exact replica of the originally encrypted part of the message. Then, by a direct comparison of the original and decrypted replica, verification of the authenticity of the sender is achieved.

This process can also work in reverse where the recipient replies to the message originator with an acknowledgment containing the recipient's digital signature, providing end-to-end user authentication.

A detailed description of the development and deployment of a digital-signature-based solution is included in the case study based on the EU-funded Information Net and Card for the Adapted Management of European Road Transport and Traffic (INCA) project. See Annex A, 'Case studies'.

Two techniques are associated with the use of encryption and keys:

- symmetric or private key systems

- asymmetric or public/private key systems.

In a symmetric system both parties use the same secret key and the same encryption algorithm. The commonest example of symmetric encryption is the Data Encryption Standard (DES).

In an asymmetric system, there is a public key, which may be known to many people, and a secret key, known only to the authorised sender. This technique can only provide authentication of the sender. The most commonly found encryption algorithm for use in public/private key systems is RSA, named after its authors, Rivest Shamir and Adleman.

There are many other encryption algorithms that are used in different circumstances. There are also issues with key management that must be taken into consideration when implementing authentication. These are discussed later in

Chapter 8
Security

this chapter. It should be remembered that encryption takes a lot of computing power and that encrypting complete messages should not be undertaken lightly.

8.3.2 Message content integrity

In a paper-based system there is no fool-proof way of examining a document to ensure its physical integrity, but with an electronic message the computation of a *seal* or *hash* number makes this possible. A seal or hash number is one which has no external value, but is computed to serve as a checksum for integrity security purposes.

The seal is computed from the complete EDI message by using an appropriate cryptographic algorithm, such as Modification Detection Code. The seal is then either appended to the message or sent separately. To check that the message has not been altered the seal is recalculated and compared.

Thus, the algorithm will produce a different and, therefore, unique hash code or seal for every EDI message. This will be sent with the EDI message and, upon receipt, the same algorithm will be used to generate a new seal based on the received message. If the new seal is identical

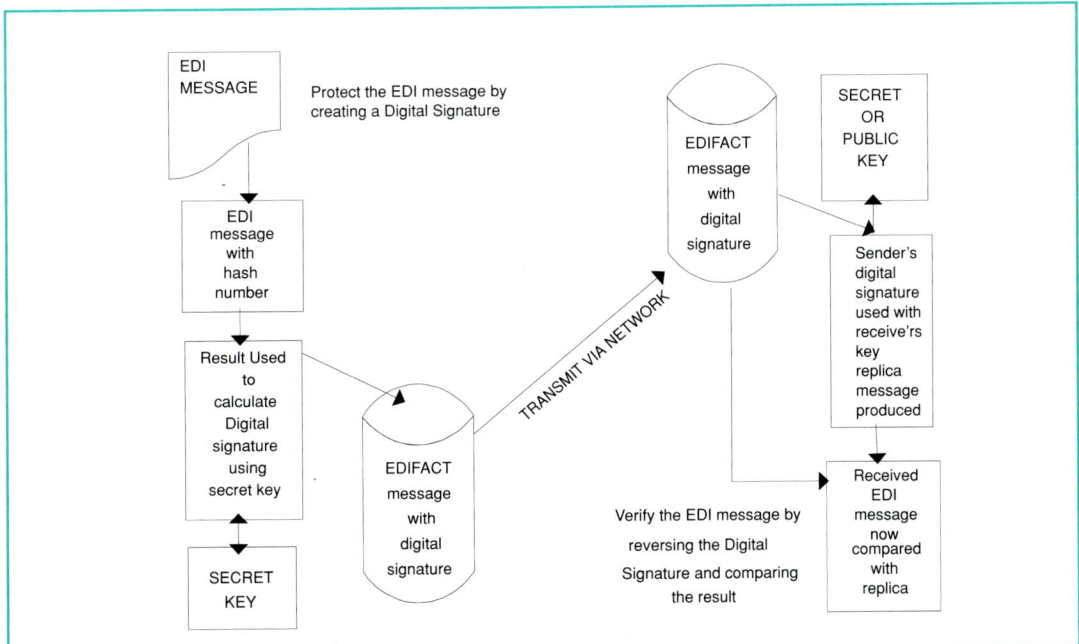

Figure 29: Authentication and integrity checking

EDI Implementation Guide

to the one sent with the message, the recipient can feel comfortable that the message has not been changed or altered in transit.

This seal is itself unprotected, so anyone having the algorithm could potentially intercept the message, decrypt it, alter it and rebuild it; therefore, it has to be encrypted using the same techniques as described for user authentication and hence user authentication and integrity-checking can be achieved using the same mechanisms and are often combined. This combination of techniques is shown in Figure 29.

8.3.3 Confidentiality

To ensure confidentiality of content, either the whole EDI message or just the information to be protected must be scrambled in such a way that it cannot be understood by any unauthorised person or application. This is identical to the encoding of a paper-based document. To do this, symmetric encryption systems are generally used (asymmetric systems are not recommended within government departments for general confidentiality purposes).

There are two main reasons for not using asymmetric systems for general confidentiality purposes:

- their relative inefficiency/speed when compared with symmetric systems – this will, of course, become less significant with increases in computing power and advanced technology

- they are in greater danger from mathematical breakthroughs in number theory.

The use of symmetric keys does require rigid key management as any disclosure of the common secret key will compromise confidentiality. Key management using asymmetric systems generally does not suffer from the inefficiency problem, but is still vulnerable to mathematical breakthroughs.

When implementing confidentiality by encryption of the data, it is normal also to implement user authentication by the creation of a digital signature, and message content integrity by the inclusion of a seal. The combination of each of these countermeasures provides a high level of security as the EDI message is protected from all threats (though no message can ever be completely safe). However, it should not be forgotten that security processing puts a heavy load on computing resources and can significantly increase costs. Thus, the level of control selected needs to be a balance between the risk and the cost of managing that risk.

8.3.4 Non-repudiation of origin

Non-repudiation of origin protects the receiver of an EDI message from the sender's denial of having sent it. In a paper-based system, the physical existence of the document can provide proof of origin, although a fake document could prove difficult to detect.

To provide proof of origin, the EDI message has to contain something that can only have originated from the authorised originator of the message. This could be, and in most cases is, the digital signature, if it has been generated using an asymmetric, key-based system where the encryption key is known only to the originator.

Providing non-repudiation of origin alone cannot fully protect the EDI message. There is the situation where the same, protected EDI message is transmitted a second time, either by accident or fraud. To protect against this occurring a system of message sequencing and date/time stamping must be implemented.

8.3.5 Non-repudiation of receipt

Non-repudiation of receipt protects the message originator from the recipient denying ever having received the EDI message.

In a paper-based system, this is achieved by the recipient returning a document such as an acknowledging receipt. In an electronic system, a similar procedure is used, requiring the recipient to return an acknowledgment message. This EDI message must contain information that can only have originated from the original message as well as the digital signature of the recipient, thus proving that the authorised recipient must have received the original message.

Both the original message and the acknowledgement message should be protected for user authentication and message content integrity check.

EDI Implementation Guide

8.3.6 Message sequencing

Sequencing an EDI message protects the recipient from loss or fraudulent duplication of that message. A message could be re-sent in its original state, which, when received, will pass any security verification, such as user authentication or message content integrity. For financial messages this may result in a double payment. Equally the loss or delay of an EDI message may cause delays such as late delivery or increased costs due to time penalties.

To prevent loss or replay, a message number is included in the EDI message. The number should be protected for message content integrity. On receipt of the EDI message, its number is verified to see that it has been incremented by one over the previous number. Any discrepancies will indicate loss or replay.

8.4   Choice of security technique

There are many trade-offs between the different techniques, encryption algorithms and key management systems, but there are few precedents that provide guidance in making the correct choices. Until recently there were no firm recommendations from the UN/EDIFACT board. This has led to organisations implementing EDI security to meet their own requirements.

When implementing secure EDI it is impractical to assign individual techniques to each type of EDI message. It is better to apply a consistent set of techniques across a department or organisation as part of a consistent policy.

There are, however, a number of factors to consider that may affect the choice of technique, such as the algorithm for encryption, the data conversions involved, key management techniques used and the role of certification authorities, if used. The choice of technique will be influenced by what is to be achieved and any acceptable compromises, for example, a trade-off could be made so that cheaper/more readily available/usable techniques are used if thresholds for such transactions are set, ie the system reverts to manual operation at a certain point.

8.4.1 Choice of algorithm

There are different algorithms for the security functions described (hashing, digital signatures, confidentiality, etc) and such algorithms may complement each other in security terms. The major point is that selection will

Chapter 8
Security

depend on the security functionality required (ITSEC issues).

The choice of a symmetric or asymmetric algorithm for encryption has an affect on the processing power required. Symmetric systems require less computing power and are, therefore, more suited when large quantities of data have to be encrypted, for example, when whole UN/EDIFACT messages require to be protected for confidentiality.

In choosing to encrypt an EDI message it is important to consider:

- capability of trading partner (do they have the same techniques or computing power?)

- is there trust between trading partners to allow the sharing of the same private key?

- cost and overhead of key management

- whether existing standards are applicable to trading partners

- any mandatory requirements (eg Government policy requiring departments to use only algorithms approved by Communications Electronics Security Group)

- legal requirements such as contractual limitations between partners

- laws governing the use of encryption (particularly in trans-border communications).

8.4.2 Data conversions

The use of mathematical algorithms to compute integrity values and digital signatures introduces two problems:

- the internal representation of the data used

- the transmission of the resultant digital signature.

The value of the digital signature calculated is dependent on the internal representation of the EDI message used. Therefore, the computation of the digital signature and its authentication by the recipient must be executed using the same internal representation. There can be no change to the internal representation of the data during its transmission, such as an ASCII to EBCDIC code conversion, hence it is important that the sender indicates to the recipient the representation used to produce the digital signature. The digital signature itself is a number with a binary value. Again, this causes problems with transmission and interpretation software. It is essential that both data and the digital signature are in the same representation prior to starting the validation process.

To avoid conversion problems it is recommended that no changes are applied to the data or the digital signatures during transmission. If, however, conversions have to take place then a technique known as *filtering* has to be applied.

Filtering is used to ensure that the data and the digital signature's binary representation are reversibly mapped using a filter algorithm. The filter converts the bit-string representation of the data and digital signature to a value that can be transmitted and converted. Once received, it is reverse-filtered to produce the original binary value.

8.4.3 Key Management

Potentially, symmetric systems have greater overheads since each pair of trading partners may require a secret key. Thus more rigorous key management is required than with asymmetric systems where the same secret key is used for each trading partner. Symmetric systems are relatively easy to manage when only a small number of trading partners are involved. However, if the community of trading partners is dynamic in its growth, then keeping the key secret becomes increasingly difficult.

The distribution of the secret key requires consideration. It can be exchanged on paper, but as the key can be complicated and extensive, this is not practical. It can be distributed on diskette or smart card. Diskettes are not really secure and smart cards are only secure if they carry encryption.

With asymmetric systems there are two keys, a private key that never leaves the sender's site and a public key that can be known to anyone. This makes the management of an asymmetric key system easier. But there is still the

Chapter 8
Security

problem of the protection of the public key. If security is not to be compromised it is essential that the receiver of a message is sure that the public key that is used to validate the EDI message belongs to the intended trading partner and not someone masquerading as that trading partner. This problem can be solved with the use of key certification and directory services and a trusted third party, sometimes referred to as a Notary Service or Certification Authority (CA), although other techniques, such as mutual exchange, may offer the same benefits.

8.4.4 Certification Authorities

A Certification Authority is a third party that is entrusted by a community of trading partners to ensure the secure and correct allocation of keys.

With a symmetric key system, where both trading partners have the same secret key, the CA may generate the secret key and distribute it to the trading partners. With asymmetric key systems the certification authority may generate and distribute the secret key to the authorised sender and the public key to all other members of the community.

There are two techniques for the distribution and management of keys:

- the public key is sent separately

- the public key is contained in a *certificate*.

8.4.4.1 Public key sent separately to each trading partner

The CA has its own public/private key pair. The secret key is never disclosed to anyone but the public key is known to all members of the community. Therefore any EDI message sent by the CA may be authenticated by any member of the community. The name and public key of a new member of a community is distributed to all members of that community in an EDI message, protected by the secret key of the CA.

The receiver will have to store the public keys of all trading partners in a community on a data base. Each time an EDI message is received, the data base will be used to look up the sender's public key. It is important that the name used to look up the public key is agreed by the community and contained within the secure part of the EDI message. See Chapter 4, 'UN/EDIFACT', for fuller

157

EDI Implementation Guide

details of where in the UN/EDIFACT standard this could be achieved.

8.4.4.2 Public key contained in a certificate

The public/private key pair for a new member is generated by the CA. The secret key is sent to the new member using any of the distribution techniques described previously. This is depicted in Figure 30.

The public key is enclosed in a certificate that contains the following information:

- name of the new member

- issue and expiry date of the certificate

- certificate reference number

- public key of the new member

- digital signature of the CA.

The digital signature of the certification authority provides integrity and authentication of the certificate. The certificate is then attached to each EDI message sent by the new member to any other trading partner. The trading partner will need to know that the key is still valid and that it has not been withdrawn. It is at this point that registration and directory services come into their own as the tools by which the CA operates. The recipient uses the public key of the CA to determine the public key of the sender, which is then used to authenticate the EDI message.

8.4.5 Key Management Recommendations

The previous sections have described algorithms, key management and the use of a CA for the distribution of keys. When implementing secure EDI, the following should be considered:

- algorithms

  Asymmetric systems should be used with hashing and other algorithms to provide integrity, authentication and non-repudiation.

  Symmetric algorithms should be used only for confidentiality, and should be implemented only if confidentiality is absolutely essential. Government departments should consult the Communications

Chapter 8
Security

Electronic Security Group (CESG) of GCHQ, who are the national authority on encryption matters, on the selection of encryption systems and algorithms.

- key management

    For small, stable communities a lead trading partner should consider becoming a CA for that community. For simplicity the public keys of each member of the community should be distributed separately rather than using certificates. This will reduce the complexity of key processing at the recipient site as the processing of a certificate requires a two-stage decryption process.

    For large or dynamic communities a certification authority should be appointed by the community. Certificate processing is recommended as it reduces the administration overhead of introducing new members to that community.

- data conversion

    To remove the need for filtering techniques, no data conversion should take place until the EDI message authentication has taken place. If this is not done, it becomes almost impossible to ensure that what was

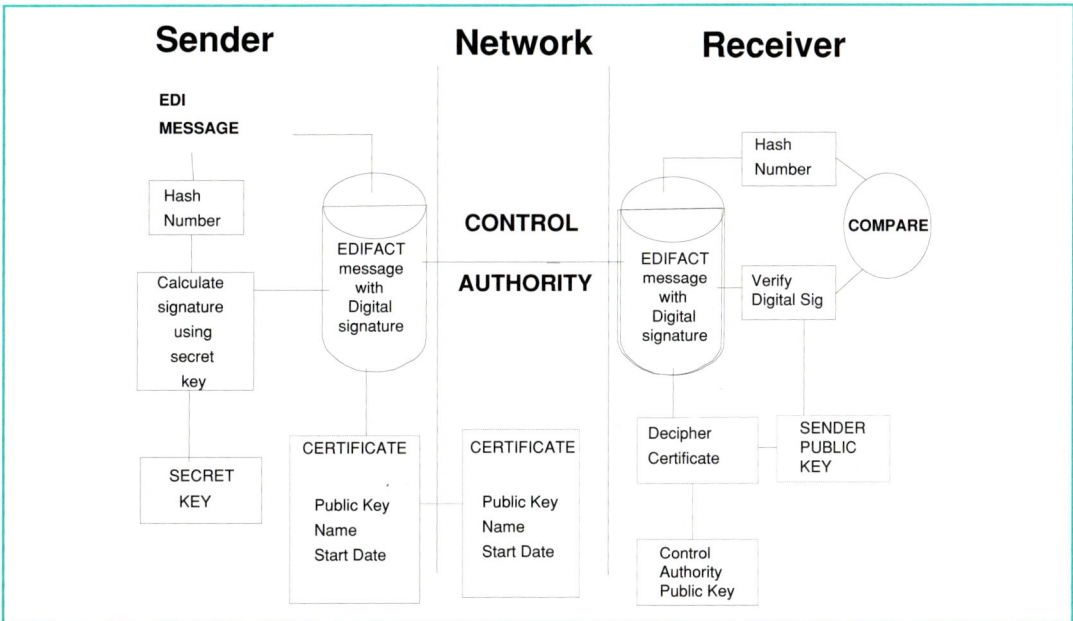

Figure 30:   Certification Authority mechanisms

EDI Implementation Guide

sent or purported to have been sent was the same as what was received.

8.5 UN/EDIFACT security recommendations

The need for an optional facility to provide security techniques in UN/EDIFACT messages has been recognised for many years. At the time of writing this Guide, draft techniques have recently been published. The UN/EDIFACT Security Joint Working Group (SJWG) has stated that the long-term resolution of security requirements should be handled syntactically, but the process for ISO approval is a lengthy one, and the immediate requirement would not be addressed. Therefore, an interim syntactical solution for security has been developed as a recommendation, and is to be adopted by UN/EDIFACT.

In addition to adopting a syntactical solution, the SJWG was mandated to convert the *FUNACK* (functional acknowledgment) message (now renamed *AUTACK*) to be a service message with its own directory set.

For more information on the UN/EDIFACT recommendations, see *EDIFACT Security Implementation Guidelines*, published by the SJWG.

To permit the required security functions to be applied to any UN/EDIFACT message, a security header and a security trailer need to be inserted into the existing message structure at the time of message transfer. The header comprises two segment groups and the trailer one segment group.

The security header segment groups are inserted immediately after the 'UNH' (message header segment), and the security trailer segment immediately before the 'UNT' (message trailer segment).

One further consideration is that, if such a message structure were presented to a trading partner's translator software without prior agreement, the translator would generate an error report, and probably reject the EDI message. Therefore, the UN/EDIFACT recommendation is that, when there are security headers and trailers within messages, both trading partners agree to use RTOx in the 'UNB' interchange header syntax identifier (data element 0001) in place of the UNOx. (See Figure 18 on p. 61 for a layout of the 'UNB' segment.)

Chapter 8
Security

8.5.1 Security Segment Groups

The UN/EDIFACT security recommendations defined the use of two security header groups and a trailer group, as depicted in Figure 31. As can be seen, this allows security controls at the individual message level as opposed to the interchange level.

Segment group 1 for the header contains a header segment, 'USH', and an algorithm segment, 'USA'. Segment group 2 contains a certificate segment, 'USC', an algorithm segment, 'USA', and a security result segment, 'USR'.

The general rule behind the design is that the first segment group identifies the security mechanisms applied to the message in which the group is included and contains:

- security technique applied to the message

- identification of the parties involved

- date of creation of the security elements

- identification of the algorithm used.

When public keys are used, at least one segment group 2 is always required. Within this segment group there will be three 'USA' segments: one for the certified public key, one for the CA public key, and one for the CA hash function used to calculate the certificate. Segment group 2 contains the signature computed by the CA in the result segment, 'USR'.

The security trailer group ends the security segment's presence in a message with a trailer segment, 'UST'. It also has a security result segment, 'USR', that contains information corresponding to the security functions specified in the 'USH' segment.

8.5.2 AUTACK

The *AUTACK* message is a Secure Authentication and Acknowledgement message, used when separate message security is required. There are two business reasons why a separate message may be used:

- to provide security for one or more messages in a single separate message

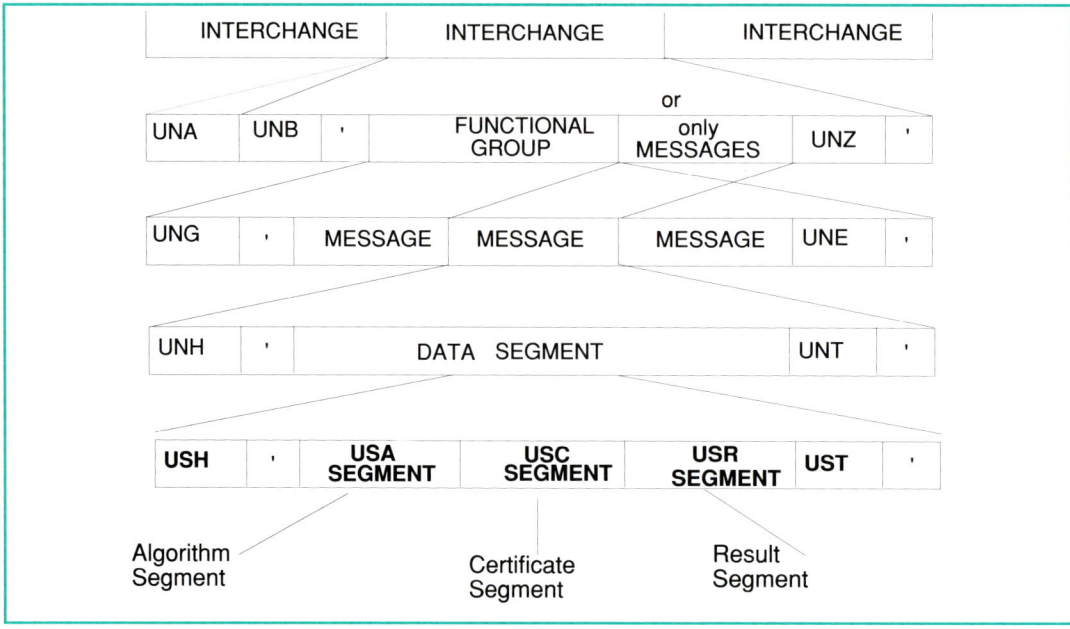

Figure 31: UN/EDIFACT security segments

- to provide a secured non-repudiation service in the form of a separate message.

It is used by the originator of a message, or a party acting on behalf of the originator, to facilitate message origin authentication, integrity of message content, and message sequence integrity or non-repudiation of origin. It is sent separately from the message to which it applies. The *AUTACK* cannot provide confidentiality services.

For a recipient, the *AUTACK* message is used to confirm receipt of the message, to confirm integrity validation and for non-repudiation of receipt.

8.6 Security hardware and software

The hardware and software requirements are determined not just by the security techniques to be used, but also by the level at which EDI messages are to be secured: department or individual user.

When securing at a department level, the EDI management software must reside in a secure environment and on a secure computer. This is because the secret keys will normally remain resident in the computer, although they could reside on a removable medium, such as a diskette, CD-ROM or smart card.

Chapter 8
Security

Removable media are preferred by Government but, as always, this is a question of defining an acceptable compromise between what is achievable, sensible and operable based on the functionality required.

When securing at an individual level, the secret key, or the information used to generate the secret key, has to reside on a removable medium, such as a diskette, smart card or swipe card, access to the fixed hardware must be controlled by a biometric or password technique.

Smart cards, small plastic cards that look like credit cards, are preferred to the traditional swipe cards. They contain a microchip instead of a magnetic stripe and can store and process larger amounts of data. Smart cards can verify that the device reading the card is in fact authorised to do so, thus providing a higher level of security, as well as sealing and signing EDI messages. They are also resistant to fraud, owing to their complexity and the need for sophisticated equipment to reprogram or reproduce. However, the key term is 'resistant to fraud'; this means that, in a normal environment, fraud is much harder to commit. The system implementor has to consider many factors, including potential attacker knowledge of card protocols, the security of the card manufacture and registration processes, the environment in which the card is to be used, and the security functionality (strength of mechanisms) provided on the card. The key point is that many current smart cards are unprotected except in the sense that attackers have not got access to readers and protocols. There is a threat to the security of systems using such cards, which comes from disgruntled employees involved/once involved in card manufacture, and electronics engineers and students. The threat will increase with the passage of time as the relevant knowledge needed to attack such systems spreads (eg over Internet bulletin boards).

To implement security techniques, it is necessary to have a translator which is capable of handling them. When implementing encryption on either all or part of an EDI message, the translator must be capable of external routine calls to allow operation of the encryption. The reverse also applies for received messages.

EDI Implementation Guide

8.7 Audit

EDI audit trails, activity logs within computer systems, fall into two categories:

- maintained on the user site

- maintained by a Value Added Network.

They are primarily used as a management tool and cannot alone be used as a security technique. They do not contain a log of the EDI message content but a summary of reference numbers and control information for the transmission, such as:

- sender and recipient IDs

- date and time stamps for both send and receive

- details from the UN/EDIFACT 'UNB' header

- information on the transmission.

This information may be used by auditors for tracking message flows. It cannot be used to establish the content of a message or for non-repudiation and authenticity checking. EDI Gateway software often makes use of these audit trails in order to build end-to-end tracking and automated control of individual business transactions. Examples of how this can be used are given in 6.5, 'EDI gateways'. Thus end system audit – who did what, what is in the transaction, etc – tends to be one of the areas that has to be defined as part of the specific implementation and is closely linked to the existing audit capabilities in the existing system/process. One of the roles of the Operational Attachment is to define responsibilities in this area. Internal Auditors should be consulted to define current best practice in this area. It is also helpful to refer to the Government Information Systems Audit Manual (published by HMSO), Section E15, which deals more fully with audit in an EDI environment.

8.8 X.400 Security implementation

Very few security features were included in the 1984 recommendations for X.400 services. Passwords were exchanged at association set-up and the 'body part' of the message that was to be exchanged could be encrypted. There was strong pressure on the X.400 authorities to rectify this situation.

Chapter 8
Security

In evaluating security issues a focus was placed on the security features to be added to the Message Transfer Service itself and not to the messages directly. As a result, the 1988 recommendations have secure techniques that are based on public and secret keys and operate in the message transfer layer. These provide protection between the User Agent and the Message Transfer Agent, and between User Agents.

All the techniques described in this chapter can be facilitated by X.400, both at the message level, eg within the EDI message, and at the X.400 level, where the digital signatures are carried in the X.400 headers.

Non-repudiation messages and certificate handling are also catered for by content integrity checks and non-repudiation services.

EDI Implementation Guide

Chapter 9
EDI in Finance

9 EDI in Finance

Electronic funds transfers have been available for many years. However, it is only recently that EDI messages have been applied to allow the reconciliation of payments to outstanding invoices to be automated. Although it is not necessary to have an existing EDI system before Financial EDI can be implemented, trading partners who have established EDI links for their supply processes consider it a natural progression to close the loop and make their payments electronically. This chapter describes some of the features of Financial EDI and highlights some of the implementation and operational issues that need to be considered.

9.1 What is Financial EDI?

There are a number of financial transactions carried out by a typical organisation. The term *Financial EDI* is, however, normally restricted to the part of the trading cycle in which payments are made to a supplier who, in turn, reconciles those payments back to the original invoices.

Figure 32 illustrates a typical trading cycle. The customer places an order for goods or services with a supplier, receives them and is subsequently invoiced for them. Once an invoice has been received and approved a financial transaction is required to pay the outstanding amount. This can be handled electronically using Financial EDI.

When payments are to be made to a supplier, the invoiced customer generates a set of electronic messages. These contain all the information required for the funds transfer and, most importantly, also include accurate reconciliation information. This information will, in turn, be used by the supplier to automatically reconcile the payment back to the original invoice.

Many trading partners will initially implement EDI links between their respective purchasing and delivery systems to automate the ordering and invoicing process. These links will normally provide the greatest initial savings to the organisations. Financial EDI completes the electronic loop by linking the accounts payable and accounts receivable systems as well.

A significant portion of the workload of any accounts receivable department is concerned with reconciling

EDI Implementation Guide

received payments and remittance advices to the original invoice. Financial EDI can be used to tie the remittance advice to the payment, thus removing one of these tasks. It also allows accurate reference information, such as the invoice numbers being paid, to be passed with the payment. This enables the payments to be reconciled automatically.

As commercial bank charges for Financial EDI transactions drop, and the inter-bank communications links spread, Financial EDI will expand in the private sector. The UK banks have established EDI links to allow this form of communication. The links are generically

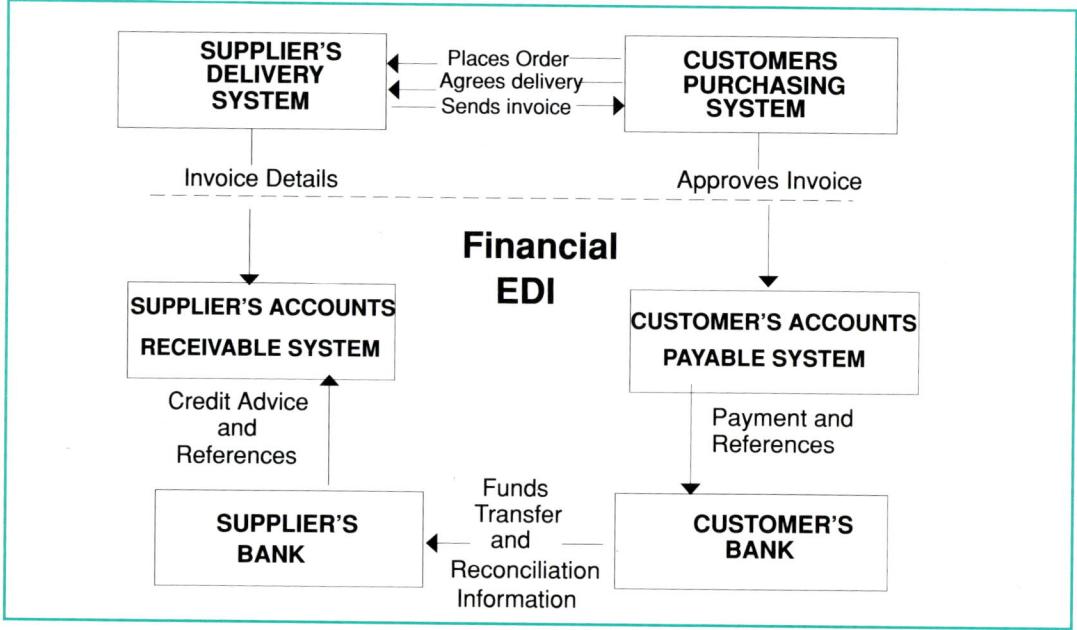

Figure 32: Financial EDI in context

referred to as the Inter-bank Data eXchange (IDX) and are mainly direct links between participating banks, although some VAN connections are also used. Most government departments, Agencies and a large number of public sector bodies use Paymaster as a common bank. They are, therefore, potentially well positioned to take advantage of Financial EDI, as will be explained later in the chapter.

9.2 Benefits of Financial EDI   Financial EDI will provide all of the advantages of any EDI-based business process. In addition to these it closes the electronic trading loop, and greatly simplifies reconciliation of payments.

Chapter 9
EDI in Finance

Financial EDI can be described as a progression from an integrated electronic supply process. There are three reasons for saying this:

- a supply process driven by EDI can deliver competitive advantage to both trading parties: reducing cycle times to just-in-time delivery; improving accuracy; improving stock control. Financial EDI produces a less balanced business case, with most of the benefits appearing in the supplier's accounts receivable function, as will be explained later in this section

- Financial EDI can involve four trading partners for each transaction, increasing the complexity of implementation. It is, therefore, better to gain experience on a simple EDI implementation before tackling Financial EDI

- the primary benefit of Financial EDI is the accurate reconciliation of payments to invoices. The best way to ensure that the reference information is correct is to supply the invoice electronically.

9.2.1 Benefits for both customer and supplier

Although the supplier will receive the bulk of the benefits, Financial EDI can be used to derive benefits for both trading parties. The following benefits may be realised by both the customer originating the payment, and the supplier receiving the payment electronically:

- settlement will become cheaper and more cost-effective as fewer queries and exceptional payments are required to complete a transaction. This, in turn, reduces the workload on the accounts payable department

- the potential for delays in receipt are reduced as transaction dates will be pre-defined

- Financial EDI completes the electronic trading loop, ensuring a higher level of data integrity throughout the entire trading cycle

- payments can be outsourced to an independent third party, who can arrange payment. This agent can then select the appropriate medium for payment, including the production of hard-copy remittance advices for suppliers who cannot operate electronically.

EDI Implementation Guide

For cross-border payments, Financial EDI confers a number of additional benefits:

- transactions will occur at a pre-defined time

- the rates of exchange can be set

- bank charges and their allocation can be pre-set

- language compatibility is ensured through international standards

- there is an increased likelihood that payment will be received as there are no manual tasks which could interrupt the process once the payment has been authorised.

9.2.2 Benefits for the supplier

Financial EDI allows a detailed list of invoiced items to be accurately passed with the payment, and thus automatically loaded into the receiving application without manual intervention or re-keying. This improves the speed and accuracy of the reconciliation process, the largest clerical effort in a typical finance department.

There may always be the need to receive paper-based payments. Financial EDI, however, greatly reduces the workload within the accounts receivable department. These staff can then focus more effectively on collecting outstanding invoices and other 'added value' activities.

Financial EDI also gives a higher certainty of payment. Trading partners using Financial EDI tend to authorise payments more quickly. These payments would then normally be held, either by the customer's payments system or by their bank, and released in time to meet the payment terms agreed with the supplier.

Better cash management is also possible. The accuracy and certainty of timing provided by Financial EDI can improve forecasting accuracy for:

- the negotiation of float times, ie the amount of time that funds must be set aside to cover outstanding invoices

- pre-advice of funds availability

- cash flow prediction.

9.2.3 Benefits for the customer

Although the customer initiating payment may not see any workload reductions, the improved accuracy of the payment cycle can be used to obtain real benefits:

- improved cash management. By using Financial EDI, the exact timing of the payment can be determined. This, in turn, allows customers to forecast outgoing cash flows more accurately

- improved trading relationship. Customers using Financial EDI can assure their trading partners that payments will be accurate and timely. This certainty of payment can be used to negotiate a discount from the supplier

- float periods can be negotiated and managed accurately through the improved payment forecasts

- the underlying processes can also be streamlined to minimise the manual intervention required. Some of these payment techniques are detailed in the next section

- overheads in stationery costs, cheques and postage are also removed.

9.2.4 Other Considerations

Although there are a number of benefits associated with Financial EDI, the technique is not by itself easy to justify. However, for those already using EDI, it can be made an extension of their existing systems relatively easily. When preparing the business case for Financial EDI it is worth bearing in mind the following points:

- there are a number of operational costs which add an additional overhead to the daily trading cycle. These overheads include additional service prices, internal administration costs and bank transaction charges

- the recipient of Financial EDI payments will usually obtain a greater number of benefits from Financial EDI. Where trading partners make payments of similar value and complexity to each other, this imbalance can be offset if both implement Financial EDI at the same time. If this is not the case the recipient may have to consider a discount or another similar incentive to encourage their trading partners to switch to Financial EDI. These costs will also have to be built into the business case

- the benefits to the supplier of Financial EDI will only be obtained if the accuracy of the reference information can be assured

- the benefits are greatest where EDI is already used for other transactions in the supply chain and where Financial EDI is a natural extension

- the benefits will be proportional to the amount and complexity of financial information to be processed, and greatest where the timing of the transaction must be assured

- it is not necessary to alter the payment cycle time when introducing EDI. Many assume that EDI will allow earlier payment, which will then introduce additional financing costs for the customer or the Treasury. This may be so, but should only be so if the overall justification makes it worthwhile. Many users simply use EDI in this environment to ensure regular and timely payment as opposed to early payment.

As with many EDI implementations, most benefits will be obtained in the long term. Financial EDI must, therefore, be part of a considered strategy. The initial costs of setting up a Financial EDI link will be greater than for other EDI implementations. This is largely due to the extra security, legal and audit controls that must be applied.

9.2.5 Remittance reconciliation

The real power of Financial EDI comes from the complex remittance information that can be passed in the extended payment and remittance advice messages. Because financial institutions charge per transaction, most organisations will batch together payments on a regular basis. Thus a payment could be received for all of one invoice, plus one item from another invoice and a part payment on a third.

This practice makes it very difficult for a paper-based accounts receivable department to accurately reconcile payments. Monies can be received without remittance notes; reference numbers can be misquoted; and documents can be mislaid.

Using the UN/EDIFACT standards for remittance advice and extended payment orders, all of this information can be passed with the payment. If the original invoices were received via EDI the ordering customer can be sure that they are quoting the correct reference numbers with the payment.

All of this means that payments can be reconciled accurately and automatically. This allows the accounts receivable department to concentrate on bad debts and gives the treasurer a clear picture of outstanding invoices.

9.3 Financial EDI in the private sector

Figure 33 depicts a simple example of Financial EDI. In the private sector, Financial EDI transactions will always require several parties:

- the customer making the payment
- the customer's bank
- the supplier's bank
- the supplier receiving the payment.

Of course, the customer and supplier could share the same bank. This simplifies the process further as there is no need to pass on the payment to a third party. In the

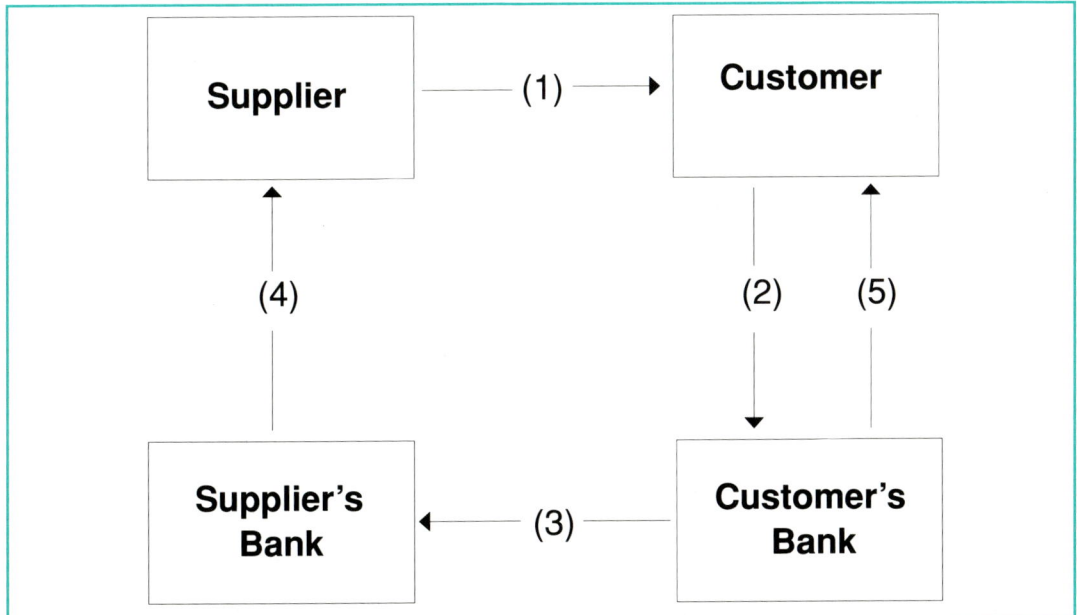

Figure 33: An example of private sector Financial EDI

example shown, all parties are capable of handling EDI messages. To minimise the number of direct connections required, the messages would normally be exchanged using a Value Added Network.

The data flows shown in Figure 33 are explained below.

1   Invoice

    The supplier's delivery system issues an invoice for goods or services supplied. The reference number from this invoice is passed on to the supplier's accounts receivable system to aid reconciliation of the subsequent payment.

2   Payment Order

    The customer issues a payment order to its bank using Financial EDI messages. In addition to the financial information this message would contain a detailed breakdown of the invoices and items to which this payment relates.

3   Value Transfer

    The customer's bank transfers the amount specified, and passes on the reference numbers contained in the payment order to the supplier's bank.

4   Credit advice

    The supplier's bank issues a credit advice for the supplier's account, including the reference numbers passed with the payment. The supplier can then use these numbers to reconcile the payment to the original invoices.

5   Statement

    The customer's bank issues a statement containing the payment details. This will normally be carried out independently of the rest of the transaction and may not even use EDI.

This is the simplest form of Financial EDI. It does, however, require both banks to pass on the reference information with the normal financial transactions. The

Chapter 9
EDI in Finance

existing UK electronic funds transfer (EFT) mechanisms, the Banks Automated Clearing System (BACS) and the Clearing House Automated Payments System (CHAPS) allow only a very limited amount of reference information to be passed with the payment. This is often not sufficient to accurately reconcile the payment to an original invoice. Also, many commercial banks do not currently offer a Financial EDI service to their customers. Those that do often charge a premium rate for each transaction.

The reconciliation information can, therefore, also be passed in a remittance advice directly from the customer to the supplier.

9.4 Examples of Financial EDI

Financial EDI may be carried out in several ways:

- the banks can handle all parts of the transaction

- the customer can transfer the funds through the banks and separately inform the supplier of the payment details

- the bank, or other third party, can act as a payments broker.

The exact strategy chosen will depend on the capabilities of all trading partners.

9.4.1 Example 1 – Financial EDI using a banking service

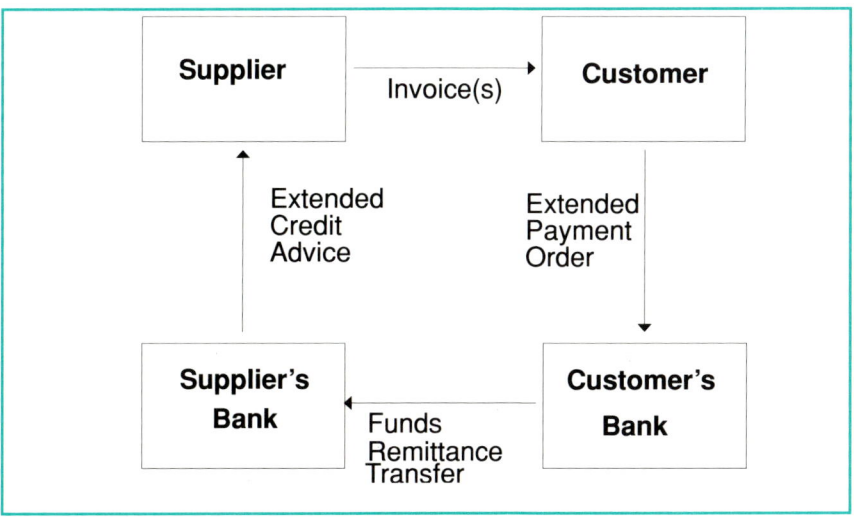

Figure 34: Financial EDI using a banking service

175

In this example, both trading partners' banks share an electronic infrastructure, allowing them to exchange EDI messages. To initiate a payment the customer sends a single message to its bank containing both the financial and remittance information. The banks will then use the financial information to set up the funds transfer, and will include the remittance information in the credit advice message sent to the supplier.

It is the bank's responsibility to release the remittance messages at the same time as the funds transfer takes effect. The supplier can, therefore, be sure that when they receive the remittance information the funds will be in their bank account.

9.4.2 Example 2 – Financial EDI using simple funds transfer

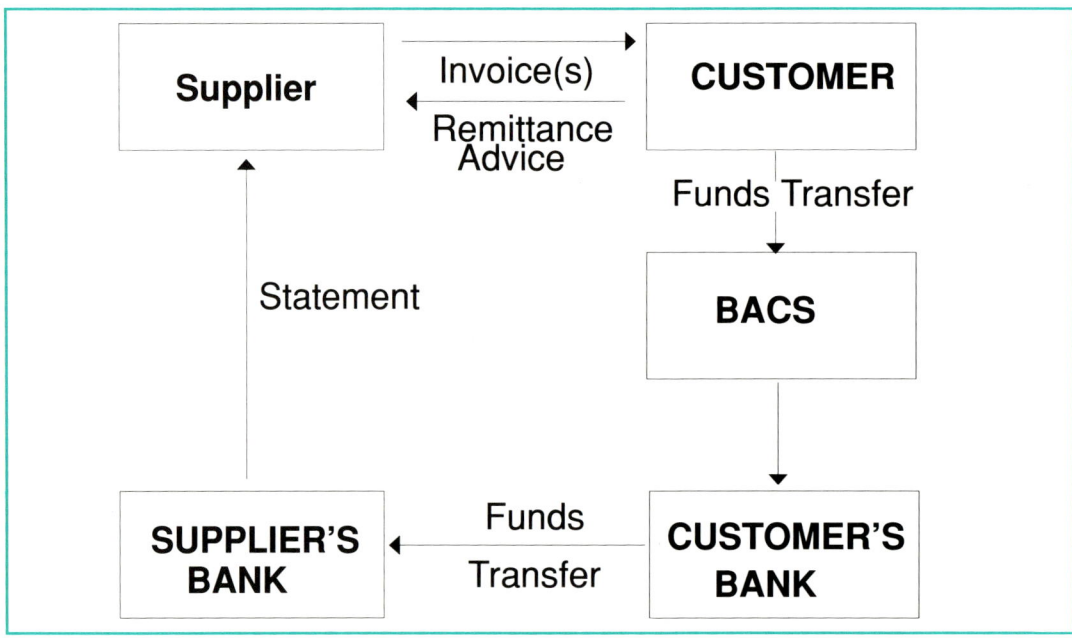

Figure 35: Financial EDI using simple funds transfer

Many trading partners may find that their banks cannot provide the sophisticated service outlined in the previous example. Financial EDI is, however, still possible in this environment. The ordering customer must, however, send two messages for each payment:

- a funds transfer message to their bank (through the BACS network, for example,)

- a remittance advice message to the supplier.

The disadvantage of this method is that the payment and documentation are not linked. The supplier cannot guarantee that, when the remittance advice is received, their account will have been credited. The expected payment date will, however, usually be incorporated in the remittance advice, and the commitment to pay made in the interchange agreement between the trading partners. The supplier can, therefore, still electronically reconcile the invoices for which payment is expected.

9.4.3 Example 3 – Financial EDI using a hybrid approach

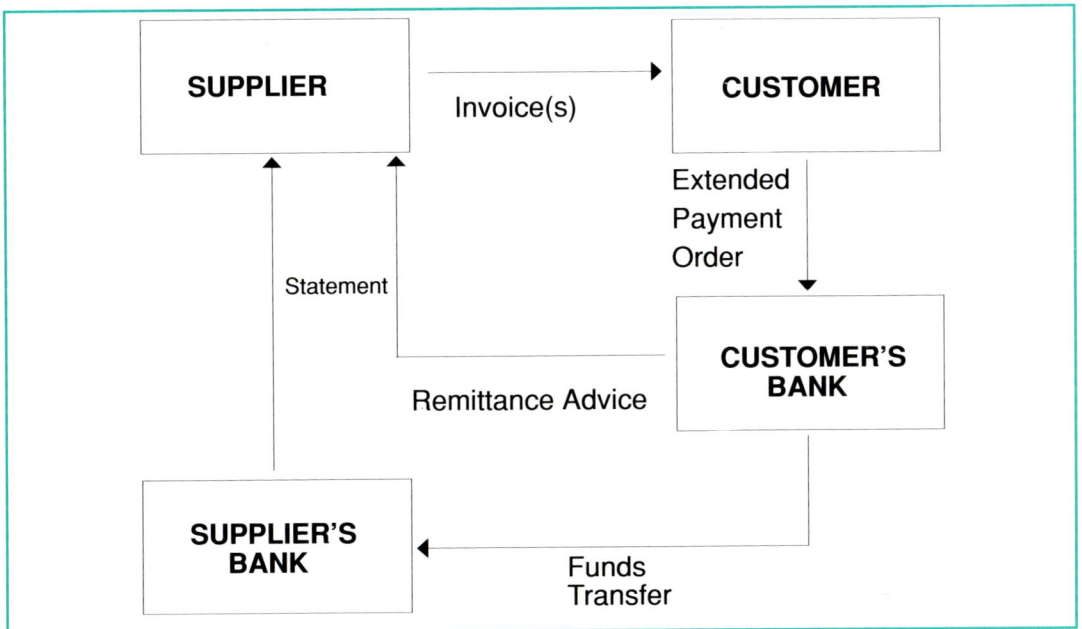

Figure 36: *Financial EDI using a hybrid approach*

In a typical trading community, some suppliers may be reluctant to communicate using EDI. In response to this situation some financial institutions may offer an extension of the banking service in Figure 34. Here the ordering customer will send an extended payment order message, containing the funds transfer and remittance advice, to their bank, thus linking a commitment to pay with the payment details. The bank will then arrange funds transfer and forward a remittance advice by the postal service to the supplier being credited

EDI Implementation Guide

The advantage of this method is that it allows the ordering customer to make all payments electronically, without having to wait for all of their suppliers to implement an EDI interface. The customer's bank maintains a profile which is used to validate the payments, and indicates the most appropriate payment method for each supplier:

- where both the supplier and the supplier's bank are capable of exchanging EDI messages, the extended payment can be passed as detailed in Figure 34

- where the supplier can receive EDI messages but their bank cannot, funds transfer can be made through BACS; a remittance advice message will then be sent directly to the supplier from the customer's bank

- where the supplier is not capable of receiving EDI messages, the bank can print out the remittance advice information and post it.

9.4.4 Ensuring payment integrity

The examples shown in Figure 34 and Figure 36 place an increased responsibility on the banks. To protect their interests the customer's bank must be certain that payment requests are valid. They will, therefore, employ many of the techniques described in Chapter 8, 'Security'. The commercial banks usually employ one of two methods:

- Financial EDI payments may have to be submitted from a dedicated workstation secured by both physical and software locks

- a Payments profile may be used. Here the bank receives a list of authorised payees from the customer's account before any payments are made. This will normally be through a separate route to the payment information to reduce the risk of attack.

When the bank receives a payment request it will check that the payee appears in the profile before proceeding. This technique is often used as part of the hybrid solution described in Figure 36, where the profile would also contain the payment strategy permissible for that supplier. In this context, a payment strategy can be considered as similar to a template used by the Paymaster, defining maximum size of payment, permissible frequency, etc.

It has to be assumed that the banks will provide sufficient separation of duties to ensure the same person is not responsible for all stages of the process. However, if only one person is responsible for the interface with the bank, then the risk of fraud will need to be countered with appropriate audit and control.

9.5 Financial EDI Payment Strategies

Financial EDI allows many payment strategies to be considered. In addition to the basic example shown in Figure 33, these include:

9.5.1 Self-billing

Traditionally a payment is triggered by the receipt of an invoice from a supplier. Where two trading partners have established a trusting relationship they may agree to alter this trigger. This technique is called 'self-billing'.

At a pre-determined time, the customer will trigger a payment, which will send a 'self-billed' invoice to the supplier indicating that payment is to be made, and initiating payment through their bank. This payment will usually occur after an agreed period, such as 30 days from receipt. To allow the supplier to reconcile the payment, a delivery reference will normally be included in the invoice and the invoice number passed with the reconciliation information.

This technique gives the customer a great deal of control over their inventory and can be a powerful tool in many advanced management processes. For example, by attaching bar-codes containing the dispatch advice number to each part, the customer could track each item's progress through their inventory. The customer may use this information to delay production of the self-billed invoice until the item was actually used, thus reducing the capital costs of their inventory.

If self-billing is considered, care should be taken to ensure that it does not affect legal ownership of the goods in question. For example, do they belong to the supplier until they are used and paid for? Who will be responsible for damage, insurance and so on? These aspects should be resolved as part of the Operational Attachment, if not covered by standard Terms and Conditions before any implementation takes place.

Naturally, if any items on the invoice attract VAT, this process must be approved by HM Customs & Excise. See Annex H, 'HM Customs & Excise guidance on EDI usage'.

9.5.2 Standing Order

A Standing Order is commonly used where regular payments are to be made for a pre-defined service. Financial EDI allows reference information to be included with this payment as with a normal transaction. However, by nature of the transaction, this information would be fixed throughout the payment cycle and may reduce the advantages of Financial EDI.

The standing order is most commonly used for goods and services which attract no VAT and for which an invoice may not be required.

9.5.3 Direct Debit

This is similar to the Standing Order, except that it is the supplier who initiates payment from a customer's bank. The customer must first set up a mandate with its bank, and have an agreement with the supplier. Payments are then made using BACS to transfer funds.

In this case the customer would be advised of the funds to be transferred via the invoice rather than through a Financial EDI message. The supplier would automatically reconcile the payment to the invoiced items when requesting the funds transfer.

There are strict rules governing the use of BACS direct debit arrangements. In addition, government bodies generally do not allow government accounts to be directly debited (as is explained in paragraph 28.3.37 of *Government Accounting*, issued by HM Treasury).

9.5.4 Factoring and Invoice Discounting

Some commercial organisations use a third party, or Factor, to recover their debt and thus reduce or completely remove the need for their own accounts receivable department. In this example the factor would receive the Financial EDI messages and reconcile them to the outstanding invoices. The factor, therefore, receives most of the benefits from Financial EDI. These savings would, however, be passed on to the client organisations through a reduction in charges.

Chapter 9
EDI in Finance

9.5.5 Netting

Where trading partners have established a closed trading cluster they may agree not to transfer funds on receipt of an invoice. Instead, each partner will record the outstanding amount in an account. After an agreed period the trading partners will then settle their account with a single funds transfer.

Government bodies are allowed to net off when settling the amount of the funds transfer, but must account gross for all the underlying payments and receipts. This technique is most commonly used where trading partners exchange large volumes of goods with similar net values, so that the outstanding balance between the partners is small. This limits the number of bank charges to an absolute minimum.

As each payment will cover many invoices the remittance advice will be large and complex. This lends itself to electronic transmission, either with the payment order or in a separate message.

9.6 Financial EDI in the Public Sector

Paymaster operates accounts on behalf of public sector bodies, through funds held at the Bank of England. Most bodies also use commercial banks for parts or all of their banking arrangements.

9.6.1 Making Payments from a Paymaster Account

There are several ways to make a payment from a Paymaster account. Details on procedures for operating the services can be found in the Paymaster *Banking Services User Guide*. The main methods are through:

- Payable Orders

- BACS transfers

- CHAPS transfers

- Request for Transfers (RFTs), ie the movement of funds between two Paymaster accounts.

9.6.2 Security of payments

Paymaster currently operates systems which have a large volume of paper input. Payments must be properly

EDI Implementation Guide

authorised. A number of mechanisms give protection, two important ones being:

- the Schedule, which contains details of payable orders issued: this is used to match the claim when the payable order is presented for payment

- the Template, which contains details of specified accounts to which payments may be made via CHAPS and Transfers (RFTs).

9.6.3 Crediting Funds to a Paymaster Account

The main methods for crediting a Paymaster account are through:

- Bank Giro Credits (special paying-in forms used to bank cheques, cash and postal orders)

- BACS

- CHAPS

- transfers from other Paymaster accounts.

9.6.4 Financial EDI and Paymaster

Paymaster supports the electronic transfer of funds via BACS and CHAPS, but currently does not provide a Financial EDI service.

The facility to transfer Schedules via magnetic tape has been available for many years. Paymaster can provide account information through its electronic 'Masterline' service, which is being enhanced to receive payment requests. It is intended that this will further be improved to facilitate Financial EDI.

Financial EDI with private sector suppliers using the extended payment messages will only be possible when Paymaster and their agents to the Clearing Services have a sophisticated EDI link.

For internal RFT payments, however, Paymaster controls all accounts in the transaction. This removes one of the parties from the Financial EDI transaction, making it far simpler to pass on remittance messages.

The strategy for public sector Financial EDI must, however, be decided centrally, for only when public

9.7 Message frameworks for Financial EDI

sector bodies have a common strategy can large-scale savings be obtained.

Financial EDI can be carried out using a variety of transfer messages.

9.7.1 UN/EDIFACT messages

A number of UN/EDIFACT messages have been developed to support Financial EDI.

The first action in the payments cycle is the customer issuing a payment order to its bank through the *PAYORD* message. The bank will then arrange payment with the supplier's bank, which will in turn notify the supplier via a credit advice (*CREADV*). Both of these messages contain details of the parties involved in the transaction and instructions to each of the financial institutions including:

- the payment release date
- the currencies to be used
- the charges to be applied.

When payment is released by the customer's bank a debit advice (*DEBADV*) may also be sent to the customer. The remittance information would then be sent to the supplier using the *REMADV* message. The *REMADV* and *CREADV* messages would be cross-referenced to ensure the supplier could reconcile the two messages on receipt.

To address the reconciliation problem extended versions of the *PAYORD* and *CREADV* messages have been created combining them with the remittance information contained in the *REMADV* message.

- the Extended Payment Order (*PAYEXT*)
- the Extended Credit Advice (*CREADV*).

In response to these messages the SWIFT banking organisation has submitted a draft message, *FINPAY*, to the Western European EDIFACT Board for approval. This will be used to pass the information between the financial institutions.

9.7.2 BACS and CHAPS

In the UK, BACS and CHAPS provide proprietary formats to specify payment details. Both of these formats specify the minimum financial information required to complete the payment and leave very little space for reference information. The remittance information would, therefore, have to be passed separately using the UN/EDIFACT *REMADV* message. BACS formats can be obtained through the sponsoring bank. Although the data required to make a CHAPS payment is standard, the format required for submission by the user is specified by their bank.

10 Managing the Implementation

This chapter describes the organisation, management process and tasks necessary for implementing EDI in a government department or Agency. The use of PRINCE project management methodology for this implementation is assumed and explained.

The chapter should be read by everyone who will be involved in the EDI implementation including, for example, key management, business process owners, IS and IT specialists, operations personnel and users.

It is recommended that Chapter 3, 'Preparing for EDI', be read before this chapter.

10.1 Overall Organisation

During the EDI Feasibility (Scoping) Study (see Chapter 3, 'Preparing for EDI'), the extent of the EDI implementation will have been decided (for example, which business processes will be converted to EDI and which technical solutions will be implemented). Depending on the extent of this implementation it may be advisable to set up, within the organisation, a permanent infrastructure for all EDI implementation projects. This infrastructure could include, for example:

- an EDI implementation programme manager, who would have responsibility for overall management of the EDI implementation and more specifically for:

    - co-ordination of the various EDI projects and working with the project and stage managers to ensure commonality, consistency and integrated planning

    - discussions and agreements with business process partners to ensure full co-operation and a good understanding of each others' roles, responsibilities and implementation plans

    - co-ordination of other parts of the EDI infrastructure to enable correct priorities to be given to their EDI project support activities

EDI Implementation Guide

- the lead role in ensuring that the EDI implementation strategy is 'sold' to the organisation and that implementation progress is continually publicised

- an EDI standards group, which would provide support and expertise to all EDI projects, especially in the mapping, use and creation (where necessary) of UN/EDIFACT messages. This group would keep up-to-date with all standards developments and could participate, as appropriate and as necessary, in external standards organisations

- an EDI technical group, which would be skilled in the understanding and use of the EDI hardware and software, including the telecommunications aspects. This group would provide expertise and support to all EDI projects

- A Business Process Re-engineering (BPR) team, if this project or programme is part of a wider BPR initiative

- Appropriate support for other technologies which are being implemented as part of the same project or programme such as E-mail.

10.2 Use of PRINCE project management methodology

As explained in Chapter 3, 'Preparing for EDI', the EDI Feasibility (Scoping) Study should have identified a number of separate EDI implementation projects (possibly one for each business process being converted to EDI) as part of an overall programme and proposed the method of implementing each project, as well as the implementation sequence, plan and resource for each project. Assuming the EDI Feasibility Report is accepted by the EDI Steering Committee, the various EDI project implementations can begin in the planned sequence.

There will be very few differences in the tasks necessary for each implementation project. The first EDI project will almost certainly be the most difficult, especially if there are many EDI business partners involved and all (or even some) of them are also implementing EDI for the first time. The major difference will be that the tasks for initial installation and set-up of the EDI hardware and software plus any telecommunication equipment installations and upgrades will be included in the first EDI project and

Chapter 10
Managing the Implementation

should not need to be repeated to any extent, if at all, in following projects.

It is unlikely that a Feasibility Study for each individual EDI implementation project will be necessary, as the overall, organisation-wide EDI Feasibility Study should have gone into sufficient detail, but this must be assessed and confirmed. It is likely that the EDI Steering Committee could fulfil the role of the Project Board for each EDI implementation project but, here again, an assessment will be necessary for confirmation. Apart from these factors, it is assumed that the PRINCE project management methodology will be followed in all respects during the EDI implementation. For example:

- each EDI implementation project will be split into the following sub-projects and stages:

  - Full Study: consisting of Initiation, Specification and Logical Design stages - Building the System: consisting of Initiation, Physical Design, Development, Installation and Operation stages

- the project organisation will include a Project Board, a Project Manager, Stage Managers and Stage Teams and a Project Assurance Team

- each EDI implementation project will produce all necessary Project, Stage and Detailed Technical and Resource Plans as well as (when the need arises) any Exception Plans

- each EDI implementation project will include all appropriate control components:

  - Mid-Stage Assessments and End-Stage Assessments

  - Checkpoint Meetings and Quality Reviews - Project Closure Meetings.

10.3 First EDI implementation for government department or Agency

10.3.1 Full Study

Specification Stage: During the Specification Stage it will be necessary to understand and to document, in detail, the differences between the old, non-EDI business process and the new EDI process. User functional specifications and user acceptance criteria for the new EDI process should be produced. Discussions should commence, even at this early stage, with the business process partners who will be involved in the EDI implementation to ensure that the new EDI process is understood and agreed by them. If the business process partners are new to EDI, some time may have to be spent in educating them and convincing them of the benefits to be gained from it.

Also, at this stage, a joint implementation plan should be produced and agreed with these business process partners. This should include:

- project objectives and organisation

- roles and responsibilities

- key implementation activities plus dates

- joint quality plans

- testing and operation cut-over methodology and dates with each partner

- agreement on which partners will participate in any pilot tests

- agreement on the sequence and time-frame in which other partners will test and cut over to operation

- joint education plans

- joint conversion plans and methodology

- joint management system and controls.

This detail will obviously need to encompass and be expressed in the appropriate Structured Systems Analysis and Design Method (SSADM) components and terminology. See 4.6.1, 'Analysis of business processes', for further detail on the use of SSADM in this context.

It may be that one or more business process partners will not or cannot agree to implement EDI. In this case, it will be necessary to define the business process that will operate with these non-EDI partners. It may be that the old, non-EDI process can continue for a time, in the hope that eventually these partners will agree to implement EDI. It may be that it will no longer make sense to do business with these non-EDI partners (if there is a choice) or it may be worth investigating other options such as EDI-to-fax solutions, which should at least ensure that the old, non-EDI process can be discontinued. In the event that the old, non-EDI process has to continue with some business process partners, the full EDI benefits will not be obtained because of the need to support both the EDI process and the non-EDI process. As a last resort, it may be worth considering the provision of EDI hardware and software support to the business process partner, if this is cost-justified against the cost of maintaining both the EDI and non-EDI processes.

Lastly, during this stage all aspects of the Interchange Agreement should be discussed and agreed with proposed EDI partners and then documented. At the same time, the security, legal and audit implications should also be addressed and all requirements documented.

Logical Design Stage: During the Logical Design Stage, the data structures and data elements for the new EDI process are defined. At this point, the detailed mapping of the data to the UN/EDIFACT message must be done (if business data is being exchanged with business process partners). If no appropriate UN/EDIFACT message currently exists, then a new UN/EDIFACT message must be created, provided it has been agreed that this is justified. Whether mapped or new, the resulting UN/EDIFACT message should be understood and agreed by all EDI partners. It may even be appropriate that one or more of the EDI partners participate in the mapping of the data or in the creating of a new UN/EDIFACT message. Better still, if any of the business process partners have already implemented EDI and are using an appropriate UN/EDIFACT message, which has already been mapped or created, then it may be possible to use this message without change or with minor modification.

EDI Implementation Guide

A detailed introduction to UN/EDIFACT standards and messages, plus the processes for creating, mapping and using them, has been given in Chapter 4, 'UN/EDIFACT'.

10.3.2 Building the System

Physical Design Stage: During the Physical Design Stage any changes necessary to IS applications must be documented. All programme changes and any changes to data bases and files must be specified. It may be that a completely new application system needs to be developed in order to implement EDI, in which case the complete application system must be physically designed and specified.

During this stage the selection (and purchase if necessary) and installation of the EDI hardware and software should be planned and documented, including all telecommunication equipment installations and upgrades. This documentation must also contain the specifications for all set-up activities required with the EDI software – for example, the set-up of any UN/EDIFACT translation tables to match the message mapping required for the implementation. As part of the ongoing joint management system for the EDI implementation with business process partners, the opportunity should be taken at this time to verify with them the consistency and timeliness of their own EDI hardware and software installation plans.

Lastly, the Physical Design should deliver all detailed development, test and implementation plans, to include:

- programme coding and unit test plans

- plans for preparation of system documentation (IS, user and operations)

- plans for preparation of the EDI Interchange Agreement

- system test, integration test and pilot test plans, including the design and preparation of the necessary test environments (the integration test and pilot test plans must be agreed with all involved business process partners)

- education and training plans.

Chapter 10
Managing the Implementation

Development Stage: During the Development Stage, the following tasks should be completed:

- all programme coding and unit testing

- preparation of all system documentation (IS, user and operations)

- preparation of the EDI Interchange Agreement, including review and acceptance by all business process partners who will be involved in the EDI implementation

- installation, set-up and test of all EDI hardware and software, including all telecommunication equipment installations and upgrades, plus any necessary network connections

- preparation of all system test, integration test and pilot test environments

- preparation of all education and training material.

At this point in the Development Stage everything should be in place for the start of system testing, which should progress in carefully controlled steps (Figure 37).

Initially, the system test should focus on the testing of the internal IS application and user processes, including security, legal and audit functions, as well as the testing of the set-up and administrative functions of the EDI hardware and software. When these are proven to be correct and working satisfactorily, the interface between the internal IS application and the EDI hardware and software should be tested, including data conversion to and from UN/EDIFACT format. This should be followed by the system test of the network connection and transmission. In this initial testing, it should be possible to use techniques for sending and receiving network transmissions internally, without involving any external business process partners. Finally, the whole system should be tested end-to-end, but still without necessarily connecting with any external business process partner.

Everything should now be ready for an integration (interconnection) test with the business process partners who will be involved in the pilot test (assuming that the partners are also ready). The main objectives of this testing are to verify:

- the network connectivity (that transmissions can be successfully sent and received at either end)

- that the UN/EDIFACT message data sent and received matches what was expected and can be successfully translated

- that all security and audit requirements can be met

- that any system and data restore-and-recovery procedures are working correctly

- that any new or modified business controls work effectively and provide the desired security of operation.

Installation State: Assuming that the integration testing has been completed successfully, the Installation Stage of the project should be ready to commence. The prime activity in this stage is the pilot test with one or more of

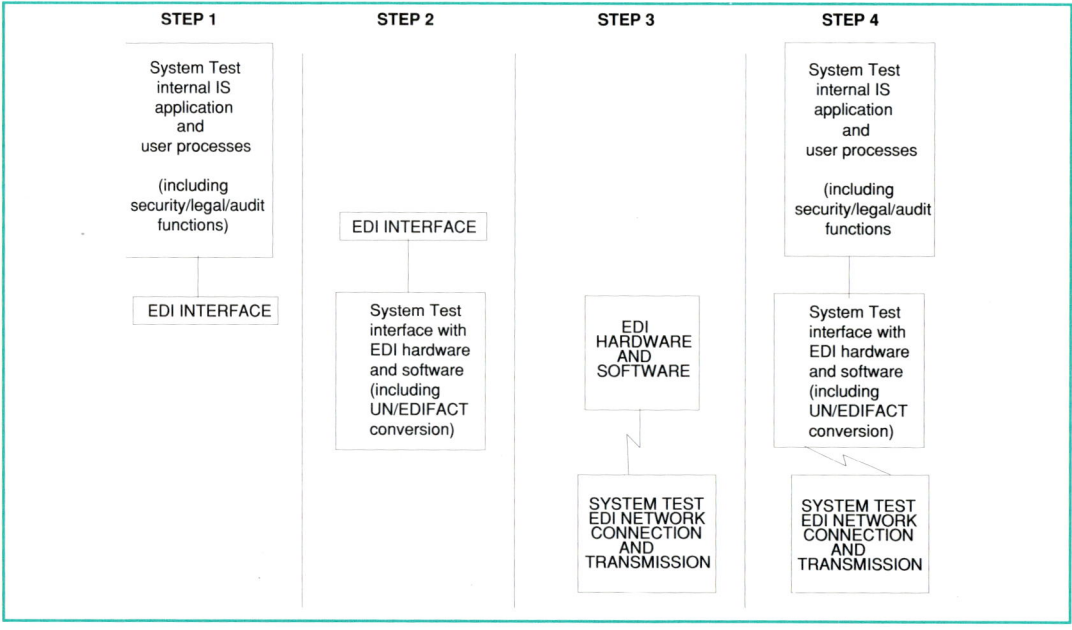

Figure 37: System test steps

Chapter 10
Managing the Implementation

the business process partners. Ideally this pilot test should take place in the operation (production) environment and this environment must be prepared. All personnel who will be involved in the pilot testing should have been fully educated and trained. Any data conversion and clean-up and all EDI set-up activities must be completed and a management system for the pilot test should be in place with all the involved business process partners. This management system should include:

- pilot test objectives and organisation

- roles and responsibilities

- detailed pilot test plan and procedures

- operation cut-over methodology and dates, together with agreed joint completion and acceptance criteria

- pilot test management and controls, for example:

    – status recording and reporting

    – problem and issue management

    – change management

    – quality controls

    – reviews and checkpoints

    – escalation procedures.

- fall-back plans and procedures in the event of a failure to cut over to full operation as and when planned.

The purpose of the pilot test is to fully test the system, together with one or more business process partners, as if it were in operation. However, the tests should be monitored and the results verified by all parties for correctness and completion. The old, non-EDI process should be run in parallel and should still be used as the operational business process. It may be possible to verify the EDI process results against the non-EDI process results if identical business data can be used (Figure 38).

In addition, potential problem situations should be tested

EDI Implementation Guide

to ensure the system and data can be restored and recovered.

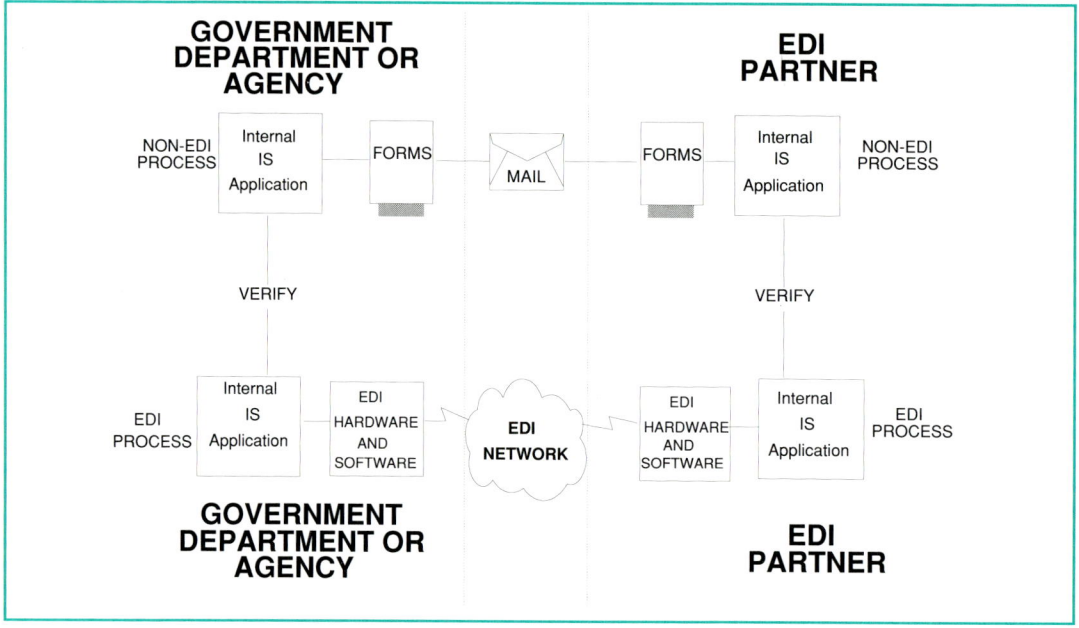

Figure 38: Parallel processing

When all pilot testing has been completed, a decision must be made whether to cut over to full operational use of the EDI process with the business process partners who have been involved in the testing. At this point the old, non-EDI process will be discontinued with these business process partners (but may continue with other business process partners who have not yet converted to EDI). However, the EDI project is not completed until all applicable business process partners have converted to EDI.

10.4 Roll-out of EDI Implementation with Business Process Partners

Following successful completion of pilot testing and operational cut-over of a new EDI implementation with one or more business process partners, the implementation roll-out with the remaining business process partners (if any) should begin. This roll-out will need to be carefully managed and controlled.

The sequence of the implementation roll-out and the time-frame should already have been agreed with the

Chapter 10
Managing the Implementation

business process partners during the Full Study. The correct balance must be found between the need to complete the EDI implementation as quickly as possible and the manageability of implementing EDI with a number of business process partners in a short space of time. The speed with which these remaining business process partners can implement the new EDI process will be largely influenced by whether or not they are already EDI-enabled and experienced in EDI.

For all business process partners it is recommended that an integration (interconnection) test be carried out as well as a period of parallel running, when the results of the new EDI process must be carefully verified. Remember that each business process partner implementing EDI for the first time is, effectively, carrying out their own pilot test and a full implementation plan and management system must be agreed with each of them to ensure that the implementation is controlled and managed properly. Sufficient time must be allowed to test and to ensure that everything is working correctly with each business process partner (especially at their end) before cut-over to full operation.

When all applicable business process partners have implemented EDI, the implementation project is finished and the old, non-EDI process can be discontinued (provided, of course, all business process partners have converted to the EDI process). It is necessary to ensure that all appropriate people within the organisation have been fully educated and trained in the new EDI process by this time.

At the end of the project a formal review should be held to ensure that objectives and completion criteria have been met and that lessons learned have been documented.

10.5 Follow-on EDI implementations in government department or Agency

Following successful completion and stabilisation of the first EDI implementation project, the next EDI implementation projects in the programme can commence. The stages and tasks necessary for these follow-on projects will be exactly the same as for the initial project, except that there may be no need for installation and set-up of the EDI hardware and software nor for telecommunication equipment installations or upgrades or network connections. The necessity and extent of these tasks should be assessed during the Physical Design Stage.

11 Operational Management

EDI systems are different from traditional IT systems and cannot be treated in the same way. This chapter introduces aspects of the management of EDI systems which make them different, but which can easily be overlooked. It is not intended to be a definitive guide, but is intended to provoke thought on some issues which, if overlooked, can cause difficulties, but which are easily managed as part of normal IT Operations good practice.

This chapter and the next address some of the new challenges which have to be faced in order to maximise the benefit obtained from an EDI implementation. All too often, potential benefits are swallowed up by the increased cost of operation and management of a process which has been 'enhanced' with the implementation of EDI.

For simplicity, this chapter focuses on the IT or DP operations considerations of an EDI environment while the next addresses the needs of the business process owner.

11.1 Operating in an EDI environment

In principle, the IT operations methodology for an EDI environment is the same as in a non-EDI one. However, there are a number of features that must be borne in mind. EDI extends certain roles and responsibilities beyond a single environment. This is explained by looking at the following areas:

- what actually changes in an EDI environment?
- inter-organisational processes
- matching the solution to requirements
- working procedures, roles and responsibilities
- application 'operability'
- 'end-to-end' service.

11.1.1 What Actually Changes?

There are three major changes that will occur:

- computing environments will be linked more directly

EDI Implementation Guide

Whereas the 'Computer Centre, No unauthorised entry' sign used to mark the border between computer operations and the business people, no such clear distinction exists with EDI.

- greater computer inter-dependencies will be created

Whereas the production of computer print-out was the end of the DP Manager's responsibility, with EDI he is responsible all the way to his customer's business application.

- the boundaries of the different roles and responsibilities will alter.

All of these implications are shown in the following diagram.

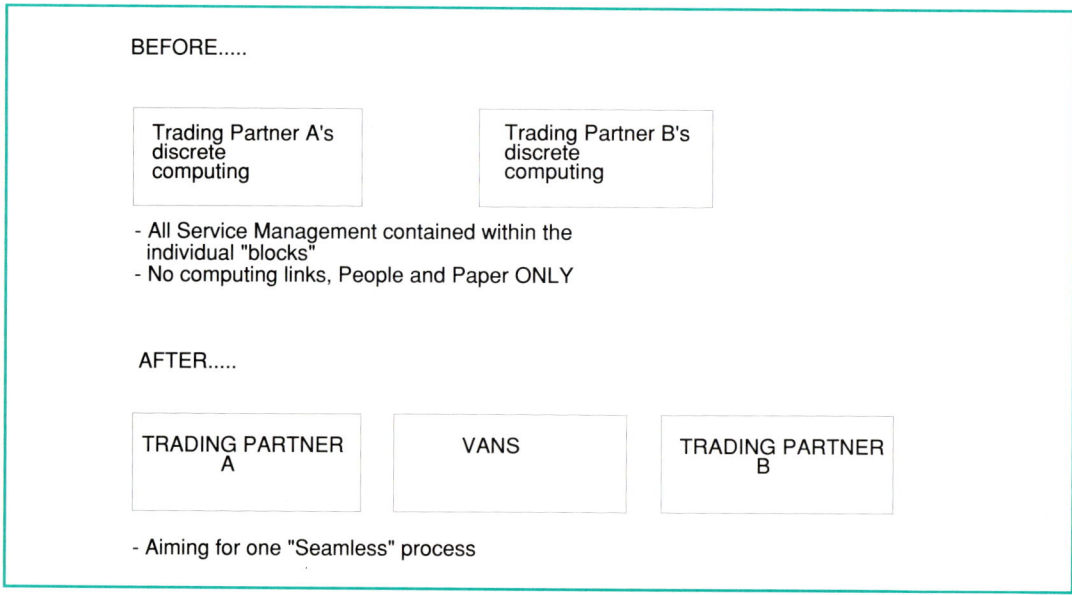

Figure 39: The computing environment BEFORE and AFTER EDI

11.1.2 Inter-organisational Processes

The scope of IT operations is often defined as the seven Service Management and Control (SMC) disciplines. The same roles exist in an EDI environment but the responsibilities change quite significantly, as is shown in the following review of the disciplines (plus monitoring, which has been added as there are significant implications in an EDI environment).

Chapter 11
Operational Management

- problem management

    In a non-EDI environment, problem management deals with those problems which are seen and can be resolved wholly within the operations environment and those which are visible outside of the group and need to be communicated and then resolved or managed to a satisfactory conclusion. This definition is adequate for an EDI environment too, but the external visibility extends much further. Instead of the person who checks the control totals in the accounts group, the problem may be perceived by a trading partner, whose translator has rejected a message or who has a code that he cannot recognise. It may be that today's 'business' contact/relationship is still the appropriate communications link between the two organisations but this should be a conscious decision and it needs to be documented.

    How should problems be handled? The Operational Attachment should define a single point of contact for each trading partner and this nominee should 'own' any problems. The actual resolution may, of course, be handled by others within the organisation, but the point of contact should be kept informed at all stages.

- change management

    All business areas that use EDI must be aware of the consequences of changes implemented – no longer are these necessarily just within the organisation. The Operational Attachment can be used as the vehicle to define change mechanisms, or at least to point to further documentation. The non-EDI concept of change management, where all changes are first tested stand alone, then as part of the overall process but outside of the production environment, and then are carefully managed into the production environment in a manner that maximises control and minimises risk, is even more important in an EDI environment, but much harder to achieve.

    If a data field that is passed in an EDI message is changed, how can the, maybe, 10,000 trading partners who use that field be protected?

However tightly controlled an organisation is, how can protection be ensured against unplanned or unexpected changes made by trading partners?

- recovery management

    The consideration here is to keep all trading partners informed in the event of recovery problems and issues and to ensure that procedures cater for those unexpected events that hit trading partners and thus affect the overall operation through the EDI linkages.

- process management

    Each side in the trading relationship will need to understand the processes and procedures of the other in order to maximise the benefits of working together and to minimise the potential problems alluded to here. This section is not designed to state the case for not doing EDI, simply to make very clear the need for impeccable management of IT operations in this environment to ensure that the benefits of EDI are achieved and operational costs are reduced rather than increased.

- communications management

    This is probably an area that need not concern trading partners if a VAN is being used for communications. If the organisation has implemented its *own* communications then this subject can become a major concern.

- monitoring

    This should be a matter of good business practice – to know what is happening with trading partners, in outline if nothing else. This may well be a joint role for the EDI Administrator and the IT service management personnel. Reports are perhaps useful to track both volumes and values of EDI traffic. This then gives some of the data needed to gain a real understanding of the benefits of using EDI. See the discussion in 6.5, 'EDI gateways', of how the correct tools can assist in this area.

Chapter 11
Operational Management

- service level management

    Are service levels, both within and outside the company, being met? Is the VAN service level agreement being honoured? This is an extension of the whole area of monitoring the EDI (and non-EDI) system.

- security management

    See Chapter 8, 'Security', for further discussion of security.

11.1.3 Matching the solution to requirements

The sorts of question that need answering here are:

- what happened to business controls?

    When the applications were predominantly manual, the business controls were also manual. Someone used to check the control totals physically, someone else checked that the cheque print run matched the tally and the storeman checked the paperwork against deliveries. Now most of these people are not needed because their roles have been automated and the information flows without human intervention. In these situations it is imperative that controls are built into the system to replace or improve on the manual controls that the system has superseded.

- what are the timing considerations?

    Does the EDI system run once a day? Once a week? Or every hour?

    This, of course, depends entirely on which process or processes have been converted to use EDI. It is a point that must be discussed by all those within the organisation who are affected, but it must also be agreed with all trading partners. Although the decision on when to run must clearly be sanctioned by the IT department, it is for the relevant business process to have the final say.

- is this a 'critical' process?

    Will the business be significantly affected if EDI

EDI Implementation Guide

transactions are not sent or received within specific times?

It may be that different departments have different opinions on what constitutes a 'critical process'. As with all aspects of EDI, this is an area for consultation and discussion but the criticality of an application will define its back-up and recovery needs and the level of action to be taken in the event of a disaster.

- what are the manual dependencies?

    EDI is all about *removing* manual intervention. Inevitably, there will still be manual dependencies. This needs to be understood clearly and documented clearly.

- what are the (additional) security implications?

    EDI in no way reduces the responsibility for having a secure computing environment. EDI gives the potential for increased security since it will be possible, though not necessarily desirable, to track all data throughout its path from one organisation to another.

- what are the recovery options?

    Is the paper-based system going to be kept as a back-up in the event of major problems? This is a vital consideration. Unlike non-EDI processes, where only one organisation is involved, the originator of EDI has to take into consideration what should happen when a trading partner has a major problem. There may have to be a paper-based solution for this eventuality.

    The options should be built into any existing recovery set-up.

11.1.4 Working Procedures, Roles and Responsibilities

Since IT support for the business processes will now cross the boundaries of organisations, there will inevitably be potential for clashes and areas of confusion. These must be understood and a method of working together must be established; again trust and partnership is the key. In different organisations there are going to be:

Chapter 11
Operational Management

- different IT cultures

- different jargon

- different approaches to basic processes

- different management structures

- different levels of professionalism

- different levels of IT experience.

How can these areas of difference be addressed?

- get talking, in detail – the sooner the better

- understand each others' needs and cultures

    Consider exchanging personnel for a short period to gain a deeper understanding of the others culture and business. This may be easy enough between two large organisations but becomes more difficult with smaller groups who may feel daunted by the prospect (and there may just be too many such organisations). The aim must always to be to find ways to increase partnership and trust. If acronyms and jargon are in use, ensure that the meanings are documented. Exchange these documents with all trading partners.

- work to common procedures

    Exchange details of the relevant procedures and decide if there are any common areas. If so, work to these; if not, decide if there is scope for change to ensure commonality.

    These may be useful as a part of an ISO 9000 series certification project.

11.1.5 Application Operability

The sorts of concern here are:

- are there additional application dependencies?

    All those involved in planning how existing systems run must be made aware of the changes that may be introduced as a result of EDI. They must understand how they are going to be affected and must be given the opportunity to raise objections.

- how can the systems be made 'hands-off'?

  This covers areas such as:

  – re-processing

  – re-transmission

  – error handling.

  It may be simple enough to stop printing a specific form and to send it via EDI instead, but the real consideration is how to handle the 'copy form' request that used to be met just by putting the original through a photocopier.

  Existing processes may already be highly automated and EDI should not introduce any further manual processes. However, in an environment which is not highly automated, EDI may also give an opportunity to look at overall process automation.

- how should back-up and recovery be handled?

  This should include everything from simple system 'hiccups' to a full disaster recovery? As noted before, provision must be made for problems at either end of a trading relationship.

- how can the process of alerts be automated?

  What sorts of alert are needed? What are the circumstances under which these alerts should be generated?

  – late data

  – data in error

  – no data

  – duplicate data

– an extremely large order exceeding the pre-set ceiling.

If there is an existing office E-mail system there may be scope for feeding alerts directly into this system.

- can standards be defined to streamline future EDI applications?

If a single EDI process is being introduced, there may be scope for defining application standards for future EDI applications. This will make later introduction easier and cheaper.

11.1.6 End-to-end Service

There are a number of areas of interest with this 'end-to-end' service, including:

- definition and documentation of the business requirement: this will have been done as part of the business analysis

- definition of the service level commitment from the VANS: this documentation should be requested directly from the VANS being considered for use

- measurement of this service: since EDI is believed to bring business benefits, these benefits need to be measured. How are the internal benefits to be measured? How is the VANS component to be measured?

- regular meetings with trading partners: setting up regular meetings with trading partners, to allow for an open discussion of problems and concerns, will prove beneficial. If these are scheduled regularly, they can always be cancelled when there are no concerns; setting up a meeting at short notice with all the groups involved will be more difficult

- involvement in any VANS user groups: these can be a very powerful tool when dealing with the VANS. They are a route for airing concerns and complaints (although complaints should, in the first instance, be directed at the Customer Service personnel of the VANS). Remember, however, that these groups are also a forum for positive, constructive suggestions to the VANS.

11.2 Role of an Operational Attachment

This is a key document for operational purposes. It defines what is happening, and when, and who should be contacted in the event of problems or questions. It is vital that a contact point be established for any trading partners to call. This point of contact must take responsibility for external contacts and must liaise between external and internal functions. As a result, whoever has this task must have the authority within the organisation to get things done – it is not a job for a junior.

Annex G, 'Sample operational attachment', shows an example of an Operational Attachment.

11.3 User Benefits

Different users will perceive different benefits. From the point of view of the IT department the benefits include:

- an increased level of automation, leading to...
- a decreased level of manual intervention, leading to...
- a decreased or re-deployed headcount, leading to...
- an opportunity to re-direct investment to other development and services, leading to...
- an increase in 'customer' satisfaction, however this customer is defined.

11.4 Fundamental Points

The following points should always be remembered:

- EDI is here to stay
- EDI radically alters the scope and boundaries of the IT role
- new cultures *will* be encountered
- ensure that the developed solution is the *right* solution
- accept the need for 'end-to-end' management – reject a parochial approach.

As stated at the start of this chapter, the aim of the last few pages has not been to give good reasons not to implement EDI. The questioning style has been used to illustrate the decisions which need to be taken and which, with the application of good IT operations best practice (an attention to detail and rigorous application of processes), can easily be managed without problem, allowing the real benefits of EDI to accrue to all involved.

12 Trading Partner Management

This chapter looks at the difficulties of managing trading partner relationships and explains the need for an ongoing overall management system with EDI trading partners. It also describes the roles that need to be undertaken, ideally by a central group which could administer and maintain this system. The term 'Trading Partner' is used throughout to describe any organisation or body with which a decision is taken to practise EDI, whether they be trading partners, business process partners or whatever.

12.1 Common practice in the private sector

Once EDI is implemented, many organisations make the mistake of relaxing and waiting for the benefits to accrue – what they then soon realise is that the management of trading partner relationships is at least as challenging as the initial implementation and, if ignored, will ensure that all of the previous efforts have been wasted.

The problems start to surface when roll-out targets are missed, and changes or upgrades to the solution are delayed by trading partners who are 'not ready' or who misunderstood the 'plan'.

The situation then worsens as it is realised that different parts of the same organisation are giving differing messages to the same trading partners; for example, different manufacturing sites are using different versions of the same message and causing confusion among the supplier community as a result.

The usual solution is to appoint a single focal point with responsibility for co-ordination and overall control of EDI activities. In the private sector this is usually sufficient and has been used to good effect by agencies such as HMSO, whose role and activity is reasonably well confined, but in many government situations, there is no logical place for a single point of control – see the NHS and CCCJS case studies in Annex A, 'Case studies', for clear examples of this problem.

Even if it is possible to define a single point of control within a community, it is often difficult to co-ordinate activities with other large partners in related communities.

The next section of this chapter outlines the role that needs to be fulfilled by the single point of control and the last section gives some guidance on how to proceed if it proves impossible to identify such a focus.

12.2 The Importance of an Ongoing, Overall Management System

To ensure maximum co-ordination, control and consistency, the management system should address the following:

- EDI 'single image'
- visibility of EDI connections
- shared EDI goals and benefits
- overall control and co-ordination.

12.2.1 EDI 'Single Image'

It will become increasingly important that an EDI 'single image' be presented, as much as possible, where EDI is to be implemented by more than one government department or Agency with the same trading partner. This EDI 'single image' should include:

- common EDI processes and technical solutions, where appropriate, to avoid the need for the trading partner to develop different solutions for each EDI implementation. If this is not avoided, the trading partner's implementation is likely to take longer and may even result in a refusal to implement

- common EDI standards, where applicable. For example, use of common UN/EDIFACT messages by government departments or Agencies will avoid the need to duplicate effort in creating new messages or message subsets

- common EDI Interchange Agreements, where applicable, to avoid the need to duplicate effort in developing and approving EDI Interchange Agreements with trading partners.

By creating and enforcing an EDI 'single image' for government departments and Agencies, the whole EDI implementation process should be made easier and quicker for them and their EDI partners. There will be the opportunity to share solutions and to learn from each

Chapter 12
Trading Partner Management

others' experiences as well as creating productivity and synergy benefits.

12.2.2 Visibility of EDI Connections

A method should be established to ensure visibility of EDI connections being planned and being implemented by government departments and Agencies with trading partners. Any government department or Agency implementing EDI should be able to use this method to see if their trading partner has already implemented EDI with another government department or Agency and to find out the EDI capabilities of this partner. In addition, the objectives of an EDI 'single image' will be supported, as this EDI connection visibility should encourage government departments and Agencies to contact each other and to share implementation ideas, solutions and experiences.

12.2.3 Shared EDI Goals and Benefits

The establishment of an ongoing, overall EDI management system with business process partners will assist in ensuring that government departments and Agencies move forward together with their business process partners in achieving EDI goals. The working relationship with these partners can be strengthened and the realisation and demonstration of visible mutual benefits should encourage a real partnership in looking for other EDI opportunities for savings.

12.2.4 Overall control and co-ordination

As part of the management system it is recommended that a single government department or Agency conceptually perform an EDI co-ordinating role with trading partners who are likely to be shared with other government departments or Agencies, wherever possible. There is a simple hypothesis behind this – the one thing that all successful EDI implementations have in common is some form of central focal point, either because it is driven by one central organisation (eg HMSO in the government supplies community or UK Customs for the CHIEF project) or a central common interest group or focus has been formed to overcome any difficulties (eg CCCJS and the NHS have both set up co-ordinating groups to help ensure progress and success). All initial contacts with these trading partners on EDI matters should be controlled and co-ordinated by this government

EDI Implementation Guide

department or Agency. Several factors may govern the selection of a government department or Agency for the co-ordinating role; these include:

- the government department or Agency which is the first to implement EDI with a business process partner

- the government department or Agency which has the highest volume of business with a business process partner

- the government department or Agency which is closest to the geographic location of a business process partner

- the government department or Agency best equipped to support the business process partner.

12.3 Role of a Central Focal Point (or Responsibilities to be Performed in its Absence)

Most successful EDI communities have a focal point of some form, whether that be a dominant or senior partner, a trade association or a user group. There are few examples where some such focus does not fill the vacuum.

Government departments and Agencies need to understand the need for this central management and encourage and support the development of such authority in whatever community centred groups which move into the role. Perhaps, a wider role is required, as performed by a Certification Authority (see 8.4.4, 'Certification Authorities').

Another important element is the use of tools to ease or avoid the problems. One international computer manufacturer which also has its own EDI capability using its global network products overcame the problems in the following manner: Central EDI Project Offices were set up in each continent, co-ordinated by a world-wide Corporate EDI Project Office located in the United States. The role of each project office was to drive the implementation of EDI in the country organisations within the respective continents.

Chapter 12
Trading Partner Management

For Europe, an EDI Project Office was established in the United Kingdom. The responsibilities of this Project Office were to:

- develop the rules and processes for ensuring an EDI 'single image' is presented

- promote and co-ordinate the shared knowledge and use of common EDI standards and solutions

- develop, administer and maintain the method for ensuring visibility of EDI connections between locations, divisions and trading partners

- develop, administer and maintain the processes for selecting a location or division to perform an EDI co-ordinating role with shared trading partners and for supporting them in this role.

In addition, this group was a central company source of EDI implementation statistics and measurements; for example, the total number of EDI connections that exist and the total number of UN/EDIFACT messages in use.

In addition, the European EDI Project Office acted as a communication focal point for EDI in Europe by organising international EDI meetings and workshops, where representatives from the companies in the European countries could get together and share EDI problems and experiences. The European EDI Project Office also published regular newsletters to publicise progress in Europe and to keep the companies in Europe informed and up-to-date on the latest EDI developments and news.

The corporation solved the problem of ensuring visibility of EDI connections between itself and EDI trading partners by creating a world-wide data base, which was available for on-line update and access by all country organisations throughout the world. This data base contained details of locations which had implemented EDI together with the EDI capability and status of these locations and their EDI trading partners. For example:

- the number and identity of trading partners with which EDI had been implemented

211

EDI Implementation Guide

- which type of EDI solutions had been implemented

- which and how many UN/EDIFACT messages were being exchanged

- volumes of data being exchanged via EDI.

This is a much simpler achievement for a large corporation, however autonomous its units, than for a government department or Agency, operating in a diverse community such as the NHS. However, thought should be given to why companies invest as much as they do in focal points, such as the one in this example, what it is that focal point does and how, in each environment, the benefits of using the opportunities available can be emulated.

13 EDI in Europe

This chapter looks at the role of the European Commission (EC) in the development of the use of EDI in Europe. Some of the significant programmes of the EC are looked at in some detail and a brief overview of EDI activity in most of the EC countries is then given.

The pace of EDI development varies dramatically in the leading economies of the European market. The UK is clearly ahead of Germany and, to a lesser extent, France, but the adoption of EDI is slower than was predicted in the late 1980s. This would not matter if there were ample time to let each country, and each business sector, develop its own timetable for the adoption of EDI. In comparison, the rest of the world is moving fast in the adoption of EDI and the USA, Australia, and the emerging economies of the Far East are now forcing the pace. The adoption of EDI in the economies of Singapore, Hong Kong and Indonesia is being heavily pushed by government initiatives. More recently, moves in the USA to push EDI and electronic trading through the government-backed super-highways programme increasingly puts Europe in danger of being left behind.

The EC has always tried to reinforce the European telecommunications and transport infrastructure in order to improve the market position of European companies. To do this, it is continuing to give a high priority to programmes in telecommunications and information policy, including EDI.

Chapter XII of the Maastricht Treaty provides a framework for the construction and extension of trans-European networks in the telecommunications sector. This direction was confirmed after the Copenhagen summit of 1993, when a statement was made that the Commission planned to invest 30 billion ECU over the next 10 years to develop the network structure, 0.5 billion in the information infrastructure and 5 to 8 billions in corresponding programmes.

The policy of the Commission in telecommunications is based on the Open Network Provision (ONP) principle. This means that everybody wanting to offer services, for example VANS, must make available open access to the telecommunications infrastructure at market prices. The adoption of this principle is a major step towards the single market in telecommunications and gives a new framework for the dissemination of EDI in Europe. These moves by the EC are putting increasing pressure on local PTTs. Under the combined threats of global competition, new technologies and the 1998 deadline for the removal of state telecommunications monopolies, the national PTTs are looking for new partners and new ways of providing services. The Commission, by enforcing the ONP principle, has ensured that national governments will put the general European economic interest ahead of their wish to protect their local PTTs. The building of trans-European networks is part of the general aim to accelerate structural industrial change and all the main IT programmes focus on this network dimension of industrial policy.

The Commission's view is that, since more and more of the market activity is computerised, and the dynamics of interchange are essential for business success, the point at which telecommunications services and information processing come together is the very nerve path of economic development. This is where EDI and Electronic Funds Transfer come into the picture.

13.1 European Commission Programmes

The Commission has supported the development of telecommunications and EDI in many of its older programmes and the latest of these, the Interchange of Data between Administrations (IDA) programme, has been set up to encourage the exchange of government and administrative information between the member states of the European Community. The Commission hopes to encourage the development of European networks and the use of EDI by this move. It also believes it can help to solve one of the real problems of the European business community by improving the cumbersome relationship between Member State and Community administration. The IDA programme will build on the results of some of the earlier programmes such as the Trade Electronic Data Interchange Systems (TEDIS), Co-operation in Automation of Data and Documentation for Imports/ Exports and Agriculture (CADDIA), Inter-institutional Integrated Services Information System (INSIS) and European Nervous System – telecommunications for administrations (ENS) programmes. The following sub-sections take a brief look at the work of these programmes.

13.1.1 TEDIS

The first phase of the TEDIS programme was launched in October 1987 as a 2-year programme and came into effect on 1 January 1988. It was set up under EC Directorate General XIII (for Telecommunications, Information Industries and Innovation) with a budget of 5.3 million ECU and performed the following activities:

- co-ordination of EDI initiatives in several major European industry sectors including:

    – vehicle manufacturing (ODETTE)

    – chemicals (CEFIC)

    – re-insurance (RINET)

    – electronics and data processing equipment (EDIFICE)

    – retail (EAN)

    – transport.

    Other smaller industry sectors were also supported.

- support for the work of setting up EDI standards by providing the secretariat to the Western European EDIFACT Board

- definition of specific telecommunications requirements for EDI, including early definitions for the X.400 requirement

- work on understanding the legal and security requirements of EDI

- many promotional activities for EDI, including surveys of European software, and identification of the needs of Small and Medium-sized Enterprises (SMEs)

EDI Implementation Guide

- co-ordination of the work being done in many of the individual member countries' bodies on promoting awareness and use of EDI. In the UK this role is fulfilled by the Simpler Trade Procedures Board (SITPRO). There are equivalent bodies in most other European countries.

The second phase of the TEDIS programme started in July 1991 and finished in July 1994. The budget was 25 million ECU and the scope of the work was much wider. The previous tasks in promotion, standardisation, legal and security were still continued but more funds were allocated to projects designed to support EDI implementations in different industry sectors with particular focus on integrating EDI across multiple industry sectors. The telecommunications work continued and concentrated on the use of X.400 and Integrated Services Digital Network (ISDN) for EDI and the interworking between European VANS.

Two calls for proposals were made in 1993. The first, in February, aimed to provide further financial support for the implementation of three central policies of the programme: standardisation, pan-European multi-sector projects and a network of regional awareness centres. As a result of this call for proposals, further support was provided to communities wishing to migrate from their own interchange formats to the UN/EDIFACT recommendations.

The Commission has, through its support for the standards process, been a leading promoter of European and international standards. The last few years have seen the EDI message development process grow from an informal body of experts into a large global bureaucracy. The growing scale of the process and its widening geographical scope has led to difficulties in co-ordination, which have caused message development to slow down and fewer messages to be adopted as United Nations Standard Messages. This partly reflects the maturing of the process. But the underlying difficulties also relate to conflicts between the needs of participants: between users who wanted stable messages and others who wanted rapid message development to meet business needs; between users who wanted messages for use in closely defined regional communities and users who wanted universal messages. The Commission's key requirement has been to prevent the formation of incompatible standards within Europe as these represent barriers to the single market.

In order to help with this process, a memorandum of understanding for the operation of EDI registration authorities was finalised in December 1993. The different conventions for identifying senders and recipients of EDI messages have for some time been a problem inhibiting interchange of messages between different sectors. The memorandum lays down a structure and procedure for the operation of registration authorities for EDI names and addresses.

The message development process of the Western European EDIFACT Board is supported through the Message Development Groups (MDGs). These groups are provided with secretariat and technical support co-ordination through TEDIS. The MDGs are listed in Figure 13.

One of the problems which have been created by the ending of the TEDIS programme in 1994 is where the support of the UN/EDIFACT message development process should be moved to. The plan is to move this work to the Comité Européen de Normalisation (CEN), which is the European standardisation body.

13.1.2 CADDIA

The CADDIA programme, which came to an end in June 1992, aimed to co-ordinate the activities of the EC Member States and the Commission on the use of data communications systems for the monitoring of imports and exports, the management and financial control of the organisation of the agricultural market, and the collection and dissemination of statistical data on intra-Community trade. CADDIA was the precursor of the involvement of the national statistical administrations and the co-operation between the three sectors taking part, customs, agriculture and statistics. It made a substantial contribution to the development of data communications networks between administrations, which was made necessary by the elimination of internal frontier controls in January 1993.

13.1.3 INSIS

The INSIS programme aims to improve communications between Community institutions and bodies, and between them and the member states, by stressing the co-ordinated and harmonised use of information technology and telecommunications. The programme's priorities are electronic transmission of written texts, systems for accessing information of Community interest, and teleconferencing systems. Although this programme has no specific interest in EDI, its work is being taken forward into the IDA programme and is, therefore, mentioned here.

13.1.4 ENS

The programme was set up in June 1991 as a two-year programme. It started work in January 1992 with a total budget of 430 million ECU.

The objective of the programme was to perform research and development, concentrating on the requirements of administrations, in the following areas:

- defining common requirements for information exchange and examining the need for interoperability between electronic information networks within member states

- carrying out studies and pre-normative research for the definition and subsequent establishment of the trans-European telematic services networks essential to national administrations for the completion of the single market, the provision of the services necessary to the free movement of persons, goods, services and capital and for increasing economic and social cohesion in the Community.

Thirteen projects covering a small but representative set of areas were launched to look at the requirements for exchange of administrative data. Each of the projects was committed to its individual objectives of setting up and running pilot programmes and to the overall aims of the programme. The experience gained in the pilot elements of the projects created a core of experience in the Member States, an identification of the broader non-technical issues requiring ongoing and possible future actions and a sound basis for the definition of the overlay network. Many of these projects used EDI techniques in their pilots to achieve the exchange of data. A fourteenth project was started late in 1993 to encapsulate the findings and actions in a handbook and to provide a core of information to take the ENS objectives into succeeding programmes.

The fourteen projects in the programme were:

- European Business Register (EBR), which demonstrated the feasibility of using networks between public administrations entrusted with the official registration of companies

- European Water Traffic Information System (EWTIS), which aimed at the design and implementation of a uniform system for real-time ship-to-shore, and inter-port communications. The project concentrated on reducing the number of calamities and safeguarding the maritime environment by reduction of illegal waste discharge and limiting the effects of pollution. EDI was used to exchange data in this project

- Information Net and Card for the Adapted Management of European Road Transport and Traffic (INCA), which aimed at providing an infrastructure for effective transport-licensing operations. The project looked at smart cards for holding licence information and using EDI to exchange information between licensing authorities. A full description of the INCA project is included in Annex A, 'Case studies'

- Computer Aided Post in Europe (CAPE), which looked at laying the foundations for an improved intra-Community postal service. The project used EDI to exchange messages between postal authorities

- Care Telematics Project (CARE), which looked at improving communications between national administrations responsible for health, environmental health, natural and man-made disaster management and medical-care-related planning, financing, administration and service delivery. The project was hosted by the World Health Organisation

- Transplant Euro Computer Network (TECN), which looked at exchanging information on the availability of organs between transplant facilities

- Social Security Network (SOSENET), which aimed to exchange information between social security organisations on pension rights accumulated in different member states. EDI was used as the mechanism for exchanging the information

- ENVIRONET, which looked at mechanisms for crisis management authorities to handle the tasks of alarming, event handling, event assessment and normal day-to-day management for river, air and coastal environments

- Income Tax Management for NOn-Resident Taxpayers (NORT), which aimed to provide tax authorities with information on fiscal operations carried out by their residents in other EC Member states. The project used EDI to exchange this information

- looked at the development of an internationally harmonised communications service suited to public administrations. This project involved several Euopean PTTs

- Certification Centre, which looked at providing an administrative focus for conformance testing and certification for ENS application pilots through the provision of registers of tested and certified products

- Retrieval and Interchange of Standards in Europe (RISE), which looked at setting up mechanisms for the exchange and retrieval of standards information from libraries

- Support for Application Pilots in ENS (SAPIENS), which aimed to provide help and support to the pilot projects and to document the pilot project experience

- Measures for ENS Administrations Services (MENSA), which was the last project to be set up, with the objective of producing the technical handbook for the ENS programme.

Several UK government departments were involved in the pilot projects of this programme.

Although the pilots finished officially at the end of 1993, the programme has been extended to look at several areas of common interest which were highlighted by the previous parts of the programme. Several of these new projects are looking at aspects of developing European communications services and one is looking specifically at legal and security issues related to the exchange of administrative data.

13.1.5 IDA

This programme started its activities in 1993 with a plan to start the main parts of the programme in 1994. The programme is expected to last into 1997. The final budgets should be around 340 million ECU.

The IDA programme will bring together the experience of all of the previous programmes and consists of two parts:

- part 1 covers Community support for projects of common interest on computerised interchange of administrative information, data and documents between administrations within the Community

- part 2 deals with measures to ensure interoperability of data communications networks and applications, increase reliability and reduce costs.

The initial documents on the programme do not mention specific solutions such as EDI but it is expected that EDI and UN/EDIFACT will play an important role in the mechanisms used for exchanging data and information.

The Commission is placing great emphasis on 'projects of common interest' in part 1 of the programme and envisages that this will take the form of feasibility studies and support for implementation.

13.2 Country Profiles

Most surveys estimating usage of EDI across Europe have looked at the number of users rather than the volume of transactions. A recent survey of the paper industry, carried out by Arjo Wiggins, looked at EDI penetration in the United Kingdom, France and Germany, based on the percentage of business transactions carried by EDI. The results of the survey are summarised overleaf:

EDI Implementation Guide

Country	Overall %	Finance %
United Kingdom	2.0	2.2
France	1.0	2.2
Germany	1.9	2.6

These numbers are still small compared to many predictions which were made five years ago, including previous reports from Arjo Wiggins. Other reports make the comment that most large organisations are taking up EDI rapidly but that resistance to EDI is larger than expected in Small- and Medium-sized Enterprises (SMEs). This is also confirmed by the Arjo Wiggins numbers which report EDI usage in large organisations (over 7500 employees) as 7%. The take-up of EDI in SMEs will probably increase as large customers increasingly mandate that their suppliers adopt EDI.

A survey carried out for TEDIS by Ovum and Xcoms of Belgium shows that most EDI traffic is carried using industry or nationally defined protocols and not UN/EDIFACT. New communities are using UN/EDIFACT as their preferred standard and many existing communities are slowly moving towards it. The estimate is that by 1997 most traffic (about 90%) will be based on UN/EDIFACT. Take-up of X.400 as the communications protocol is not expected to be as rapid and will constitute only 60% of the traffic by 1997.

The TEDIS report, and other reports from PFA Consultants in the UK, all indicate that the UK and the Netherlands are the countries which lead Europe in the adoption of EDI. The Netherlands has the largest number of projects but the UK has the largest number of fully commercial projects operating. The estimates for both countries is about 2.3% penetration. Belgium, Sweden, France and Switzerland follow with between 0.9% and 1.4% penetration. Of the other European countries, most surprisingly, Germany sits at the bottom of the list with a reported penetration in the TEDIS survey of 0.4%, along with Spain.

Chapter 13
EDI in Europe

A brief summary of activity in some of the mainland European Countries follows. Further examples of activity in the United Kingdom and elsewhere are given in Annex A, 'Case studies'.

13.2.1 Austria

There is one large EDI project in Austria, known as ECODEX, which is sponsored by the Article Numbering Association. It uses the German standard, SEDAS, for retail, and UN/EDIFACT for other industries.

13.2.2 Belgium

Two banking communities account for the majority of EDI users and although Belgium has an estimated EDI penetration of only 0.4%, most of the activities have an international bias. The two banking projects are: CIRI for the national banking system and SWIFT for the international banking settlement system. The RINET project is also based in Belgium and is working on EDI systems for European re-insurance companies. There is some overlap between this community and the LIMNET community based on Lloyds of London.

13.2.3 France

EDI in France has been given strong support by the French Government with an initiative led by the Prime Minister in 1991. The French parliament has more recently voted to eliminate paper from government administrative routines and EDI projects have been launched in important areas of public administration. Projects include the exchange of EDI messages by civil courts and lawyers, customs, the exchange of EDI messages between the Ministry of Finance and its private sector partners, the use of EDI for public procurement, and the collection of VAT and statistical data.

In the commercial sector, the use of EDI has been led by the major multinationals acting as 'hubs' exchanging messages with their numerous smaller 'spokes'. GALIA, the French automotive association, supports EDI in that sector, providing a VAN which carries messages to its own and ODETTE standards. The retail sector uses its own standard and provides a VAN service for its members. The transport and logistics sector also uses the retail standard for commercial and logistic transactions as well as a French standard specific to transport and based on UN/EDIFACT syntax.

EDI Implementation Guide

There are many EDI user groups in France, which provide a great deal of support to their members. EDIFRANCE was created in 1990 by the French Government under the umbrella of AFNOR, the French standards body. EDIFRANCE draws its members from both the public and private sector and aims to promote the use of EDI in all sectors of industry throughout France. A French awareness centre has also been created by the Chamber of Commerce using TEDIS funding under the awareness programme. French EDI users are active in many EC-funded projects and have helped to found many pan-European EDI groups.

The current French EDI user base is estimated to be 5000, double that in 1990, and it is estimated to be growing at about 10–15% annually. Usage of UN/EDIFACT messages is estimated to be over 50% of the total EDI traffic and use of X.400 accounts for about 55% of traffic. This makes the support of international standards in France relatively high compared to the rest of Europe in general.

13.2.4 Germany

Germany has a long tradition of EDI, using industry-specific messages since the 1970s. Two national standards have dominated EDI development in Germany: SEDAS for the retail and distribution sector, and VDA for the automotive sector. In transport, insurance and banking EDI has started later, but still with industry standards. Only the chemical and electronic industries and the Bundespost Telekom use UN/EDIFACT standards alongside their own. It is estimated that there are about 2500 users of EDI in Germany.

German companies have been sceptical about UN/EDIFACT since the 'Quality Control Review' in 1990. This review was undertaken by the UN/EDIFACT Board, when it was perceived that the UN/EDIFACT standards were being extended by different Message Development Groups in a way which made them incompatible. The review resulted in tighter controls being applied to the message development process. German companies regarded this process as puttting the whole standard into disrepute. Only recently have they started to show greater interest in the more regulated standards development procedures, which have given them more confidence in UN/EDIFACT. This view of UN/EDIFACT may have caused the reluctance to report usage to a TEDIS survey, which the Germans perceived to be biased towards UN/EDIFACT. This may well have resulted in the unexpectedly low penetration of EDI in Germany.

The German user group DEDIG was created only in the summer of 1993, through the initiatives of the Economics Ministry, the German Chamber of Commerce and DIN (the German standards institute), to promote and support EDI. The Bundespost Telekom is offering very competitively priced X.400 services and this may help to support the wider use of EDI.

13.2.5 Italy

In relation to other major European countries Italy has been a late starter in the use of EDI and most companies only started implementing in the 1990s. The moves towards EDI have been led by the large multinationals which have imposed the technology on their often reluctant trading partners. There are estimated to be about 1200 users of EDI and this is expected to grow at about 15–20% per annum. The volume of EDI messages being transmitted per user is very low compared to other countries. The most significant and largest user of EDI in Italy is Fiat with its automotive suppliers.

UN/EDIFACT messages account for about two thirds of the transmissions, the only other message standard being ODETTE in the automotive industry. There are very few X.400 communications users. This may be because many of the organisations are using PC implementations, which have been offered as complete packages by the VAN providers. The provision of VANS has been restricted in Italy and there are only three providers: GEIS, INTESA (a joint venture between Fiat and IBM) and SARITEL, which provides a service on the public sector network.

There has been a general lack of support for the use and promotion of EDI by the Italian Government and EDI is not being adopted for large-scale use within public administrations. The customs and some port authorities are the only active users of EDI. EDIFORUM Italia was established in 1988 as a special interest group of the Italian Telematics Forum to promote the use of EDI in public bodies and administrations but so far has not been very successful.

EDI Implementation Guide

EDI is not being promoted effectively in Italy. It is being approached at the organisational level rather than the community level and users are failing to benefit from community experience. Without direction and impetus from government and user groups, the development of EDI in Italy will occur in a less than supportive national environment.

13.2.6 Netherlands

The Netherlands is probably the EDI success story of Europe. The Dutch EDIFORUM user group is very active in promoting EDI in both the public and private sectors. Public organisations account for about 50% of the estimated 10,000 users in the Netherlands and many EDI projects have received government financial and promotional backing. The opening speech of the annual EDI conference in November 1992 was made by the Prime Minister with the title 'EDI – What does it cost and what does it bring me?' Since 1990 the EDI user population has increased six- or seven-fold, giving the Netherlands probably the largest user base in Europe and certainly the largest base per head of population. It is estimated that there are 135 active EDI communities.

Several factors may account for the success in the Netherlands but consistent standards, VAN interconnectivity and extensive government support are among the major ones.

Because the Dutch started later with EDI than many other of the major countries, there was no large existing base of organisations using community or national standards. In 1988 they decided to move the TRANSCOM retail community away from the national standard to UN/EDIFACT. This move has not yet been achieved in Germany, France or the UK. There is an almost total adoption of the UN/EDIFACT standard in all Dutch communities. The single focus of EDI through EDIFORUM provides a consistent approach to developing and using UN/EDIFACT messages.

The largest VAN in the Netherlands is run by the Dutch PTT and is X.400-based. The PTT adopted an early policy of interconnection to other VAN services. Under the government-backed VEDI project, designed to develop the EDI market, a particular sub-project (VEDET/400) has been set up to link the VANS using X.400.

Chapter 13
EDI in Europe

Interconnection is particularly important to the Dutch market because the main EDI communities do not sponsor a particular VAN or set up their own services. This has resulted in sophisticated EDI software packages designed to connect to multiple VANS and has encouraged a very flourishing software market. This is a very different approach from many communities in other European countries.

The support and usage of EDI in the public sector is extensive. In November 1992 there were reported to be 2800 users in the health sector, 460 in social security and 400 in government. One of the social services projects uses EDI as a tool for easing the administrative burden on employees and banks by handling sick-leave payments. The largest of the Government projects links 700 municipalities to 300 government offices for recording change of residence and other personal data.

There are many other significant private sector projects including: EDIFLOWER for supporting the Dutch flower industry, INTIS for supporting transport in general and the port of Rotterdam, the DIY retail sector and insurance led by Assurantic Data Netwerk (ADN).

13.2.7 Norway

The Norwegians believe that, living on the edge of Europe, close links and modern methods of communication between government and industry are necessary for national survival. They have created the National Infrastructure for Information Technology programme to simplify the exchange of information between different public sector information systems. This programme is supporting projects in: the National Insurance Administration, for exchanging invoices and information between GPs and employers; the Norwegian State Railway, for exchanging documents with its customers; the Public Roads Administration, for exchanging invoices with its vendors; and the Ministry of Justice, for exchanging information with the police. The health sector is also involved in some projects.

13.2.8 Sweden

There are an estimated fifteen EDI communities in Sweden. Open EDI islands have been developed in several industry sectors, including banking and finance, and construction. (In this context 'Open EDI Islands' is the term used to describe the EDI communities operating within Sweden – they are separate but aim to do things in an open and common manner, hence the term which has nothing to do with 'Open-EDI' as described in Chapter 14, 'Future directions'). Each of the emerging communities have drawn up implementation rules for using UN/EDIFACT standards in their own sector. The most active of all the EDI communities is based on Volvo. They were pioneers in using EDI in the automotive industry and in the development of ODETTE standards.

13.2.9 Other European Countries

All the other European countries have set up bodies to promote the use of EDI and UN/EDIFACT and they are all actively getting involved with international and national EDI projects. Spain has a number of communities now, as does Portugal. Greece is still in the very early stages but has taken part in EC projects in ENS and DRIVE. All of the newer countries will adopt UN/EDIFACT standards from the start with the possible exception of the automotive industries, where ODETTE is still the most widely accepted European standard. However, ODETTE messages are now available to work with UN/EDIFACT syntax.

13.2.10 Further Details

Further details on developments in mainland Europe are given in the following publications:

- Electronic Trader Magazine

- ENS 1993 Report

- Ovum Report on VANS Market Europe 1993

- PFA Research Reports on Europe 1994

- TEDIS reports for 1990, and 1994 and other survey reports

- The European Public Sector EDI Newsletter.

14 Future Directions

Hopefully, this Guide has provided a thorough grounding in the principles and practice of EDI. This chapter aims to add an understanding of forthcoming changes and developments in the EDI world and to explain business trends and emerging technologies which will affect the way in which EDI is used.

It would be easy to end this Guide with a long list of promising technologies which will ensure that EDI is widely used and its perceived benefits become pervasive. But that would ignore probably the most important message in this book – that EDI is more than just a technical tool. It is a tool which, when utilised properly, can facilitate a whole new cultural approach, based on partnership and inter-relationships between trading or administrative groups. It is also as well to remember that EDI is not the simplest of tools to implement and, as a result, its usage encourages a resistance to change.

Thus, at the EDI90 conference, Jack Shaw, President of EDI Strategies, said:

> *In North America, a few forward-thinking companies are now integrating their use of EDI with other advanced Information Technologies. Companies are using artificial intelligence, or expert systems, to eliminate human intervention from the processing of routine incoming transactions.*

It should come as no surprise that the aspirations of more than half a decade ago are still no more than that in many cases. (It is also worth noting that those 'Future Technologies' of yesteryear, such as expert systems, now have a clearly defined, small and relatively unimportant niche in the grand scheme of things as their limitations have become understood. Though this is not to belittle the potential for expert systems, it is simply an observation based on current performance.) Similar examples can be found in the conference proceedings of every EDI event during the last decade explaining that EFTPOS, X.400, X.500, CALS, and many others were each the missing piece of the jigsaw that would ensure incredible success for all when harnessed with EDI.

EDI Implementation Guide

Therefore, while this section does attempt to appraise the likely effect of a wide number of technical advances upon the use of EDI and also to explain some of the developments in the EDI community, the key element which will determine the future direction and success of EDI usage is the business and cultural one of perceived benefit.

14.1 Usage Today

It is widely believed today that only 1–2% of businesses in the UK use EDI. This is a higher percentage than the rest of Europe and comparable with North America. Of this small minority, figures from PFA Research (*State of the Nation Update*, 1994) suggest that as few as one in a 100 companies using EDI have fully integrated it into their business processes and are achieving significant benefits. See the discussions in Chapter 13, 'EDI in Europe', for a fuller discussion of relative usage of EDI across Europe.

The percentages for usage and penetration are lower outside the business community, in areas such as public administration. So, is EDI a small niche activity with a few devotees or is it really an immensely promising tool, which has been ignored or overlooked for so long?

The successful users tend to be large corporates, which have been able to invest the necessary resources to implement EDI and which have the organisational magnitude that encourages attention to process and process improvement in order to survive. In this environment, with a focus on logistics, supply chain management, stock utilisation and cash flow, it is easy to see why one or two converts to EDI have been able to achieve so much.

Conversely, the vast majority of users are the small ones, often referred to as SMEs (Small and Medium-sized Enterprises), for whom the use of EDI has been dictated by a larger partner. For these users, the concept of EDI is often alien – allowing automation of their business is not cost-effective and introduces risks which are too great. Thus they are faced with three options:

- rejecting the suggestion to use EDI
- reluctantly adopting just enough EDI to satisfy the partner
- fully embracing and implementing EDI.

Chapter 14
Future Directions

These options are not distinct but should be viewed as points across a spectrum. What is clear, though, is that for a SME to choose the first option risks losing the business which that partner brings. Thus the SME is left with the question 'How much EDI to *do*?' Often the simple answer is the second option, as this is the lowest cost and lowest risk scenario – if the partner changes his operation, it will not unduly affect the SME whereas, if EDI were fully integrated, it might.

The second option also has the benefit that, when several larger partners arrive with slightly different proposals for EDI, each can be accommodated.

Thus the real challenge for the future is to find a way for SMEs to overcome their natural reluctance to adopt EDI. To do this, EDI must be made simpler to implement, with greater encouragement for its usage and more obviously achievable benefits from so doing. Otherwise, EDI risks being relegated to the ranks of a niche technology and a real opportunity to change the business psyche from a combative one to one based upon partnership will have been lost.

There are examples of success: the London Insurance Market (LIMNET) has adopted the use of EDI for its insurance claims processing and because they have operated as a community, developing solutions that are acceptable and beneficial to all, they have created an electronic marketplace where it is quicker, easier and more sensible to transact business using EDI than to contemplate use of the old, manual processes. Indeed, it is becoming clear in this example that to stay in business it may be necessary to accept that there is no longer a manual alternative to EDI which is acceptable in this community.

When planning to implement EDI in or for a government department or Agency, the ability to ensure a solution in which everyone benefits gives a far greater chance of success for all concerned, simply because, by definition, any government initiative will be community-wide and thus have the benefit of easily becoming pervasive. However, this does not mean that it is, therefore, not important that the solution is compatible with other initiatives in the same environment.

14.2 Overcoming the Current Difficulties of EDI

14.2.1 Use of Subsets

One of the major difficulties inherent in EDI as used today is the concept of standards and their usage. The complexity of agreeing data format and content with every trading partner has to be avoided, as this would increase costs and reduce benefits, so that EDI would probably become untenable. This is achieved by agreeing to use a common format.

To make this format or standard widely acceptable, it is made as comprehensive as possible, so that, for example, an invoice used for a drum of preservative in the UK is equally applicable for a bill for crane hire at a remote location overseas with associated customs information or education and consultancy services over a period and, indeed, as a telephone bill in Italy – with multiple tax bands, amounts in thousands of lire and individually itemised calls.

Once a common standard has been developed that meets all of these needs, it is found to be too extensive and complex for any individual need; so subsets are developed for individual uses. Then it is discovered that the particular community in which an organisation operates is not distinct and that there will probably be a need for several versions of a message and subsets of it. (And all of this without considering the implications of data content and what 'Total Amount' means to one trading partner as compared to another.)

To help overcome this complexity, EDI translation software is purchased, which facilitates the selection and set-up of appropriate message formats and subsets for a particular partner and transaction, but does not automate this activity. The translation software is only one component of the whole solution and on its own performs a very limited function. That is, it translates from one file format to another. It has no bearing on trading partner tables or standards selection.

Chapter 14
Future Directions

So what has been achieved? The cost and overhead of developing and agreeing formats individually with each trading partner would not have been cost-justified. To avoid this, an individually agreed format with each trading partner has been retained, but the cost and complexity of using a very comprehensive standard has been added, rather than just agreeing a simple format based on the transactions exchanged today; and complex and expensive software has also been introduced, which needs to be maintained, operated and managed.

To be fair to those who spend so much time developing subsets, it is worth reiterating the major benefits that they bring:

- a complete review and documentation of business information to be used in the subsetting operation that can be used in future implementations (whether EDI or not)

- using a standard subsetting methodology means that only one need be learnt and that it can be a common methodology spanning a number of organisations (if based on an agreed standard)

- one standard as the base for subsets means that the commonality of underlying components, eg syntax, elements etc, need be learned once only, thus saving time and investment.

So, is the average organisation any better off? Most SMEs are not – that is why they go for the lowest cost, least investment option. On the other hand, the large users clearly benefit.

The only way this can be overcome is if all of the participants work together to agree common implementations within a particular market and, ideally, ensure that the market is a large enough community to enable the majority to avoid multiple implementations.

No physical change is required here – though there are initiatives which will alter the marketplace – merely a change of attitude to ensure that the benefit of EDI is realised and thus EDI is implemented for its benefit, not merely for its own sake. It is worth remembering that

EDI Implementation Guide

there are a number of organisations which seek to overcome these problems by providing some guidelines as far as usage is concerned, including migration strategies and best practices. (The *ECA Information Service*, Volume 1 Section 5, provides information on migration.)

14.2.2 Messages and MDGS

The same problems that exist with subsets exist with messages. There appears to be a natural inclination on the part of EDI implementers to believe that their business need is unique and novel and so a new message is needed as nothing extant can meet their need. This is particularly evident in administrative implementations, where a whole series of paper forms is replaced by at least as many EDI messages whereas, with a little lateral thinking, it is not difficult to envisage them all as, say, queries or responses to queries and, as such, to use the same existing message for all (*QRYRSP* in this example).

Similarly, in the retail distribution sector, what is the difference between 'Advance Shipment Notification' and 'Pre-Notification of Delivery' (other than the perspective of the developer)? Does either of these really differ from the UN/EDIFACT *DESADV* (Dispatch Advice) message, except perhaps in the way in which they are used?

The increasing number of Message Development Groups within the UN/EDIFACT process risks exacerbating the problem, unless effective co-ordination across the groups is introduced into the process and the overall aim of the groups changes from one of confirming syntactic acceptability and functional applicability to one of focusing on simplification of the plethora of options currently available. Only in this way will the *raison d'être* for standards, that of simplification of usage, actually be achieved.

14.2.3 Directory usage

Most of the comments relating to subsets and messages can also be applied to directories. In addition, there is the difficulty of encouraging users to use codes in place of free text in their messages, as only then can full automation be contemplated, and once they start to use codes, to do so in a way that uses existing directories without the need for new code development (which moves away from standard usage again).

Chapter 14
Future Directions

14.2.4 Lack of Change or Version Control

One of the major weaknesses of the UN/EDIFACT approach to EDI is that it is totally passive, providing guidelines and syntax for messages and standards, but absolutely no control on how they are used. This is particularly apparent when it comes to updating a standard – there is no change management in the system and it is, therefore, up to each user to decide when or even whether to update the version of the message in use. For someone using EDI with just 100 partners, this means that either a global announcement of message change is communicated or 100 different agreements are negotiated and made. It is rare that the former case can be achieved even by the most dominant of partners, simply due to the logistics of systems or application change. For a government department with potentially hundreds of thousands of partners, this aspect of EDI could prove very expensive to manage.

However, the UN/EDIFACT board is not to blame for this – the above is simply one example of this oft-overlooked area of EDI. Typical application development practice says that, when something is changed, all the affected modules are tested to ensure compatibility and their introduction is carefully managed so as not to impact any other elements. This is fine within a closed DP environment, but if changes affect the data which is used to format the EDI messages to be sent to trading partners, should the partners be involved in the application testing? Should they even be aware of planned changes? There is no simple answer, but this whole area is one which will need careful thought if a huge overhead of testing, update and alignment is to be avoided. See Chapter 11, 'Operational management', for a fuller discussion of this aspect and the remarks on Open-EDI which follow for a possible solution.

14.2.5 X.435

X.435 is explained in Chapter 6, 'Software', and has long been promoted as the missing component in the standardisation process. However, to accept this is to miss the point of X.435 and to misinterpret the role of the VAN.

The availability of X.435 allows a large user of E-mail with an X.400 infrastructure to implement EDI without the need for new investments at this level. There will still be a need for all of the high-cost items such as software and the resource to define messages, produce mappings, test implementations and manage roll-outs.

X.435 also provides a common access to multiple VANS, instead of using VANS proprietary access software for each connection – one piece of software per connection. Bearing in mind that the VANS tend to give their proprietary access software away to users and that each X.435 implementation is likely to be as individual as a standard X.400 set-up, this again is a debatable benefit.

However, there are a number of developments in the pipeline which should improve the lot of the EDI user and these are detailed below.

14.3 Encouraging Developments

14.3.1 Information Highways

There has been much press coverage of Information Highways, Electronic Commerce, the National Network Infrastructure and the Internet since the early days of President Clinton's tenure of office, when Vice-President Gore sent an open letter to heads of government departments, instructing them to build plans for a National Network Infrastructure, which would allow technologies like E-mail and EDI to become pervasive.

This subject has broadened to encompass the increasing usage of the Internet (a collection of loosely coupled servers forming a world-wide network of mixed ownership, which has grown out of the US defence industry and academia), which now has many millions of regular users world-wide, originally for E-mail, but increasingly for access to data bases, servers and conferences.

Business has started moving into the Internet environment, making it easier to use by introducing tools and facilities such as the 'World-wide Web' and using them to build 'CommerceNet' within the Internet community. CommerceNet is one of the Internet options which can be used for EDI traffic and, as such, is encouraging and enabling a much wider community to reach and to use EDI.

However, because of its significantly different user base and totally different technical origins, it is not unrealistic to imagine that EDI on CommerceNet may soon diverge or develop in different directions from that which is

Chapter 14
Future Directions

practised today. As long as the UN/EDIFACT board is able to keep up with this process of change, this may not be a bad thing in the light of the challenges outlined in the previous section.

14.3.2 CALS

In addition to the network developments, there have been a number of initiatives which have aimed at mandating the use of EDI in the logistics process in order to achieve real change. The largest of these initiatives have always been defence-based and the largest of all is the US Department of Defense Continuous Acquisition and Lifecycle Support (CALS) initiative.

The aim of CALS is to improve the quality of systems and products, to reduce lead-times or time to market or deployment, and to reduce lifecycle cost.

This is not a simple supply chain automation project but an attempt to re-engineer the whole process from initial design using CAD/CAM data exchange to hand-over of on-line manuals and reference literature with the completed product. In this way, the drawings which are developed during the design stage are the basis for the subsequent stage of the development and can be traced right through to the maintenance drawings which the final user of the product receives.

Initiatives such as CALS overcome the SME problems described at the beginning of this chapter because the whole industry has to change to fit in with the new process and all participants can thus share the benefits – this is the real power and benefit of government department or Agency-led initiatives; if they are properly implemented they can become pervasive, not just in the direct relationships with that Agency or body but throughout the whole community, and the benefits, once this happens, far exceed those that can be shown in the business case for any particular participant, transaction or relationship.

Note: A fuller description of CALS is contained in the EDI93 Conference paper 'Why would you want to use CALS?', given by Michael Potter of Applied Network Research.

14.3.3 Utility Billing

A change which is not as powerful as CALS but which could be as effective a catalyst is utility billing. Many utilities find themselves having to compete to keep their existing business customers, and one way in which they can do this is by providing better and more accurate information – for example, consolidated bills across all of a customer's sites, greater detail of telephone calls made and received, fuel consumption details and statistics. All of these are examples of information which will allow a customer to control their business better and so remain a more satisfied customer. To achieve any of them, a utility is committing itself to huge amounts of paper and administrative effort, or simple and regular EDI transmissions. EDI is often the only way in which this level of support and information exchange can be achieved and it has the additional benefit that it allows the utility to work closely with the customer and understand what the information is used for, what information is needed and, thus, how better that customer can be supported.

Again, the relationship between a utility and its customers is not that dissimilar to that between a government Agency and its customers or clients.

14.4 Diverse and hybrid EDI solutions

Most of this Guide has focused on how to implement EDI in the same way that others have done to date. This is a very effective way to remove paper, manual intervention and all of the other aspects mentioned in Annex B, 'Preparing an EDI business case'. However, it takes no account of some of the hybrid forms of EDI which are being implemented to simplify start-up, particularly for SMEs, or some of the new areas in which EDI is being used or is likely to be used.

14.4.1 Hybrid forms of EDI

Often the initial justification for EDI or the short-term aim is to automate an existing process. This can best be achieved if as many trading partners as possible adopt the solution as quickly as possible. As can be seen from earlier sections of this Guide, a decision to use EDI is not to be taken lightly and implementation cannot be expected to take place overnight. Thus various hybrid forms of EDI have arisen to allow organisations which want or need a fast roll-out of EDI to achieve their aim without the need for trading partners to move as quickly.

Chapter 14
Future Directions

A simple example is EDI-to-fax. The leading partner sends out annual statements as EDI messages. There can be no hope for 100% take-up at the first attempt, but initially the justification may be in the cost saving of removing the old process. This can be achieved by sending the statements as EDI messages, and having a third party translate, reformat and send them on as fax transmissions to all of those partners who are unable to receive them as EDI. This can bring only first-level benefits, as it is, by definition, only applicable or suitable for outbound transmissions, but it is an effective aid to speeding the take-up of EDI and can be used to help trading partners up the learning curve.

Other forms of hybridisation currently available or widely discussed include EDI-to-post (the Royal Mail EDIPOST service being a prime example) or the telephone-to-EDI solutions being trialled by various organisations including, for example, a well-known chemical company, which is using it to allow non-EDI enabled customers to report on arrival and status of hazardous materials.

14.4.2 CAD/CAM

As defined in Chapter 2, 'Basic concepts', technical EDI is the transfer of technical drawings using EDI. The difficulties here relate to finding a common way of representing drawings produced by different packages and converting from one package to another. However, a number of initiatives are under development, which will increase the use of EDI for this form of data transfer, not least the CALS initiative mentioned earlier.

As these techniques become more easily accessible, the breadth and scope of EDI usage will grow.

14.4.3 Image

An alternative to developing standards to represent technical drawings is to use existing standards with images (of whatever form) appended. Thus, an insurance claim message may have, instead of free text describing a damaged ship, an appended video clip of the ship and the damage sustained.

None of the standards organisations is currently developing message syntaxes to handle this type of example, but some users are experimenting in just the way described.

EDI Implementation Guide

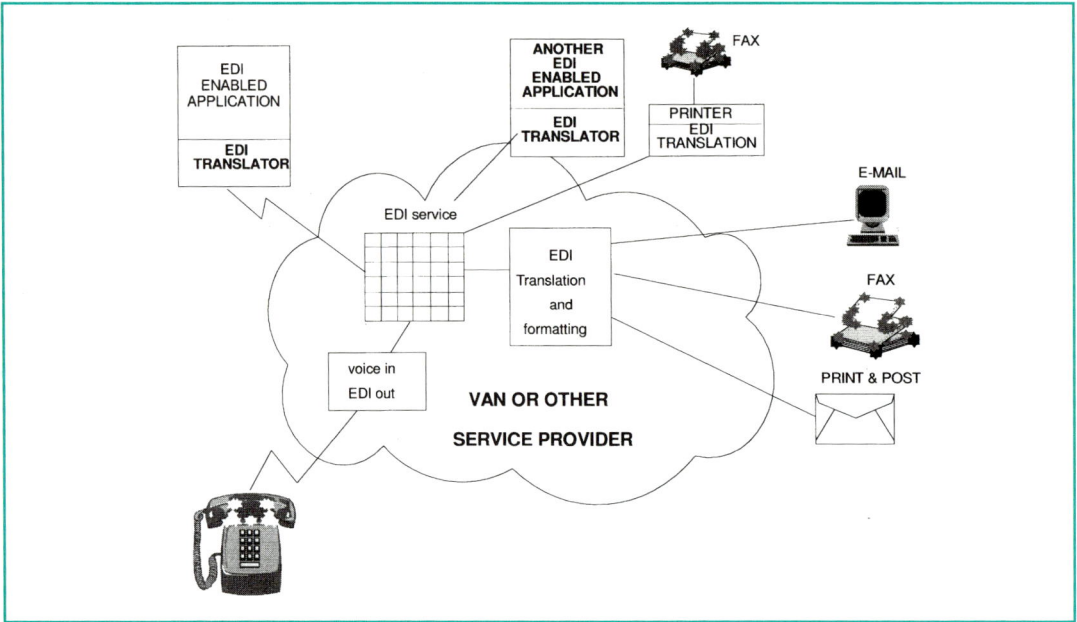

Figure 40: Hybrid EDI options

As with all of these examples, in order to be successful, EDI needs to fit into the business activity and practices of those who use it and to blend with the other technologies that the user decides to implement. Thus, as long as the standards organisations continue to support new developments and initiatives such as these, the use and application of EDI will continue to grow and expand.

14.4.4 Technological Advances

The previous section gave examples of some of the ways in which EDI is beginning to be used. This section gives some short examples of where the benefits of using EDI in this way are likely to be seen.

14.4.4.1 Multimedia

Multimedia is a widely used term, referring to the combination of video and sound in computer applications, ranging from being able to see someone at the other end of a telephone line to displaying pictures transmitted by the Hubble Space Telescope. Where does EDI fit? Generally, in support of multimedia applications: the motor dealer who has a sophisticated multimedia application for guidance through the servicing of a new model, provides remote question and answer support and similar consultancy and details lead-times and prices for the various parts involved. This is an imaginary solution

Chapter 14
Future Directions

which is likely to be available in the near future and to be similar to many other applications in many other industries and areas. In all of these, EDI provides the capability of simple update and automated management.

14.4.4.2 Kiosks

Once multimedia applications become widely available, the ability to make the applications accessible to the ultimate end-user, the general public, will be feasible and sensible. Already, retail kiosks containing multimedia displays of goods which can be ordered are appearing in some stores and airport lounges. Others are being produced for tax and social security guidance and support. In all of these, the benefits of using EDI to provide simple update and automated management, coupled with the ability to buffer the central or server application from the end-user or client application, will ensure continued growth and success. For further information on this subject, see Case Studies 1–4 in *Information and the public*, available from CCTA.

14.4.4.3 Airborne shopping

The concept of the kiosk may be taken one stage further, by addressing the sophisticated entertainment systems which are becoming increasingly common on passenger aircraft. If an aircraft operator is to provide a system which allows passengers to shop with any of a number of retailers, specify delivery requirements, pay by credit card, collect or browse news and information, gamble, select and view a film or other programme or any of a number of other activities – how does that airline handle the mass of orders and delivery instructions, updates to information, billing, credit checks and so on? There appear to be two choices: either many individual agreements and developments with many suppliers and third parties, or EDI.

There are many developments of airborne shopping currently being piloted and developed and at least one is starting to investigate the benefits of using EDI for all of the 'back end' communications and information distribution. It will be interesting to see which solutions prove most successful.

14.4.4.4 Cable television

A final example – if an airline operator is able to provide the solutions and services described above for its passengers, why then should a cable television operator not do the same for its subscribers? The same solutions

EDI Implementation Guide

will be needed, the same problems will need to be overcome. The simple conclusion is that, with EDI, it is feasible; without, it is no more than a nice idea and a potential management nightmare.

14.4.5 Groupware and others

Of course, there is always the possibility that EDI will stand still and be swept away by some newer, simpler, cheaper, better way of doing the same things. Or, alternatively, some totally different solution.

There are examples of new communities deciding to use E-mail to agreed and simple formats in order to avoid what they see as the pain of full, standard EDI. There are cases where this is the correct thing to do, as discussed in 14.2.1, 'Use of subsets'; however, as usage grows, these solutions tend to develop into full EDI solutions or end up with greater problems than they sought to avoid by not using full, standard EDI.

Other implementations, such as those utilising groupware products such as Lotus Notes, grow out of the formalisation of person-to-person E-mail communications and provide alternatives to EDI, but miss many of the benefits that can be achieved (see Chapter 2, 'Basic concepts').

These are examples of new solutions where EDI could have been used but has not. In each of these examples, it is easy to see that EDI is a better long-term solution. However, this need not be the case. It is not inconceivable that the benefits that EDI allows could be achieved by some totally original alternative that avoids the difficulties and costs associated with EDI – for example, a simple device driver (like a printer definition), which will take information passed to it and structure it in such a way that it can be handled by the equivalent component on the partner's machine.

The challenge is for the EDI community to understand this potential and either look for this better alternative or develop the solution they have into something that can withstand such a challenge. The natural reluctance to change once EDI has been implemented is understandable, but must be resisted if long-term benefits and improvements are to be gained.

Chapter 14
Future Directions

14.4.6 Interactive – EDI

One potential area of significant progress, advance and change is that of interactive EDI (I-EDI). The need it is being develped to address is that of constrained supply. There are many such examples: booking space on a ship, in a container or on a plane, booking lorries or delivery runs. All of these tend to need an immediate response stating availability information upon which a decision can be made.

The most commonly quoted example is the travel agent who is arranging a travel itinerary for a customer. The agent needs to find one or more connecting flights, vacant hotel rooms, available hire cars and various other items to provide a complete picture for the customer. The customer will then accept them all as a package or request changes, which will involve the agent in another iteration.

If and when the customer accepts the package, it is imperative that all of the flights requested still have a vacant seat or seats, depending upon the number in the party. It is of no use knowing that there were vacancies when the enquiry was made if now, five minutes later, they have been booked by another agent for another customer. What is required is for the seats, the hotel rooms and the hire cars to be locked when the agent enquires and either unlocked (released) or booked, depending upon the customer's response.

Historically, this has been achieved with proprietary solutions such as the Computerised Reservation Systems (CRS), which the airlines have developed and into which the hotel community have had to develop access. This has been very successful but it is expensive and, with 3–4 CRS systems, it is not as cost-effective as a generic solution, such as EDI would provide, if it were suitable.

I-EDI is a definition of EDI which allows a 'conversation' or 'session' to take place, whereby two or more applications communicate over a sequence of operations, like a conversation. In the airline example, the initial request checks to see if there are sufficient seats available on the preferred flight and these are locked so that no other enquirer can book them until this conversation has finished and they have either been booked or unlocked. In this scenario, one application (the travel agent's) would

EDI Implementation Guide

have a number of I-EDI sessions active with the applications of the airline, the hotel and the car-hire company and, only when a complete and satisfactory picture had been created and accepted or rejected, would all of the individual conversations end with either multiple confirmations of bookings or cancellations, freeing the constrained resource for the next enquirer.

The UN/EDIFACT Board has been working on I-EDI definitions since the late 1980s and progress is slow, partly due to the complexity of the task and also to the lack of an urgent need for progress, as the most obvious beneficiaries are already catered for by the CRS systems. This is changing, as smaller transport companies and shipping organisations become aware of EDI.

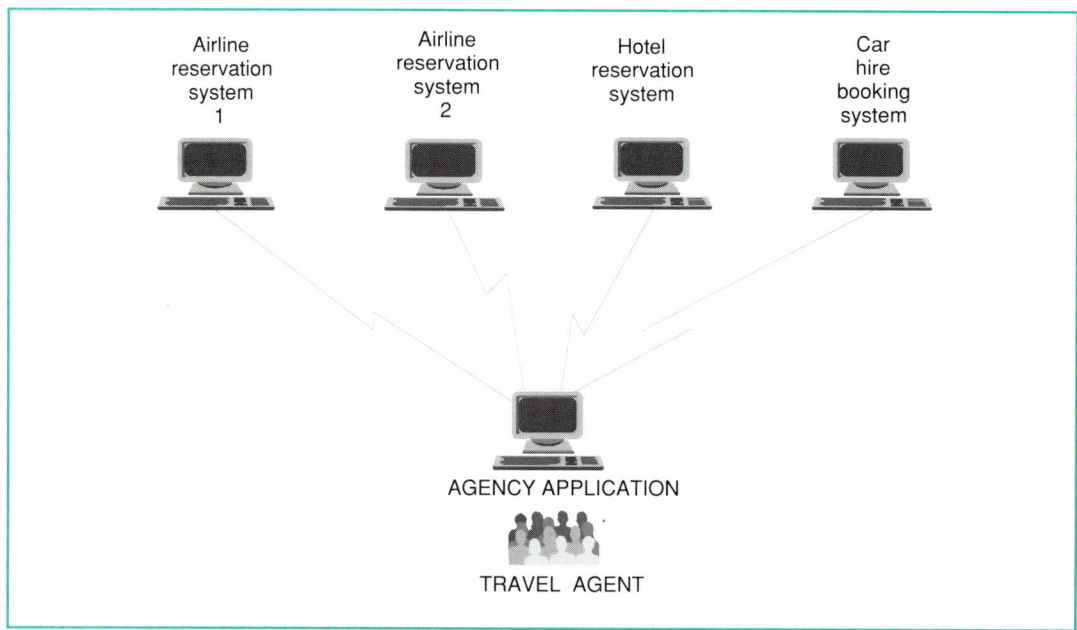

Figure 41: Example of an Interactive EDI application

14.4.7 Open EDI

This chapter consists of two halves – a list of difficulties which could render EDI a failure in the history of business development and a range of options which may accelerate the take-up and usage of EDI and the benefits that can be achieved through its use.

There is one initiative which seeks to overcome most of the difficulties outlined in the first half of the chapter. It is run under the auspices of ISO and is known as Open-edi. (If successful, it has the potential to overcome all of the difficulties outlined previously.)

Simply stated, it aims to redefine EDI and its usage so that EDI becomes wholly rule-based and testable, in order that changes in the mode of operation of one party will not affect another and usage of standards is wholly predictable and testable without the need for individual discussions or debates.

The aim is to develop an EDI solution by means of which any user can trade with any other user without the need for individual agreements or established relationships. Thus (a simplistic example from the Internet community), an organisation could use EDI to place an order for a pizza to be delivered from its local pizza company. The pizza company would need to know nothing of the organisation in advance and the organisation need never have dealt with the pizza company before. Both will be using standards, formats and processes which are commonly accepted and each will be a recognised member of the overall EDI community. (It may well be necessary for a Certification Authority – see Chapter 6, 'Software', for a fuller description – to be used in this environment to ensure that all members of the community can be verified as bona fide by reference to this agency.) Although it is understandable in the light of the previous pages, this is no small undertaking and should be regarded as a potential increased benefit on the horizon rather than an excuse to delay.

14.5 Summary

The items identified as difficulties in the future of EDI are challenges which must be overcome and it has been shown that there are encouraging developments on the horizon for greater penetration and diversification of EDI usage. But it must be remembered that EDI on its own is of little value – it is the effect it has on the way business is done that is so important.

Sir Angus Fraser, President of the EDI Association (as the Electronic Commerce Assocation was then known), made the point very clearly as long ago as 1989 at a conference held in Brussels and entitled, 'EDI – 1992 and Beyond':

In the EDI field, the stakes are colossal: EDI bids fair to change the whole concept of how business will be run in the years ahead. The implications are much more fundamental than the economies and improved service which flow from the fact that EDI is a mechanism for taking what is on one company's computer and putting it directly on to another organisation's computer with no print-outs, errors or rekeying, with no waste of staff time, no postal delay and no misunderstanding because of language barriers, so that it can be as easy for a firm in Perugia to order goods from a supplier in Sheffield as from one in Milan. These benefits are important and should not be minimised. But there is more to it than that. EDI's immediacy can change the structure of a market. In some sectors, EDI is already a prerequisite for doing business at all. It often changes the relationships between organisations and their trading partners. Those who fail to embrace it face the prospect of exclusion from their markets as they lose competitiveness.

The major challenge is not a technical one; it is one of effecting a cultural change within organisations . . . We already have a modern electronic structure in many ways, but the capacity to use it is still very limited.

Maybe the missing incentive has been the example and encouragement of government. If so, has there been a better time to start?

Annexes

EDI Implementation Guide

Annex A: Case Studies

This section gives a brief summary of the current status of EDI in the United Kingdom and four case studies from the UK and European government sector: each highlights a different example of the use of EDI and focuses on a range of aspects of the solution in order to give practical examples of the key points in this Guide.

A.1 EDI Status in the United Kingdom

Several examples of the use of EDI and its development in the UK have been referenced earlier in this Guide. The fact that UK usage started in the retail sector (as pure EDI, using the old United Nations Trade Data Interchange (UNTDI) standard) and evolved from file transfer techniques in the automotive industry (using what became accepted as the Organisation for Data Exchange by Teletransmission in Europe (ODETTE) standard) has been covered.

Subsequently, other sectors have followed, notably insurance and, more recently, government and education. It would be possible to devote a whole guide to EDI usage in any one of these sectors, but an important consideration in any EDI solution is that any two implementations of EDI are no different in concept (as discussed at some length in Chapter 14, 'Future directions').

Probably the best indicator of current interest is the activity of the Electronic Commerce Association: of late, the Special Interest Groups which are most active and which enjoy the largest attendance at their meetings and events have been the Government, Health and Pharmaceutical and Education sections – so it is obvious that EDI has arrived in the public sector.

A.2 Selection of the Case Studies

The case studies which follow were selected because:

- they are current examples of the use of EDI within the (wider) public sector – whether a government department, a public agency or some other non-private organisation

EDI Implementation Guide

- they are actual – they have happened – all have bad news as well as good, none has been a total success (and no EDI project ever could be), yet, on balance, all have provided far more benefit than 'cost' (see Annex B, 'Preparing an EDI business case', for a fuller discussion of this concept)

- each is a significant project or a component in a major programme of projects which shows the scale of EDI penetration with the government sector already

- collectively, they provide a balanced view of the range of implementation options open to any organisation considering EDI, the wide set of choices which can be made and the fact that there is no single, correct way to implement EDI other than 'that most appropriate for the organisation concerned'.

These case studies are not intended to be examples of implementations which should be copied without full consideration of the facts. INCA, for example, has many characteristics which may not now be ideal, as the understanding of the problems and the viable solutions have progressed since it was conceived. However, it still merits inclusion simply because of the clarity it brings in understanding the problems to be overcome.

A.3 Introduction to Case Studies

A.3.1 NHS

The National Health Service (NHS) covers a huge range of organisations and processes from NHS Supplies and procurement through to GP funding and pathology activity. The procurement EDI activities have been covered in the previous guide in this series, *Electronic Data Interchange in Government: The Business Opportunities*, so this guide looks in greater detail at developments in the area of pathology.

A.3.2 CCCJS

The Computerisation of the Criminal Courts of Justice Systems (CCCJS) is a mammoth task. Interlinking the processes, systems and paperwork of a multitude of barely related public and private organisations, from the various types of courts to prisons, police authorities and the probation service, is an immense undertaking.

This study summarises some of the key steps taken by the Home Office and some of the processes that have been developed during the first five years of the project. Yes, five years – CCCJS is a prime example that revolutionary change to an operation does not occur overnight.

A.3.3 INCA

The Information Net and Card for the Adapted Management of European Road Transport and Traffic (INCA) project is one of the research projects funded by the European Community (see Chapter 13, 'EDI in Europe') to determine the best approach to implementing EDI between driver and vehicle licensing systems in different countries.

This project was very complex to manage: it was multi-national, required new messages (or so it seemed), and had particularly rigorous security requirements, involving the conveyance of personal data. Upon implementation, it became apparent that the real beneficiaries were not the various licensing authorities which entered the research expecting to be beneficiaries, but the various police and customs authorities which suddenly were able to contemplate modes of operation (process improvements) previously inconceivable within the limitations of the information available to them.

While all of these aspects are discussed, the key focus is on the approach to and the need for message design and the implementation of security.

This case study has been written by an author who was involved in the INCA project from its inception. As with all the other case studies in this Guide, permission to publish was sought from the appropriate authority. Unlike all the other case studies, however, permission has not been received because the INCA project is complete and the relevant authority has been disbanded. We believe the description given to be accurate and include it here because it provides a wealth of technical detail not available yet from the other case studies.

A.3.4 MOD

The last case study involves the Ministry of Defence (MOD), which has decided to adopt EDI for firm, business reasons. The implementation is less advanced than in the other case studies, but a thorough business case has been prepared, which shows convincing arguments for its adoption throughout the organisation.

A.4 NHS

A.4.1 Overview

Every year in the UK, about 50 million specimens of blood etc, are sent from 25,000 General Practitioners (GPs) to 1000 pathology laboratories for analysis and report back to the GP. The use of EDI for the specification of the tests required by the GP, and for the reporting back of the results by the pathologist offers some important opportunities for improvements in efficiency, cost-effectiveness and quality of health care. Examination of the issues and problems encountered in the introduction of EDI for pathology messaging in the NHS offers valuable experience and insight, much of which is applicable across the whole of government and public sector.

A.4.2 Introduction and Background to EDI in the NHS

The growth and manner of EDI usage within the NHS cannot be controlled through a top-down centralised management process, because the NHS is an evolving and decentralised environment. Nevertheless, this growth could not have been achieved without a central commitment to development and the use of standards.

A.4.2.1 *The NHS Environment Relative to Public and Private Sector Generally*

The NHS has never really been an 'organisation' as such; it has always functioned more like an 'industry' or 'sector' – and all the more so since the advent of GP Fundholder status and Self-Governing Trust Hospitals. These entities have removed most of the top-down 'organisational' direction which used to be applied from the NHS Management Executive (now known as the NHS Executive) through the old Regional structure and enforced through control of purse strings. Top-down control has been replaced by the 'internal market', in which the various units organise themselves into 'supply-chains' and buy and sell health-care as 'purchasers and providers'.

So, within this increasingly decentralised 'market economy' environment of the NHS, EDI is never going to be introduced successfully by way of a centrally imposed dictate; it has to be encouraged and nurtured from the grass roots for each of the applications for which it is appropriate.

Annex A
Case Studies

The NHS presents virtually all of the EDI implementation problems and issues typically found throughout the Government and Public Sector.

The issues encountered in the NHS have in many cases been raised by the need for 'pioneering', since EDI development in the private sector has concentrated on commercial rather than administrative transactions of the kind needed in health care and other public sector functions. Implementation of EDI within the NHS involves resolution of all of the following types of problems and issues, which are examined in more detail in this case study.

- availability of suitable application software systems

- communications infrastructure

- integration of applications with respect to EDI usage

- EDI message standards

- coding systems

- legal and security issues (with particular regard to the Data Protection Act)

- management of 'information exchange communities'

- business case and cost allocation issues.

A.4.2.2 The Overall Status of EDI Development within the NHS

The focus and priority for EDI usage within the NHS has been shifting from supplies to contracts and, more recently, towards clinical applications.

The first application area to which EDI was applied in the NHS was medical and general supplies. This started in the late 1980s, but the restructuring of the NHS in general, and the supplies authorities in particular, resulted in a hiatus in its development and widespread usage. These NHS 'reforms' have resulted in an increased focus on 'contracting' to support the introduction of the internal market. It was recognised in the early 1990s that the creation of purchaser/provider relationships was going to result in a vast increase in the number of financially oriented transactions centred around the

253

Contract Minimum Data Set (CMDS), which is the transaction corresponding to an invoice in the secondary care environment (hospital and health authority or 'commissioner').

To begin with, the CMDS sent by hospitals to claim payment from the Health Authorities has been a 'block' transaction, covering a whole category of episodes over a whole contract period. As the implementation of the reforms progresses, however, the CMDS will become increasingly detailed and will eventually refer to a specific episode carried out for an individual patient. It will also need to contain contractual information, including quality measurements in support of contractual conditions relating to the Patients Charter. This will result in an enormous volume of transactions, which can only be handled effectively through an automated process such as EDI.

The growth in secondary care CMDS requirements is in addition to growth of the use of EDI for the primary care contract-related messages, namely the 'Registration' messages, which indicate the number of patients served by a particular practice and the 'Item of Service Claim'. At the end of 1994, there were over 1000 GP practices using EDI to send these contractual messages to the relevant Family Health Service Authority (FHSA), of which there are currently nearly 100, and over 3000 dental practices using EDI to communicate with the Dental Practice Board. The relatively greater penetration in dentistry is examined in A.4.3.3, 'The issues and problems'.

Although the concentration at the level of the Department of Health and the NHS Executive has shifted towards contracts, the focus of the clinicians at the primary and secondary level has been more on the ways in which EDI can be used to improve the efficiency and quality of health care itself. As the locus of authority and economic power has moved away from the old central and regional structures and towards the self-governing trust hospital and particularly the fundholding GP practice, so the emphasis has shifted towards the applications that are more important to the clinicians who exert large amounts – if not all – of the control over priorities.

Annex A
Case Studies

The three basic requirements for EDI implementation are only just becoming available: message standards, enabling application software packages and communications infrastructure.

EDI message standards are converging on UN/EDIFACT, which has received a clear endorsement from the NHS Executive. However, the development and acceptance of UN/EDIFACT messages has been a long and arduous process and the key NHS-specific (CMDS and clinical) messages have been published only in the second half of 1994. There have been a number of 'Executive' and 'Management' letters issued setting deadlines. Owing to a number of factors, including delays in the development of an agreed UN/EDIFACT CMDS message, these deadlines have not so far been met, although most relevant units have development programmes under way, which have resulted in widespread use of EDI CMDS messaging by the end of 1995.

The communications infrastructure for the NHS is still in a process of evolution. Many of the old Regions had implemented their own wide-area networks linking the major units. To integrate and supplement this capability, a contract was awarded by the NHS to provide 'Healthlink', which provided a national 'spine' linking these regional networks together, as well as an overlay structure providing local access for GPs and FHSAs and a central message-handling capability. The usage of this structure did not become either universal or consistent across the country and, in 1994, a decision was taken by NHS central management to withdraw endorsement of Healthlink and, instead, to award a contract to provide a centralised Message Handling Service (MHS). A related contract to provide a communications infrastructure will be awarded shortly. In all cases, however, the contract determines the nature of the services and the conditions under which they are offered; there is no 'mandate' which compels any NHS unit to make use of a particular service, and indeed there is still fierce competition among the would-be suppliers and corresponding confusion within the NHS units.

A.4.2.3 Motivators and Inhibitors to EDI Development within the NHS

Some of the motivators for the use of EDI in the NHS are common to all sectors, while some are NHS-specific and have been partly due to the 'reforms'.

Generic motivators include:

- greater efficiency, removal of need for re-keying, avoidance of paper, reduced staff costs

- improved accuracy, fewer errors

- increased opportunity to process transaction data automatically to produce management information; avoidance of need for additional demands on clinical and management staff to generate and process information specifically for management purposes

- higher quality of service.

Specific emphasis in the NHS comes from:

- increased focus on budgetary control through trust status for hospitals and fundholder status for GPs

- enormous increases in contract message volumes (CMDS)

- increased focus on measurement of, and adherence to, quality standards under the provisions of the 'Patients Charter'

- target dates set by the NHS Executive for hospitals and health authorities to be able to send and receive CMDS messages electronically based on an UN/EDIFACT message

- the growing awareness on the part of self-governing trust hospitals and GP fundholders to exercise the internal market and to 'shop around' for better service; this is particularly evident in pathology, where the ability of fundholding practices to switch labs has been a stimulus to the development of pathology laboratory links, where the threat of losing the business of large fundholding practices has encouraged many laboratories to implement EDI.

Annex A
Case Studies

The major inhibitors to EDI development in the NHS have resulted from standards development and technology supply problems, but have also been concerned with organisational issues; most of the inhibitors have now been overcome, however, and in some cases the inhibiting factor has turned into a motivator.

Standards: The development of NHS-specific messages has required a certain amount of 'pioneering' (see 'Message Standards' in A.4.3.3, 'The issues and problems'). The absence of agreed messages, or even a credible commitment to UN/EDIFACT, for a significant period resulted in an unwillingness on the part of application systems providers to invest in the development of EDI-capable systems. In the case of pathology, central endorsement was perhaps given prematurely to a non-UN/EDIFACT standard, resulting in developments which are now seen as 'non-strategic' and will at some stage need re-investment to bring them into line.

Applications software: Hospitals use a variety of software systems, based on a variety of packages and 'home-grown' applications, with varying degrees of integration across the various units within the hospital. The pathology laboratories within the hospitals tend to use one of a small number of packages, but so far the providers of these systems have not been willing to invest in UN/EDIFACT-enabled solutions.

The FHSAs all use a base system supplied by the Family Health Services Computer Unit (FHSCU) in Exeter, which has been UN/EDIFACT-enabled.

The major problem, however, has been the provision of UN/EDIFACT-capable software for the GP practices.

Communications: The absence of a clear communications strategy accepted across the NHS has undoubtedly been an inhibitor to the development of EDI. However, the competitive pressures which may have contributed to this situation have now started to act as a motivator. A contract was awarded in 1994 to provide not just a Message Handling System, but also a 'Catalogue' of products and services associated with networking and messaging and providing components within 'solution sets'. This includes GP and Pathology software systems, thereby putting a spotlight on those products which are conformant with the NHS standards (X.400, UN/EDIFACT, etc) and those which are not. It also provides a far easier mechanism for users to compare function and price. The development can be expected to result in a downward pressure on prices as well as an acceleration of appropriate EDI-related development on the part of the system suppliers.

A.4.2.4 The Positioning of Pathology within the Health Care Process

The information flows are driven by the clinical and analytical processes within the GP practice and the Pathology Laboratory; the handling of the information raises issues of accuracy, authorisation and confidentiality.

When a GP decides that a pathology test is appropriate, the first action is for the GP to construct a test request, specifying the nature of the test to be performed and indicating to the pathologist any special circumstances, medications which the patient may be taking, etc. The request details are appended to the patient notes and copied to the practice nurse who will collect the appropriate specimen from the patient. The specimen bottle will be labelled appropriately and placed in a bag together with the request form, which is usually colour-coded to indicate the kind of test required (haematology, biochemistry, microbiology, etc), and batched ready for collection by an appropriate courier.

On arrival at the laboratory, the samples are sorted out according to the process required (aided by the colour coding). The first task is to 'register' the patient on the pathology system, and in particular to determine whether or not a record for the patient already exists and, if so, to identify accurately the appropriate patient record. This is so that the pathologist can evaluate the result in the light of previous results for the patient in question. The tests are then carried out, reviewed and authorised by the pathologist, and sent back to the correct GP.

In all of the above processes, the confidentiality and ethical issues are paramount, all the more so with increased social and legal focus on cytology and HIV testing procedures.

Annex A
Case Studies

It is not immediately obvious that EDI is necessarily the best medium for pathology messages, or that EDI on its own is sufficient for all pathology-related communication.

Most GP practices and pathology laboratories use computers for keeping records and for other administrative functions, but, whereas the majority of pathology laboratories already use a computer system for administration of the test requesting/reporting process, GPs maintain mainly manual patient records and administer pathology test procedures manually. While practice culture might account for this behaviour, it is likely that a far more significant factor has been the medium for the receipt of clinical data, namely paper.

The merits of storing patient data in a computer record include instant retrieval and the ability to automatically analyse and process information held on the record, such as an analysis of a patient's blood sugar level. The problem to date has been that in order to incorporate clinical details into the computer held record, these details have had to be keyed in. The transmission of clinical data using EDI removes this need. Because of the structured nature of both pathology test requests and reports, the high frequency with which they are transmitted and the considerable administrative effort associated with current manual practices, the adoption of EDI will benefit both parties.

The increasing use of computer systems by GPs in their clinical procedures will lead to a recognition that only EDI can deliver these benefits because, unlike electronic mail or fax messages, EDI messages can be generated, read and understood directly by computers. Unfortunately, some laboratories have promoted the use of electronic links to GPs on the basis of speed of response, and have implemented fax or electronic mail links with resultant disenchantment on the part of the GPs, who gain no real benefit simply from increased speed.

The pathology laboratory clearly benefits from EDI pathology requests, since the EDI request avoids the need for re-keying and the consequent exposure to error, although there is still the need for some paper documentation to accompany the sample (if only the label on the bottle), not least to provide the opportunity for colour-coding. The benefit to the GP is less obvious, unless the GP is making use of computer-based patient records for clinical purposes, in which case the result message will have precisely the patient identification details included on the original request – which means that the result can be filed with confidence in the correct patient record without the need for checking by practice staff and the resultant exposure to human error.

Pathology EDI offers some clear benefits to GPs and to Pathology Laboratories.

- Reduced GP practice administration

    Automatic creation and re-creation of pathology test requests: The availability of complete and up-to-date computerised patient records will assist the GP in generation of the test request and help to ensure efficient provision of relevant supporting information to the pathologist. The use of EDI for test requests should reduce the problem of lost documentation, but in such cases the request can be re-generated automatically.

    Automatic updating of computer patient record with pathology test request and result detail: Once a test request has been generated on screen and sent via EDI, the computer patient record can be automatically updated, guaranteeing the upkeep of accurate and complete patient records. GPs can incorporate incoming structured EDI test results directly into the computerised patient record, once they have screened them to ensure and validate quality.

    More efficient flow of result information to GPs: The presence of a GP identifier in the test request enables the routing of results to the originating GP. This removes the manual administrative effort associated with sorting through results and allocating them within the practice.

- Reduced pathology laboratory administration

    The machine readability of EDI pathology test requests means that they can be automatically booked-in, thereby reducing administration and clerical effort.

- Improved pathology laboratory data quality

    The automated and error-free transmission of unambiguous data from the GP patient record to the pathology laboratory record, together with enforced completeness of the computer-generated test request, will help in getting the information right first time.

- Improved health care

    Improved test result interpretation: By providing the pathologist with complete clinical information, the chances of more accurate test recommendations and correct interpretation of test results are improved.

    Availability of processed historical information: The machine-readability of results information transmitted via EDI means analyses of past results can be automatically generated and manipulated by GPs. Pathology service usage can be automatically audited for operational and budgetary purposes.

    Reduction of uncertainty in the timing of results provision: The increased certainty associated with automated test reporting means that GPs are better able to advise patients as to the likely availability of results.

- Improved audit

    The conducting of pathology test requesting and reporting using EDI will enable the automated audit of activities by both the GP and the pathology laboratory. GPs will be able to audit pathology service usage automatically, while pathology laboratories will be able to produce automated activity reports and GP billing information.

EDI Implementation Guide

A.4.3 The Status of Pathology EDI in the NHS

A.4.3.1 Summary of status

According to one of the leading practitioners, 'Pathology reporting is the only form of clinical EDI being done on a meaningful scale in the UK'. By the end of 1994, over 100 GP practices were exchanging pathology messages. The vast majority of these were still using the American ASTM 1238 message standard, with only ten or so using UN/EDIFACT. In addition, there were another 100 or more GP practices using other 'sub-EDI' electronic exchange media which did not allow complete integration with practice computer applications. Most laboratories were still in pilot mode with only one or two large fund-holding practices, although a few were well into widespread implementation (the John Radcliffe laboratory in Oxford was servicing 47 GP practices).

Under the auspices of the National Networking Project, three pathology laboratories have recently been identified as 'pathfinder' sites: Preston, Ipswich and Oxford. Being pathfinders means that these labs are implementing applications using E-mail as well as EDI. Two of the GP systems suppliers have committed to support the project in its use of the new national standard UN/EDIFACT clinical messages. In the case of Preston and Ipswich, the GPs involved in the pilots are also using X.400 and UN/EDIFACT messages to transmit their items-of-service claims to the relevant FHSA.

The pioneering work in pathology EDI was conducted in two projects: the Oxford (John Radcliffe) initiative and the South West project, based around Southmead Hospital in Bristol. The objectives of these two projects were different – a point reflected by the choice of messaging standard. At the time of the conception of the Oxford project, ASTM 1238, a specialist American standard for the transfer of clinical data only, was chosen on the grounds that it was proven and in the public domain. The Oxford project has successfully demonstrated that benefits to GPs can be realised as a result of transmitting pathology results using EDI. The objective of the South West project, however, was to build upon the experience of the Oxford team, firstly to implement pathology reporting using the UN/EDIFACT standard and then to extend the application to include test-requests.

A.4.3.2 The Oxford RHA and John Radcliffe Project

In 1985 the John Radcliffe started to collaborate with the suppliers of one of the most popular GP systems. This project showed that half of all haematology and biochemistry reports could be returned on the day that the specimen was collected, with no human intervention at either end.

The Oxford RHA project started in 1991, building on the earlier work at the John Radcliffe by transmitting pathology reports to GPs over Healthlink, using the ASTM 1238 messaging standard. The project now covers 302 GPs in 47 practices, receiving biochemistry, haematology and immunology reports from all the Oxford hospitals.

The GPs participating in the project use systems supplied by five different software providers. Real benefits to GPs have been realised during this project, but the level of benefit has been largely dependent upon the ability of GP systems suppliers to upgrade their systems to make full use of the EDI capabilities.

The SWRHA pathology data transfer project: This 'National Pathology EDI Demonstrator' is the first UK project to exchange patient clinical data using UN/EDIFACT. The project involves the Haematology and Biochemistry Laboratories of Southmead Hospital, Bristol and 17 General Practices using 4 types of GP systems. The project started in October 1993 with close co-operation from the Oxford project, and initially involves the transmission of pathology test results to GPs.

Upon successful completion of the pilot, implementation will continue across the Region. Future projects will implement other UN/EDIFACT-based clinical and administrative messages using the same physical and message handling infrastructures.

A.4.3.3 The issues and problems

Application software systems: The availability of GP systems able to support UN/EDIFACT - or indeed any form of EDI – has itself been a major issue (the past reluctance of GP systems suppliers to invest in speculative development in the absence of a committed standards strategy has been addressed in A.4.2.3, 'Motivators and inhibitors to EDI development within the NHS').

At present, the majority of pathology laboratories are supplied by a handful of pathology systems suppliers, at least some of which already have EDI-capable products on the market or are well under way with development. It is not yet clear, however, whether all of these systems will have UN/EDIFACT (as opposed to ASTM 1238) capability from initial availability. It is likely that the EDI product offerings will normally take the form of a stand-alone PC linked to the existing laboratory information management system. The PC will be dedicated to EDI and will handle the tasks of extraction, translation and communication. At least one company is marketing an EDI front-end system which is said to be able to 'bolt-on' to virtually any laboratory information management system and which 'comes in at well under £20,000'.

Communications infrastructure: The issues leading to some confusion at the user level are explained in A.4.2.3, 'Motivators and inhibitors to EDI development within the NHS'.

Integration of pathology with other GP applications: Unless applications are integrated at the GP level, the full benefits from allowing the information to 'flow through' cannot be realised, and the costs are less easy for the practitioners to justify. The major inhibitor to application integration has been the functionality of the available practice systems packages. The release of national standard UN/EDIFACT messages (see 'Message Standards' below) will accelerate application integration, mainly because of the impetus it will provide to the GP systems suppliers to provide application systems which make effective use of these messages.

Most of the GP systems suppliers are now producing fund-holding packages and EDI modules to integrate with their other GP software. Prices of systems depend on the number of users, but the maximum cost for an EDI upgrade is around £500 (some suppliers include it in the standard charge). Encouragingly, most of the GP practices now adopting EDI for pathology messaging are coming from amongst those already using EDI for FHSA links, of which there are over 1000.

Annex A
Case Studies

Message Standards: The development of UN/EDIFACT messages has been a somewhat tortuous process, largely due to the need for widespread consultation and endorsement by professional bodies such as the Royal Colleges. As a result, the national standard message designs for pathology were published only in the last quarter of 1994. In the case of pathology (as with several other applications), the availability of UN/EDIFACT messages came some time after the user need, so the majority of installations are currently using ASTM 1238.

Recently, a group of national standard UN/EDIFACT messages has been released, including Pathology. The full list includes:

- Pathology Request and Result, covering haematology, biochemistry and microbiology

- Radiology Request and Result

- GP/Hospital Message, covering referral request, discharge summary, death notification, outpatient attendance report

- Acknowledgement messages corresponding with the above, where appropriate.

These clinical messages were developed with the full involvement and authority of the appropriate Royal Colleges. They have also been aligned with international health care message development processes operated by MD9 and CEN Working Group 3. In particular, the UK Pathology messages are a valid subset of the Project Team 008 of Working Group 3 Laboratory Services messages. This authoritative status is expected to accelerate their complete acceptance as representing approved 'best practice', thereby removing debate and confusion and encouraging the software suppliers to invest in associated system development with the confidence that the resulting products will meet the market needs now and in the future.

Coding systems: Much of the work in creating usable EDI messages has in fact been required to produce clinical and administrative coding systems – many of which are needed for other purposes in any event. There is a great deal of co-ordination work in progress, aimed at converging and rationalising clinical codes at a national, European and global level. These clinical codes cover descriptions of parts of the body, procedures and treatments, as well as medications. Administrative codes are principally concerned with identification of patients, practices, hospitals and other organisational units, as well as identification of contracts and terms.

Legal and security: The use of EDI for pathology messaging raises issues of security and confidentiality under the Data Protection Act. Many of the issues surrounding the use of networking for clinical applications are under active discussion between the NHS Executive Information Management Group and the British Medical Association.

It would appear at present that Department of Health regulations require the continued use of paper, since GP contracts can be interpreted as requiring the maintenance of paper patient notes. Another regulation appears to require that the GP 'signs' the items-of-service claim. Yet another area of concern is the requirement for pathology results to be 'authorised' by the pathologist, since this has normally been taken to involve a signature.

It is recognised that the technology exists in the form of RSA encryption and digital signatures to cater for all the above requirements. The issues are:

- Is a digital signature acceptable in place of a written signature in all cases?

- Is the use of RSA to ensure confidentiality acceptable to the national security agencies?

- Can a 'trusted third party' structure be established in an appropriate timeframe to support the administration of public encryption keys?

Management of an Information Exchange Community: EDI is a 'pack' activity, but in a complex environment like the NHS, it is not always clear who should lead the pack. Who will call the initial meetings, who will ensure everyone is up to the same level of awareness and education, take the minutes, provide advice and

Annex A
Case Studies

assistance . . .? Under the old Regional structures, there may have been an obvious candidate (although many would say that it needs to be someone more directly involved). In the evolving NHS environment, should that leadership role fall to a hospital? To an FHSA? Or to a Health Authority?

More recently, there have been examples of several practices in an area getting together and demanding that their 'supplier' laboratory should equip itself to supply electronic results; typically these are large fundholding practices which are keen to realise the benefits of IT. Even so, it is one thing to start an initiative – and quite another to manage the initiative through to successful implementation.

More recently the NHS has created a number of 'local' co-ordination groups to encourage 'natural communities' to take ownership for their communications requirements. The Local User Requirements Groups and Local Communications Management Groups have yet to prove their appropriateness as 'community managers'. It is perhaps still too early to draw firm conclusions, but some see these groups as a continuation of the old 'regional thinking', since they each cover a large area of the country and are perhaps therefore not 'local' enough. Certainly, the principal focus of activity is at the very local level of the individual laboratory and its community of GP 'customers'. To quote one prominent practitioner:

> In some cases laboratories have implemented pathology links with their GPs without the knowledge or approval of their own trust hospital, let alone any input from the regional level!

For the pathology application alone, it is clear that the pathology laboratory will be acting as the natural 'hub' in the centre of its community of GPs – and hence is the natural leader of that community. This still leaves the more complex issue faced by the GP practice, namely the fact that the major benefits of EDI come from integration of multiple applications, only one of which involves the pathology laboratory. Who will ensure that the pathology laboratory liaises effectively with the radiology department and with the FHSA? Considering just the community centred around the pathology application,

EDI Implementation Guide

there are a number of issues to be considered by the pathology laboratory:

- Should pathology laboratories concern themselves with their GPs' choice of software – or even encourage them to enquire vigorously of their systems suppliers when an UN/EDIFACT EDI capability will be available?

- Will the pathology laboratory offer advice, education or even active support to GPs in its role as hub of the EDI community?

- Should the pathology laboratory contact and generate interest among its GPs. If so, how? (An option is the use of a promotional document or brochure which explains the potential benefits of pathology EDI to GPs.)

- How should the pathology laboratory convert interest shown by GPs into action?

- What should be the role of the pathology laboratory in making 'community' decisions about joint pilot objectives, a joint implementation plan, the use of codes?

Business case and cost allocation issues: An assessment of the business case for messaging within the NHS for each of the 'old' regions was commissioned by the NHS National Networking Team. It is called the 'Networking Investment Appraisal Study' and has recently been completed.

At the beginning of the pathology EDI pilots, the GPs' system and messaging costs were subsidised from NHS central budgets and/or by the FHSA. The GP costs now have to come out of practice budgets, but the promoters of the Oxford project were very encouraged by the fact that none of the practices involved dropped out once funding was cut – they felt that the project had stood up well to its first 'free market' test, and that the principle of cost-effective use had been validated.

Many of the benefits to the pathology laboratory are difficult to quantify in financial terms. Others cannot be realised until a significant proportion of GPs are linked to the pathology laboratory and until test requesting is implemented as well as reporting. The pathology laboratory business case should initially attempt to focus on the tangible benefits to the pathology laboratory associated with pathology EDI. This is not to say that longer-term and less tangible benefits are not relevant. Where the business case for pathology EDI remains unproven, it may well be the appeal of less tangible factors, such as more accurate patient records and availability of accurate and complete historical data to pathologists, that swings the verdict. Ultimately, however, it is likely to be the demands of the GP 'customers' who are prepared to 'vote with their feet' that will make the business case for the laboratory – provided they have a way of getting themselves together into a 'buying consortium' with a critical mass of commercial muscle.

A.4.4 Experience Gained from NHS Pathology EDI Pilot Implementations

- The interaction of people raises more issues than the interaction of computer systems

  The particular issues to emerge, and lessons to be drawn, from the pathology EDI messaging pilots during 1994 have been more concerned with the interaction of people than with the interaction of computer systems.

  The first lesson has been the need for wider co-operation between the various parties involved. The GPs already need to communicate with multiple departments in multiple hospitals, as well as with their FHSAs. As long as each GP was only focusing on a single application with a single FHSA or hospital department, there was no great pressure for co-ordination between these various organisations and units. Once multiple applications are involved, and there is the opportunity of justifying a move to EDI against a number of applications, there is a greater requirement to ensure that these multiple opportunities are convergent and mutually reinforcing rather than conflicting and incompatible.

  The second lesson comes from a recognition of the need for co-ordination *mechanisms* on at least a national basis. At the early pilot stage, the users consist of tightly knit groups, in which all participants know each other and can agree on such things as procedures, addressing conventions, coding systems, security procedures, as well as the basic issue of who is prepared to send and receive what kinds of messages to and from whom. As the participants start using EDI on a wider basis, the need soon emerges for some kind of central sender/recipient registration, Interchange Agreement procedures, 'Trusted Third Party' for encryption key management in support of digital signatures. These are currently only at the discussion stage, and there is a certain amount of reluctance to abandon local arrangements in favour of supporting a national mechanism. There is also a corresponding danger of 'reinventing wheels' rather than adoption of standardised approaches such as EDIRA.

- Availability, ease-of-use and cost of end-user software has been a key factor in the take-up of EDI in the NHS

The relatively rapid take-up of EDI by dentists for items-of-service claims has been in large part due to the fact that the Dental Practice Board made a standard software package available to dentists – and subsidised its cost. Because dental practices in general only use computer systems for financial and administrative, rather than clinical applications, the problems associated with EDI application integration are very much reduced compared with the GP situation – but so are the corresponding opportunities for fundamental improvements to the processes and quality of health care.

The availability of suitable end-user software (or otherwise) has been the key inhibitor to the uptake of any EDI application involving GPs, including pathology. This is true in the sense that this software must necessarily come from a range of software providers, who will all need to see a sufficiently secure marketplace for their products before they are prepared to come up with the necessary investments.

A secure marketplace will only result from an unambiguous commitment to a standards strategy, and from an organisational structure mature enough to enable the potential users of that software to obtain and invest the necessary funding, confident that the *status quo* will remain long enough for them to reap the potential returns.

It has taken some years to achieve, but EDI pathology messaging in the NHS has now reached the point where all of the major inhibitors are just about removed and an exciting period of rapid growth is just starting.

A.5 Recent Developments (March 1996)

Report of the Efficiency Scrutiny into bureaucracy in general practice: *Patients Not Paper* **(PNP); June 1995**

This report, commissioned by the Prime Minister, has made a number of recommendations to the NHS Executive, including support for implementation of 'clinical links', EDI.

Arising from the report, the *Patients Not Paper* (PNP) programme has been implemented by the NHS Executive, including the recently initiated (December 1995) *GP/Provider Links Project*. The GP/Provider Links Project is highly focused on ensuring the provision of EDI (NHS Standard Message) enabled clinical healthcare applications in order to allow take-up of this technology. Tied to this enabling of applications are 'Trailblazer' implementations, which will examine the use of the NHS standard messages.

The NHS Executive level of concentration is, therefore, now on clinical EDI. The PNP programme and associated GP/Provider Links Project reflect the shift towards a primary-care-led NHS.

Clinical Message Programme Board

One of the major products from the initial tranche of message development is the management structure itself. The management structure consists of the Clinical Messages Programme Board (CMPB), on which the Royal Colleges are represented, and the Clinical Message Development Groups, which directly manage specific messages – for example, pathology and radiology.

This structure is now being utilised for further clinical messaging development, including Cytology and

Pharmacy, as well as continuing its role with the delivered messages standards in terms of version control.

NHS-wide Networking

A number of areas have moved on with respect to networking, including award of contract for WAN services, connection of Healthlink and the NHS MHS service and the initial phase of the NHS-wide Networking Management (NWN) pathfinder projects.

- WAN service contracts have been awarded to BT and Mercury. Both networks will offer data and voice services, with connectivity to the BT Syntegra X.400(88) MHS.

- In recognition of the migration issues surrounding especially large-scale GP use of the RACAL-supplied Healthlink network, the NHS Executive has contracted for a P1 protocal link between the BT Syntegra MHS and Healthlink. The Syntegra MHS services are still seen as the strategic direction.

- The NWN pathfinder projects are now nearing completion of the initial phase. The most significant outcome from the two pathfinders (Preston and East Suffolk) which entered into contractual relationships via the BT Syntegra catalogue for clinical application functionality and EDI integration has been the lack of progress with suppliers. This has included issues of development timescales, supplier commitment – especially to GP systems – and contractual relationships with BT Syntegra. This further emphasises the importance of the NHS Executive's concentration on EDI-enabling clinical applications via the PNP GP/Provider Links Project.

Local User Representative Groups (LURG): Natural Community Groups

These organisations have made significant progress in developing 'Natural Community Groups' within their geographical sphere of influence. These smaller, trading-partner-focused groups are now providing an appropriate community management mechanism.

At the same time, the merger of the old District Health Authorities, with their secondary care focus, and the FHSAs, with their primary care focus, is resulting in the Health Commissions becoming increasingly important as the lead organisation in EDI development.

NHS-wide Clearing Service (NWCS)

The NHS-wide Functions and Manpower Review means that Regional Health Authorities (RHAs) ceased to exist as of 1 April 1996 and were replaced by the NHS Executive Outposts.

Previously, RHAs had been responsible for the collation of contracting data contained in CMDS and its supply to the Department of Health. To ensure the continuation of this information flow, the NHS Executive has contracted (via the Private Finance Initiative) for the provision of a NHS-wide Clearing Service (NWCS). All secondary care providers and (non-GPFH) purchasers are required to implement EDI links to NWCS by April 1997. Subsequently, all Contract Data Sets will flow via this service, using national standard EDIFACT messages developed during 1995 to allow transport of both the CMDS and the additional, locally agreed contracting data.

The period 1996-7 will, therefore, see a rapid take-up of EDI among providers and Health Commissions (note that by April 1996 almost all FHSAs and Health Authorities had merged to form Health Commissions). NWCS services will be extended to GPFH practices from April 1997.

A.6 CCCJS

A.6.1 Overview

The Initiative on Co-ordination of Computerisation in the Criminal Justice System (CCCJS) is intended to promote the efficiency and effectiveness of the Criminal Justice System, by automating the exchange of information between Criminal Justice organisations. The Initiative should deliver substantial financial benefits to the Criminal Justice System by, for example, reducing the cost of re-keying information as cases pass through the system, and reducing the number of adjournments by ensuring that more accurate and timely information is available at court hearings. There will also be important benefits which improve the quality of the service, such as reducing the time victims and other participants have to wait before cases are resolved and reducing the time people spend on remand.

Work began in 1992, with the aim of ensuring that the forthcoming computerisation of many of the organisations within the Criminal Justice System (CJS) happened in such a way as to ensure compatibility between the systems and the inter-linking of processes, as appropriate.

Since its inception, it has been facilitated by a unit based in the Home Office. In this instance 'facilitated' is the correct term because the unit is not in a position to mandate developments or activities.

The main CCCJS stakeholders are:

- Government departments:
    - Home Office
    - Lord Chancellor's Department
    - Crown Prosecution Service (CPS)
- Executive Agencies:
    - Prison Service Agency
    - Driver and Vehicle Licensing Agency (DVLA)
    - Court Service
- Locally managed organisations:
    - Police
    - Magistrates' Courts
    - Probation Services

Annex A
Case Studies

- Other national bodies:

    – Bar Council

    – Law Society.

As can be imagined, many individual processes link a community of this size – today, a Crown Court will produce various types of 'Court Listing' (daily, warned, fixture and running lists), detailing which cases are to be held in which courts on a particular day, typically on paper.

These court listings will need to be communicated to police, probation service, prison service, lawyers and others so that all necessary attendance, prisoner movements and the like can be arranged. If anyone cannot make the scheduled appearance, the case is reorganized – wasting a huge amount of court and supporting person time. A current pilot seeks to remove this high overhead of adjournment by feeding Crown Court listings to appropriate recipients via E-mail.

A similar, current pilot is looking at communications between the DVLA and other CCCJS partners. 1.4 million driver related cases pass through the courts each year and for each one, it takes two to three weeks for the court to get the necessary licence details from the DVLA. If the DVLA has no match on the requested licence, then there is a delay. Tens of thousands of cases are adjourned each year due to the lack of necessary paperwork. The current pilot allows courts to request licence details three days in advance and also, to request immediate details should they be needed. Each Magistrates' Courts Committee will eventually have this solution. This scenario presents a huge business justification for EDI when the costs of paper-handling (stage 1 benefits), reduction in adjournments and knock-on effects on other organisations (stage 2 benefits) are taken into account. As always, it is difficult to predict stage 3 benefits in advance but one of the potential areas will be the ability for the police to operate differently based on the better information on drivers and vehicles that will be accessible.

The organisations most closely involved in EDI interchanges are the following:

- Crown Courts
- Crown Prosecution Service
- Magistrates' Courts
- Police Service
- Prison Service
- Probation Service.

In addition, there are three key data repositories used by CJS organisations for which EDI links are planned:

- driver and vehicle records (DVLA)
- criminal history (Phoenix – Home Office)
- various statistical databases (Home Office).

There are also a number of other organisations which are part of the CJS business environment, with which E-mail and EDI links will be developed over time, such as the legal profession, non-CPS prosecutors (such as Customs & Excise and TV Licensing) and the Legal Aid Board.

A Criminal Justice IS/IT Board represents all the key stakeholders and a number of projects run on PRINCE programme/project management lines which deliver parts of the infrastructure, such as the network service, data and message standards, and which focus on piloting specific interfaces between organisations. These include:

- Data Standards
- Data Protection and Security
- Networking

- Interface Pilots:

  - Drivers Data

  - Court Appearance Statistics

  - E-mail

  - Plus many more soon to start.

A.6.2 CCCJS Technical Strategy

1.96 million defendants were proceeded against in magistrates' courts in 1993.

The CCCJS initiative needed to have an approach which could accommodate the variety of existing technical environments in different organisations and allow them to retain their independence in future hardware and software selection. This meant the definition of a flexible strategy based upon *open systems* for the information transfer and communications elements.

For information transfer, this has been accomplished by passing all data in the form of messages. Any organisation can pass information out to the network in a standard message format for which all recipient organisations have a common understanding – irrespective of whether their computer is a new strategic system or an existing system. Two key types of message which are used in the CJS are EDI and E-mail.

For the communications network, independence is provided by the requirement to conform to international open systems standards. These are clearly recognisable, as they all start with an X (eg X.25 or X.400). X.400 is the international standard for handling EDI and E-mail messages and defines how the messages should be handled by the sender, recipients and any network service provider, such as the Criminal Justice Network (CJN), which provides electronic 'sorting offices'.

EDI messages are designed to be sent between computer systems with little or no human intervention. (For example, a Magistrates' Courts system may send an electronic request to DVLA, whose own computer systems will automatically generate and send a response.) The content of the message has to be structured and

EDI Implementation Guide

follow certain pre-defined rules so that each computer can correctly interpret the information exchanged. The rules used to structure CCCJS messages are those defined in UN/EDIFACT. This approach is currently being trialled on the Drivers Interface Project, and on one other Interface Project relating Magistrates' Courts Appearance Statistics.

E-mail messages on the other hand are usually sent between people. There is no need to define any structure to the content of E-mail messages as they are read by people who can interpret the meaning of the message rather than simple computers which need to obey message structure rules. E-mail systems often have the ability to attach documents or other files (such as spreadsheets) to the main body of the message.

A.6.2.1 Theory

The basis for the architecture is to logically separate the different components into distinct modules which can then be physically implemented as best for each organisation.

For example, Case Management has an EDI module added to extract and convert the data from that application into a form from which it can be translated into the UN/EDIFACT syntax before being passed through communications software out to the CJN (or vice versa for the receiver). These EDI modules will have a range of management functions to ensure their passage across the network is controlled.

A.6.2.2 Practice

The physical implementation of these modules could take a number of forms. Some organisations may put all of the functions on a single machine, some may use it as a front-end processor to handle the functions outside the core CJO application, and some may prefer to use a third-party Value Added Supplier (VADS/VANS) to perform most of the functions.

Thus, there is a wide range of options for each organisation to utilise the system components and technologies most suited to their internal organisation and processes, while exchanging data in a form acceptable to all other players. Some systems may choose to implement the majority of the functions on their core strategic system (eg MASS – MAgistrates' Courts Strategic System), whereas others may find it more appropriate to utilise a free-standing computer to handle the EDI conversion and communications functions. Communications into the CJN could be direct by X.25 connection or through a dial-up service such as ISDN.

An alternative is where only the core application is on the user systems and a central VAD service undertakes all the conversion, translation and communications functions, receiving the data from and passing it to user systems via a range of supported protocols.

In practice the solution for most CCCJS users will be a mixture of these approaches, quite possibly using VADS for some of the central control and audit functions, while retaining some of the conversion and translation functions on local equipment.

A.6.3 What are the Stages of an EDI Project

Experience from the EDI projects undertaken so far has shown a general pattern to the work. Initially, there is a need to set up the project, agreeing who is involved, the scope of the work and producing plans. This is followed by some investigative work, possibly to establish the feasibility and then to specify the content of the data to be passed and the requirements for the processes which handle that data. Experience from the early projects indicates that this is also an important time to consider whether the business processes themselves can be improved or redesigned – before they are automated.

These data structures and processing requirements can then be more comprehensively defined and used as the basis for a set of interface specification products. These include not only the message and process design but also hardware and software requirements and interface agreements.

In parallel with the design, some procurement activities may be necessary, for example to obtain third-party software or services.

The computer interfaces can now be physically built and tested, and together with other activities such as user training, a move forward can be made into implementing that interface and running the trials. For each interface a cost benefit analysis will be undertaken to establish that a national rollout of the interface can be justified.

A.6.4 CCCJS Developments – Policies and Procedures

CCCJS has identified more than 200 information flows that will benefit from automation.

The CCCJS initiative differs from conventional computer development programmes, owing to the multiplicity of organisations involved and the resulting need to ensure compatibility, consistency and efficiency through shared standards and the setting out of best practice gained from experience.

The CCCJS Unit has long provided an element of this data standards, which ensure that the data passed has consistent meaning. Similar support will be provided for all other aspects of interface development and the early drafts of some of these are now available in production. These include:

- Interchange Agreement Format

    This sets out all the details needed to fully specify an interchange, such as detail of the message content, the parties involved, the events affecting the data transfer and a series of annexes with agreements between the parties – particularly, the Data Protection and Security Agreement required by DPS (Data Protection and Security) policy.

- Message Development Guidelines

    Drawing on experience to outline the steps to take and things to look out for.

- Testing Strategy

    Setting out how testing of interfaces should generally be performed and recommending the format for detailed test plans for each development.

- Project Planning Templates

    Being continually revised with experience, these templates show the products, activities and resource requirements for typical development projects.

Other policies will follow in the future, covering such areas as change control and the management of new versions and releases.

Annex A
Case Studies

A.6.5 E-mail

As well as the specific interfaces that are being developed within certain CCCJS projects, the benefits of providing an E-mail service between CJS organisations are also being studied. This is being done for two reasons:

- a belief that a general E-mail service will enhance communications and working relationships between CJS organisations

- a concern that those areas which come at the end of roll-out timetables should be offered an interim method for improving local exchanges of information.

There are currently two pilot areas (Suffolk and Hampshire) and, with the help of colleagues in those areas, information exchanges where E-mail is likely to be beneficial have been identified. Technical requirements have been identified and guidance produced. Testing of these pilots began in September 1995 and evaluation will take place in 1996.

A6.6 How are CCCJS Developments Managed?

The majority of activity carried out in the CCCJS is managed as projects, with a standard structure normally used for the management, control and user input to these projects.

Each project is run by a Project Manager, controlling a mixed team, drawn typically from staff in involved CJS organisations, CCCJS Unit staff and consultants.

The Project Manager's terms of reference and the overall direction of the project are controlled by a Project Board, drawn from senior representatives of some or all of the organisations involved. Each Project Board has overall responsibility for an Interface Project, and the Project Boards all report to the IS/IT Board.

Finally, the views and interests of the various users of any potential interface are obtained through a series of working groups. Many projects have a dedicated Project Assurance Team, which can provide input to the plans and review the products of the project. The pilot project also has two groups made up of representatives from most stakeholders, with a broad remit covering all project areas: the User Panel, covering broad end-user input to issues such as interface priorities; and the Technical Panel, allowing more technical representatives to comment on development approaches, computer system constraints and so on.

A.7 INCA

A.7.1 Overview

The European Nervous System (ENS) programme of the European Commission DG XIII was set up to look at the feasibility and requirements for exchanging information between many Administrations and Agencies within the European Union, as well as some European Free Trade Association (EFTA) countries. The subproject run by the INCA consortium is concerned with the exchange of UN/EDIFACT formatted data between driver licence and vehicle licence registration offices and police forces within Europe.

The consortium started its work at the beginning of 1992 and completed its pilot implementations at the end of 1993. The licensing authorities participating in the INCA Network pilot are UK, Greece, Spain, Portugal and Sweden. The police forces of Kent County Council in UK and The Ministry of Public Order in Greece also took part.

Each country is able to send enquiries to all other participating countries and to receive responses to those requests automatically. Enquiry and response messages were specially developed for the project using UN/EDIFACT syntax. The messages use early versions of security techniques recommended by the UN/EDIFACT board in January 1993 (these recommendations have since been updated and the new recommendations are covered in Chapter 8, 'Security'). Each message is protected by a digital signature which is created and checked by the gateway to ensure integrity of the message and authentication of the sending authority. The security uses public/private Rivest Shamir and Adleman (RSA) key techniques.

A decision was taken to base INCA on the IBM Information Network VAN. The continuous receive capability of the EDI mailbox service ensures that enquiry messages are forwarded to administrations with the minimum possible delay. The automatically generated responses are returned in the same way. This technique combines the application independence and security advantages of EDI while still achieving responses to enquiries which meet the requirements of the administrations.

Each of the country administrations uses a PC-based gateway to link to their existing data base applications. The gateway also performs all the EDI message-handling functions and connections to the mailbox. The gateway was specially customised for use in the project.

A.7.2 Functions of the System

The principle behind the INCA communications architecture is to allow each administration authority maximum autonomy in how it organises its internal systems for the registration and control of licence data. The INCA architecture only specifies how the information is transferred between administrations, how it is structured and what functions are being requested. The architecture, therefore, defines the interface rules for an authority and does not specify how that information is to be processed or used by the authority within their internal systems.

The INCA architecture and message structure have been designed to support the following functions, which were identified as broad requirements:

- exchanging of data between licensing authorities for the purpose of maintaining the data bases held by that authority

    The data sent to the authority would be information that is required by that authority to update its data, eg a vehicle has been exported and re-registered in another country; a suspected stolen vehicle has been identified in another country; a driver holding a licence from another country has committed an offence. This could allow court systems to put updates on to a data base, and is referred to as *data exchange*.

EDI Implementation Guide

- accessing of the data held by a licensing authority for enquiry purposes

    This could be required by a control authority, eg the police or customs, to check on the validity of documents presented to them.

For the pilot project, only the accessing of data for enquiry purposes has been used. There are two types of user:

- Licence Administration authorities which own licence data bases and make them accessible automatically to other INCA users

- Licence Administration and Control Authorities (eg the police) which access these data bases for enquiries.

A.7.3 Implementation considerations

Most of the national administrations allow updates and enquiries to licence information via screens which are directly connected to their applications. The style and layout of the screens is controlled by the data base applications. The application puts out prompting information to the screen and requires data to be entered in a particular way. This works well if the users only need access to their own national data bases but if other countries' applications were directly accessible (regardless of security and political implications) then each user would need to be aware of the characteristics of every other system and would also have to cope with national language problems. This would probably be impractical unless the screen presentations of all administration systems were standardised – a difficult political proposal.

However, it is also the case that the data stored on each country (or regional) system varies according to national (or local) requirements. Unless the whole licensing system across Europe were standardised this would be a very difficult problem to solve.

The amount of information which is sent inside a message may vary according to country legislation and the requirements of the administration. This variation in data content should not require any changes to the structure of the INCA UN/EDIFACT messages. Each administration can, therefore, specify what data it is prepared to release in a service agreement without requiring any changes to be made in any receiving administration's system. Should changes in legislation allow more, or less, information to be sent this can be implemented by an individual authority without needing changes to be made by all other authorities or changes to the architecture. Given the unstable nature of legislation surrounding INCA this consideration was very important.

EDI messaging for the exchange of information between licensing authorities has been proved to offer several advantages, which must be weighed against the disadvantage of potentially increased response times to enquiries. The advantages of using EDI can be summarised as:

- it is independent of national languages

- the data structures (the EDI messages) which are exchanged between the authorities can be standardised and need not be consistent with any processes currently being used internally within an administration.

A.7.4 The Use of EDI Messages

One of the most important parts of the work done in developing techniques for the exchange of licence data was the development and testing of the EDI message structures. The new messages defined for the INCA pilots use a majority of standard UN/EDIFACT segments, data elements and codes. However, some new segments had to be defined as well as many new codes for the existing elements. To help in this work and to provide good message documentation, use was made of a documentation tool from a Dutch company, EDITIE. This tool has proved invaluable since it has allowed many changes to be made to the structure of the messages without having to consider the considerable time that would then have followed in changing documentation.

Separate UN/EDIFACT messages have been defined for each type of licence that has been exchanged between the authorities. For the pilot two messages were defined:

- a Vehicle Licence message
- a Driver Licence message.

The structure of each message is designed to be sufficiently generic that it can be used to perform more than one administrative function. The UN/EDIFACT structure is the same for each licence message, eg a driver licence message can be used to update or enquire on a particular driver licence. The designated function is controlled by codes within the message, which specify what data the message contains and how it is to be treated by the receiving authority.

More messages may need to be defined if the INCA community expands its function but it is hoped that new functions can be added simply by the introduction of new codes to the existing messages rather than by designing completely new messages. For example, information on stolen vehicles is already identified as a high priority by the administrations. This may require specialised message structures but it is hoped that the details on a stolen vehicle are the same as for a registration and the only new item required is a code to specify it as stolen.

The application data definitions are the highest level of agreement between the authorities in INCA. These definitions cover how the elements are identified and the exact meaning of any coded data or function. For example, the colour of a car is represented by a code in the UN/EDIFACT message. This code does not correspond to any which is currently used by the administrations. Each administration translates these codes and structures into a format which can be processed by their own applications. This process of 'translation' is unique to each administration since it converts the standard UN/EDIFACT structures into unique in-house files for each administration.

New data codes have also been agreed to cover things which do not currently need to be coded in any national country system, eg a unique coded name for each national administrative authority. The functional use of the message is specified by codes contained within the message; eg 'This list of vehicles is requesting re-registration in my country; please confirm they are valid in the country of origin'; or 'Please confirm the status and validity of a driver's licence'. These data definitions could also be the basis of harmonising the structures and formats of the licence applications, which would then allow more interactive access techniques to be used in the long term.

The quality of documentation and description of the message elements and codes cannot be underestimated in such a project, where the messages are being used to carry information which requires exact and sometimes legal definition. Good documentation and code definition is even more important when it is taken into account that the actual data being held on the data bases varies from country to country and the selection of the correct data to include in the message is dependent on the definitions.

The decision to use EDI and UN/EDIFACT messages for the project has proved to be advantageous and the benefits expected from this architectural decision have been realised. Data is being exchanged between the data bases of many different countries and the enquirer is not aware of the many different structures in which that data is being held in each country.

There are some questions over the handling of country-specific character sets but so far the data has been exchanged using only Roman characters and while this does limit the way in which data is being presented it has not proved a major problem.

The message structures defined for the pilots have shown themselves to be capable of carrying data from the different countries. There appear to be some problems over the number of codes required to carry driver licence compound types but this requires only the addition of new codes and not message restructuring.

The documentation of the UN/EDIFACT messages for the project proved to be adequate but the documentation of the associated 'in-house' file formats, which were originally provided only as examples, was not found to be good enough and many discussions between the implementation teams could have been avoided if this job had been performed more thoroughly.

A.7.4.1 Use of the UN/EDIFACT Syntax

An *interchange* is the name given to the basic unit of exchange between partners in UN/EDIFACT. An interchange can contain more than one message addressed to a single recipient; it may be considered as roughly equivalent to a file containing one or more messages. The UN/EDIFACT interchange can contain either single messages, specifying a single update or enquiry, or batches of messages, specifying a series of updates or enquiries. INCA specifies that:

- only one message type is sent in a UN/EDIFACT interchange – ie an interchange cannot contain messages relating to both driver and vehicle licences

- the message type contained in the interchange is carried in the interchange header (the UNB segment) in the Application Reference element

- for the pilot, only one message is allowed per interchange, eg only one enquiry or response.

These specifications represent a limitation of the capability allowed by the UN/EDIFACT standard but it has meant that the implementation of the INCA gateway has been achieved more easily and it has also simplified the work required to interface the gateway to the data base access applications.

A.7.5 Implementation of the INCA Concept

All EDI messages are processed and controlled by a gateway in INCA, called a Country Control System (CCS), located on the site of each administration. Only Country Control Systems are allowed to communicate with other CCS's. The CCS provides the implementation of the architecture. The physical implementation of a CCS could vary, depending on the requirements of the administration and what systems they already have in place. However, for the pilot, a CCS has been built on a PC DOS platform and this has been used by all of the administrations.

The original concept of the INCA architecture was that any control authority (eg a police force) entitled to make checks upon international licences would always send their enquiries, or data, to their national licensing administration system using whatever mechanisms are normally used. The national licensing administration would route the message via a CCS to the appropriate CCS in the receiving country. The advantages of working in a hierarchical way were seen as:

- the way of making international enquiries would be the same as for national enquiries, ie they would be in national language and information would be presented in the same way

- in countries where the internal systems are well developed and internal communications infrastructures already exist for making enquiries they would largely remain unchanged

- control of security and privacy of data would be easier to manage if a minimum number of CCS's were specifically authorised to exchange information with other countries. Each country administration would be responsible for securing the data of its opposite numbers in the other member countries. Each country administration would ensure that only authorised enquiries were forwarded to the other member countries

- routing enquiries and information to the correct country via the network and mailbox would be easier to manage since they would be based only on the country and licence type. Each CCS would not need to be aware of internal arrangements for routing messages within other countries.

In the light of further work done during the pilot, it has been found that there are many control authorities and private enterprises (such as insurance companies) that might wish to participate using a direct connection into INCA. This has caused a re-examination of the original concept of the CCS and the security mechanisms that surrounded it. It is now accepted that any system which conforms to the architecture and is an 'approved' member of the user community, ie owns a security key distributed by the Certification Authority (CA), could access data from licence administrations.

In countries where there are regional administration systems for licences, they could send their requests via a CCS or they could become members in their own right.

The communication mechanism between the regional authorities within a country could be entirely internal to that country or could be based on the INCA exchange architecture.

Opening the INCA community to more potential members brings into question some of the original concepts of a hierarchical community with only a small number of authorised users. The technical implementation of the CCS, which should now be renamed to an INCA gateway since this name more closely reflects its function, remains largely the same but the management of the security aspects become very different. The control and distribution of security keys through a CA becomes a very different job if there are potentially hundreds of users instead of the original concept of about 20 users.

If a Control Authority belongs to the INCA community in its own right, eg a police force or vehicle inspectorate, then it could well require a single terminal implementation which would conform to the INCA gateway architecture. In order to test the feasibility and usefulness of this, the project built a single terminal gateway with a user interface. This stand-alone version of a CCS provided all of the function needed by a police authority and has also been used by some licence authorities to provide an enquiry capability. The single PC implementation has proved a useful first step by allowing the administrations and control authorities to gain experience of using EDI techniques, as well as bringing confidence in working with their peer group, at minimum cost.

Individual authorities may wish to develop more sophisticated implementations in the future to provide better access to their existing terminal users and this can be done without requiring other country licensing authorities to change their implementations. Each country can, therefore, move at its own pace while still being able to participate in the INCA community.

Building the translation and construction functions for the EDI messages directly into the licence application systems and working directly with the data elements defined in the messages provides faster response times than using

Annex A
Case Studies

the currently accepted EDI techniques involving batch processing of files containing the EDI messages. This type of implementation requires a lot more effort on the part of the authorities and provides less flexibility if message structures are changed. Before anything like this is undertaken, the message structures should be stable and tested. The INCA messages are not currently stable enough to recommend that anything like this is done.

The work being done by the UN/EDIFACT board on interactive EDI and defining new versions of the UN/EDIFACT syntax to cover real-time exchanges may be relevant to INCA when looking to provide application-to-application transfers in 'real-time' but currently INCA is probably not sufficiently advanced to pursue this work.

A7.6 Security and Integrity of Messages

All data exchanges between administrations are made using EDI messages; by definition, therefore, there is no direct access by a user to another administration's data bases. There is no possibility that an otherwise authorised user, eg a control authority, can perform non-approved functions or is allowed to have direct access to data. Any response sent out by an administration contains only information which it is prepared to release to another INCA community member.

A.7.6.1 Identification of requirements

The INCA project identified that there was an undeniable need to provide secure means of data interchange between the administrations.

After discussion with the administrations it was decided that whether there are national or regional control centres was not relevant to the INCA security architecture; each national or regional entity could be considered as a secured domain, whatever the entity, eg a stand-alone terminal or a complex internal network with an attached administration data base. The important point coming out from these discussions was that for security purposes a 'user' is defined as an 'administration' and not an individual person within that administration. In practical terms this means that the INCA gateway is the boundary of the domain which is to be secured. Since the gateway resides on the administration's site, it is assumed to be physically secure. Any person or machine within the administration is assumed to have legitimate access to the gateway. Any restriction of access to the gateway is the responsibility of the administration and is outside the scope of the INCA security implementation.

The exchange of EDI messages takes place between these entities (the INCA gateways) through a public network, and it is this part of the process that needed to be secured by the INCA architecture. Once the data has been received into an administration's systems environment it is considered to be secured by the normal security environment of the administration.

Having clearly identified where the threats may come from, and what part of the INCA network architecture needed to be secured, the next step was to detail what level of security was required during the transfer. This depends upon the type of data that each EDI message is carrying and falls into the following categories:

- authentication

- integrity

- confidentiality

- non-repudiability.

Authentication: Authentication allows an authority to be sure that any message received has come from an authorised source. After having sent an enquiry, it is also necessary to be sure that the answer is coming back from the right authority.

Integrity: Integrity checking allows the authority to be sure that a message that arrives in a gateway has not been modified during the transmission.

Confidentiality: Confidentiality ensures that no one, other than an authorised body, can look at the data while it is in transit.

It may be necessary to have confidentiality for exchanges containing private data, such as the number of remaining points or a list of offences on a driver's licence, However, it was thought that this was not required for the network pilot, and it was not implemented at this stage. Of course, confidentiality could be implemented later but it was considered as being out of the scope of current INCA implementation.

Furthermore, to implement confidentiality would mean that some, or all, of the data would need to be enciphered. In order to use this technique there are legal issues which need to be addressed. In some countries authorisations must be obtained from government in order to send encrypted communications.

Non-repudiability: Non-repudiability means that the sender of a message cannot later deny having sent the message, or the receiver cannot deny having received it. This is normally required if the message is an order for a financial transaction. For INCA, it is believed that messages about offences may require a non-repudiation mechanism, but in most cases non-repudiability is not required as long as authentication and integrity are ensured.

In summary, the INCA consortium decided that the following security functions were required:

authentication	always required for all messages
integrity	always required for all messages
confidentiality	only required for some aspects of some message types – it is not included in current implementations
non-repudiability	may be required in the future for some messages.

A7.6.2 Selection of Security Techniques for INCA

The choice of the security mechanism had to take into account some practical and organisational issues, among them:

- every gateway must be able to deal with every other gateway
- the addition of a new gateway must not cause practical problems for existing users of INCA
- it must be possible to send and receive messages at the same time
- some mechanisms have legal issues.

Authentication service: Authentication requires the use of keys being used in combination with an algorithm to produce a digital signature. The choices of algorithm to be used are non-reversible (eg public/private key) or reversible (secret key, eg Data Encryption Standard (DES)).

As INCA required that the addition of a new gateway to the community could be easily achieved without requiring changes to existing systems, the use of a non-reversible (public/private) algorithm was more suitable. Such algorithms offer a higher security level than reversible but, for practical purposes, they require a CA to distribute the key pairs.

INCA has selected the RSA algorithm. The Zero Knowledge algorithm, although newer, is more suited to interactive access techniques than EDI.

Integrity service: To ensure integrity, a seal (digital signature) is computed from the contents of the message. This is carried with the message and can be checked by the receiver to ensure that the message content has not been changed.

The computation of the seal may be done in several ways. Some mechanisms use keys (eg DES) and others hashing algorithms. For INCA the use of keys would mean public and private keys because of the requirement to add new gateways easily. Using public/private key mechanisms to compute a seal from a complete message would take a lot of computing power and a long time to process because of the complexity of the algorithms being used. Consequently, INCA specifies the use of a hashing mechanism to compute the seal.

It is possible to achieve both integrity and authentication of messages using a technique that encrypts the result of applying hashing to the message thereby producing a digital signature. The INCA architecture specifies this technique to be used to calculate the digital signature.

A normalised hashing algorithm, GOC (Generateur d'Octets Chiffrants, ie Ciphering Bytes Generator), is used on the whole message to generate a few bytes of data. These few bytes of data are encrypted with the secret key of the sender to produce a 'digital signature', which is sent with the message.

The receiver uses the public key of the sender to decrypt the digital signature and recover the result of the sender's hashing of the message. This is compared to the hash result produced when the receiver applies the same hashing algorithm to the message just received. If the results compare then the message has been both authenticated and validated.

In order to be able to verify incoming messages, the receiver needs to know the public key of the sender. There are several mechanisms which could be used to allow this to happen:

A.7.6.3 The role of the certification authority

- the keys could be held on the receiving CCS gateway and looked up, based on the address of the incoming message. The keys would be distributed by bilateral agreement

- all the public keys for the community could be stored on a central data base and retrieved by the INCA gateway, when required

- the public key of the sender could be sent with each message.

The last has the advantage that no central or distributed data base is required to hold keys and new users can be added without needing to inform existing users of the new public keys. It also means that keys can be replaced quickly if security has been breached in any individual site. However, it does mean that the receiver has to be able to 'trust' the public key of the sender to be genuine and know that it belongs to an authorised authority.

The role of the CA is to distribute public and secret keys to authorised members of the INCA community and to provide a security certificate to that authorised user. The certificate is a file in UN/EDIFACT format containing:

- the public key of the authorised user

- the name of the authority, in full, and the allocated short (code) name for the owner of the public key; this is the unique code name which is used to identify the sender in the UN/EDIFACT messages sent by that authority

- the expiry date of the certificate

- the digital signature of the CA based upon hashing of the above data. This signature is created using the secret key of the CA.

The certificate data could be copied into the sender's message and transmitted with every message or it could be sent as a separate message from the CA to each member of the INCA community. The recipient uses the public key of the CA (known to everyone) to validate the certificate. The public key of the owner of the certificate can be extracted from the certificate data and used to validate any message coming from that sender.

For the pilot, one of the members of the INCA consortium acted as the CA and distributed the certificates, containing the public keys, to each member separately. The certificate data is stored in a table in the gateway. This mechanism has worked well for the pilot since the number of users is small and fixed. In the future, however, INCA may have to look at sending the certificates attached to each message. The processing overhead is much smaller if the certificates are distributed only once since it saves having to authenticate the certificate each time a message is received before the public key of the sender can be used to authenticate the rest of the message.

For INCA, the security information, signatures and certificates are carried within the UN/EDIFACT messages, according to the UN/EDIFACT Security Implementation Guidelines of January 1993.

A.7.6.4 Considerations When Carrying Digital Signatures in UN/EDIFACT Messages

EDI data is carried in character format as specified by the UN/EDIFACT syntax. Digital signatures are binary numbers and, therefore, must be treated carefully if they are to be carried inside UN/EDIFACT messages. If data is sent from a machine working in ASCII (eg a PC) to a machine working in another format (eg EBCDIC on a

Annex A
Case Studies

mainframe) a conversion has to be performed somewhere. This is sometimes done in the network mailbox or in conversion software on one or other machines. This is fine for normal UN/EDIFACT character data but does not work with binary fields.

Any data which is in a format other than character, such as the digital signatures, must be manipulated in order to ensure its correct transmission to the receiving party. In order to achieve this, INCA specified that binary fields should be treated in the following way before transmission and in reverse upon receipt.

Known binary fields are converted to hexadecimal using a specified code page function. Each of the two characters of the hexadecimal data is carried in character format in the body of the message. This doubles the length of the data when compared to the binary format but it ensures that, regardless of any character conversions (eg ASCII 8-bit to EBCDIC, or ASCII 7-bit to 8-bit) done within the network, or the transmission modules, the binary value is preserved. More importantly in some cases, it ensures that no binary field is interpreted as a control character by any of the transmission modules or translator functions.

In order to use this mechanism, the data element 'Filter Function coded' 4721, and 'Code Page coded' 4731, must be used. It is the job of the security module to use this information to manipulate the outgoing and incoming data.

In the same way, when validating incoming messages using hashing algorithms, it is important to know what character encoding the original message was in when the hash algorithm was applied. The original encoding may have been changed during the transmission process. The security module must perform any character conversions on the UN/EDIFACT message before calculating the hash number and comparing it with the result transmitted with the message.

In the case of the INCA pilots, where all of the implementations are currently based upon PCs using the INCA-supplied implementations, this may not be important, since all data is sent and received in 8-bit ASCII encoding. However, in the future it may not be possible to guarantee this.

EDI Implementation Guide

A.7.7 Implementation Details of the INCA Gateway

The functions of an INCA gateway are to:

- communicate with the application systems which access and update the administration data bases; the structure of the data which is passed to and from the administration's application is called the 'in-house file'

- convert INCA UN/EDIFACT messages to, and from, the in-house file structures: this process is normally called 'translation'

- provide the mechanisms to meet the INCA security architecture and, therefore, protect the data base applications from unauthorised access

- provide network access and data transfer functions to the INCA network implementation; this function provides physical connections to the network and the VAN-provided mailbox services

- provide management and control of the flow of messages in order to meet the service-level objectives agreed to by the administration

- provide audit functions for all messages flowing through the system. This is particularly relevant for messages which provide information to update data bases.

A gateway could be implemented on a separate machine from the administration's data base access application or it could be built into the same machine. It provides the implementation of the INCA architecture.

The INCA gateway for the pilot projects has been built using a PC designed to be attached directly to the licence administration's data base access application. One of the advantages of this approach is that the first implementations could be carried out using affordable PC front ends. The software was put together centrally for all the pilot administrations and was based on the products of the Dutch company, EDITIE. This approach brought several advantages:

- the implementation software could be standardised,

Annex A
Case Studies

> thereby keeping the development cost for each administration down to a minimum

- the messages and sample translation routines to the in-house files could be standardised along with the security implementations, giving fewer possibilities for error in individual implementations.

- only the connection to the data base application would be individually built by the administrations. This could use a simple file transfer technique, thereby keeping the changes to existing systems to a minimum.

The project also built a user interface, running on the same PC as the gateway, which allows enquiries to be keyed in and responses viewed. This stand-alone version of an INCA gateway provides all of the function needed by a police authority and has also been used by some licence authorities to provide much of the function and keep the customised development work to a minimum.

The implementation is designed to move an EDI message, or batch of messages, between two gateways via a mailbox system. In order to use the gateway, an administration application must pass it a file containing a batch of information to be exchanged with another administration, or a file containing an enquiry it wishes to make against another administration's data base. In the case of an enquiry, a terminal user will have keyed the request parameters into a mainframe enquiry application, or put the enquiry into the special PC application provided by the project. The file must be in a special format, which has been defined to the gateway. This format is known as the *in-house* format.

There may need to be modifications to the normal mainframe enquiry application to allow fields which are only relevant to international enquiries to be entered. For example, there would need to be an indication of the country code for the licence enquiry, which would not be relevant for a national enquiry system. Other fields may need to be converted into the codes specified by INCA before translation can take place. For example, the colour of a car is represented by codes in the INCA UN/EDIFACT message, which are not used by any

EDI Implementation Guide

administration's internal systems. The in-house files are converted to and from UN/EDIFACT messages in the gateway. This process of translation is unique to each administration since it converts the in-house files into the standard UN/EDIFACT message structures and also converts the received UN/EDIFACT messages into unique in-house files for each administration.

After the translation process the UN/EDIFACT message goes through the security module in the gateway. The details of this process are included in A.7.11, 'Details of the INCA security implementation'.

The UN/EDIFACT messages are addressed and routed over the network to the mailbox of the recipient. The UN/EDIFACT messages are received into the recipient's gateway where, after checking the digital signature, they are turned into in-house files. The in-house file is passed to the administration's mainframe data base application, which interprets the enquiry and gets the response data required. The response data is then formatted and returned. In the INCA pilots the processing of received enquiries was completely automatic.

A.7.8 Networking Functions

The INCA architecture differentiates between the physical transmission of the data over a network and the logical movement of information between the administrations. The architecture specifies the logical movement of the EDI data between administrations by specifying the use of UN/EDIFACT messages. Physically, these messages could be transferred directly over a telecommunications network or by using store-and-forward techniques. The networking implementation chosen for the pilots has little effect on the application interfaces or the UN/EDIFACT messages. Changes would be required in the gateways to accommodate other transfer protocols and audit controls but these changes would not affect the work done in establishing the data exchange between authorities. The objective of INCA was to separate as much as possible the decisions about networking from the decisions about data exchange.

In order to implement INCA, three aspects of providing network services had to be considered:

- the provision of a backbone carrier service and the

connection of the administration sites to the backbone network

- the value-added service functions to be provided on the backbone network

- the management and delivery of the service to the administrations.

A.7.8.1 *Network connections for the pilot*

All transfers of messages between INCA gateways go via a message routing store-and-forward application, which is provided on the IBM Information Network, to which each of the administrations is connected by a leased line. The physical connections of the administrations to the backbone network varies according to the specific requirements of the countries and the regulations governing provision of telecommunications services. The network connections have used a variety of connection types, X.25, asynchronous, and SDLC, at different speeds, using digital and analogue dedicated connections as well as dial-up.

In Greece, where the use of Hellaspac (the PTT X.25 service) is required for all internal data connections, INCA has used a gateway between the IBM Information Network service and Hellaspac. Similar gateways from national PTT X.25 networks exist in other countries and have been used where direct connections to the IBM network are not appropriate, such as in Spain.

A.7.8.2 *Store-and-forward services*

The INCA pilot implementation uses the IBM Information Exchange store-and-forward EDI mailbox service, which also acts as a message-routing function. The continuous receive functions of Information Exchange are used via the leased lines to provide a store-and-forward function, which passes enquiries to the gateways as soon as they come into the recipient's mailbox. If a gateway is temporarily unavailable then the messages are held until the gateway comes back on-line.

There are some advantages to be considered in using a message mailbox service and store-and-forward techniques:

- the implementation of the gateways is simpler since they do not 'talk' directly to each other; they do not

- require a message rescheduling function to allow messages to be resent if the target system is temporarily unavailable; the messages are held in the recipient's mailbox until the target system comes back on-line

- since the line protocol and the application protocol supported by each of the systems in the community are not identical, a combination of the network service and the store-and-forward service handles protocol conversion. This has allowed each of the administrations to choose a protocol which is most convenient to them without having to achieve agreement between all the parties involved. It also allows parties to change the protocol they are using without affecting all of the existing administrations. This provides a migration path from many of the existing proprietary standards being used towards international standards

- if the INCA community is connected via multiple network services in the future, then the easiest way to achieve interworking between networks will be to provide interconnection between the store-and-forward services

- if archiving or audit trails are required to be held centrally for security then this service could be built around a store-and-forward application.

A.7.8.3 Addressing and routing of messages

Routing of enquiries to the correct gateway is based on the addressing information contained in the UN/EDIFACT UNB header segment. The store-and-forward service checks this header and routes the message via the mailbox address to the correct physical network address. Should the physical network address of the gateway be changed, the logical mailbox address remains fixed.

The pilots have highlighted an important consideration of the maintenance of routing and addressing tables in communities such as INCA. Routing of enquiries and information to the correct gateway assumes that the gateway holds a table of all nicknames and conversions to their mailbox address. In order to be able to work this way, each administration must be allocated a coded name or nickname which is known to every member of the community.

If the hierarchical principle of CCS's is followed, as described earlier, all enquiries for a country are routed through one or a small number of regional gateways. CCS's only need to be aware of the addresses of other CCS's. Any changes to internal arrangements within a country do not need to be known. If individual control authorities are given direct access to other country administration systems, the maintenance of routing tables in all of these systems becomes a much more difficult task. In the long term this would probably require a directory service to manage the updates.

A.7.9 Response Times

One of the concerns which was considered in the pilots was the trade-off between direct access to a data base and using EDI with store-and-forward when it comes to response times to enquiries.

The response times experienced in the early stages of the pilots were extremely variable and depended largely on the implementation set-up in each of the administrations' systems. The following table looks at the variability of the response times and considers the component times which make up the total response times. The response time considered here is from completing an enquiry screen to getting the answer back on the screen. The process involved in getting back a response to an enquiry consists of going through a gateway four times; twice on each site. However, it should be remembered when looking at these times that the system can be used to send batches of enquiries as easily as single enquiries and that the processing time for a batch only varies marginally from that of a single enquiry.

Function	Response time (seconds)
Process UN/EDIFACT data for sending and receiving	32
Handle digital signatures	24
Prepare for sending and receiving and audit log processing	40
Network transmission, including log-on and application protocol handling for mail box	8
Mailbox handling time	2
Application processing time (dependent on administration's implementation)	Variable
Average total time to process (with minimum delays)	113

EDI Implementation Guide

It can be seen from this summary that by far the largest times involved are in processing data in the gateways. The actual network times, even using store-and-forward, are not so significant. Preparing data ready for sending, and handling the incoming messages takes a considerable amount of processing and this is largely due to the error recovery systems and audit trail functions which have been implemented, plus the requirement to load and unload the actual transmission software for line handling.

The loading and unloading of transmission software was required because of the 640 Kb memory addressing limitation of DOS. There was insufficient storage available to have all the software memory resident. This could be improved by changing the operating system on the gateway to one which could multitask, eg UNIX or OS/2.

The construction and checking of digital signatures also adds a large amount of time to the overall response. The time taken for this function could be reduced if the digital signature could be carried in UN/EDIFACT at interchange and not message level. This would allow digital signatures to protect more than one UN/EDIFACT message and would reduce the overhead. This mechanism is not currently supported by UN/EDIFACT guideline standards.

One other factor has an effect on the total processing time required in the gateway. All processing takes place serially and no multiprocessing is supported. Each of the functions is, therefore, loaded and unloaded for each message that is processed.

In summary, it is possible to reduce the response times for processing single enquiries even if the EDI processes remain similar to the present implementation. However, the times are not likely to be reduced to the levels which could be achieved by direct access to the data bases unless more drastic redesign takes place, using interactive EDI techniques. This would involve the administrations in more complex implementations and this trade-off would need to be discussed in more detail with the INCA user group.

A.7.10 Provision of an INCA Service Management Function

One of the outcomes of the pilots and the project has been an identification of tasks which need to be performed on behalf of INCA users.

These tasks have been performed for the administrations in INCA by other members of the INCA consortium. In the future, these functions could be performed by a body which represents the users of INCA and works closely with the network carriers and VANS. For convenience, the body is called the INCA Service Provider.

The Service Provider is there to support the INCA community in its implementations, ongoing maintenance and enhancements of the service and its acquisition of the network carrier services. The Service Provider specifies service levels and function to be delivered by the network carrier services.

This area is still the subject of ongoing discussions in the INCA consortium but the sorts of job which could be performed by the Service Provider are:

- supporting the INCA community users in the selection of the required carrier services and specifying the required function to the carrier service providers. The Service Provider would be responsible for service levels and ensuring that they are met on behalf of the members

- providing or specifying any networking services required by the INCA community, ie directory services, networking security functions, message transfer functions. It must be responsible for administration and control of network addressing (particularly in the case of interworking) and ensuring the consistency and compatibility of addresses

- supporting the users in the selection of software and implementation components by specifying the user interface architectures. This job could be extended to working with software suppliers to build generic software which conforms to the required interfaces and approving this software for use in the community. This function is not intended to prevent users from

- controlling and specifying the interchange agreements which each INCA member would sign. The interchange agreements would specify the obligations of each INCA member and would be designed to protect the members of the community. By specifying and controlling INCA interchange agreements to cover legal, security and operational obligations of members it would save each member from needing to draw up such agreements on a bilateral basis

- specifying and documenting the use of INCA EDI messages and ensuring that these messages continue to support the expanding requirements of the community. An important aspect of this task is to specify and document the use of data elements in these messages in order to be able to cope with the existing variations in the way this data is held by the administrations. This job also involves understanding any new requirements from members and to consolidate these requirements across the community. The INCA Service Provider would work with the standards bodies to ensure that new messages conform to standards and also that any new standards changes are incorporated in INCA messages

- ensuring that any new member of the INCA community conforms to the message standards and interchange agreement (particularly in security) by running a 'validation centre'. The validation centre is capable of sending and receiving test messages from the members to ensure that a member's implementation and use of messages conforms to the INCA community requirements. This ensures that when new members, or new messages, are introduced to the existing community, they do not cause problems or errors in existing members' systems

- acting as CA for security keys and distribution of security certificates. This function is extremely important to members of the community since it provides their protection from unauthorised users of the INCA services. This function is closely associated with the validation centre function since the last stage of validation is to issue the new user with a certificate which becomes an entitlement to use INCA services and access existing members' systems

- ensuring the uniqueness of coded names for use in network communications and EDI messages and to ensure this is in line with smart card uses. This administrative function is related closely to network addressing and directory functions

- expanding the INCA community, in line with its members' requirements, into new areas and to include provision of new services both to administrations and the commercial sector. The INCA Service Provider must also ensure that the service is capable of meeting new legislative requirements that may be placed on the administrations and would involve the networking of the administrations.

The Service Provider role is both technical and administrative in its functions and must be directed towards meeting the requirements of its members.

A.7.11 Details of the INCA Security Implementation

The CCS gateway contains a table of certificates for each of the members of the INCA Community with whom it exchanges data. This table is keyed on the certificate identifier number of the authority owning the certificate (data element 4718 in the UN/EDIFACT CER segment). This number is allocated to the certificate owner by the CA. The body of the table contains other elements from UN/EDIFACT segment groups 2 and 3, and the certificate, such as:

- certificate identifier: CER 4718 (used as the key to the table)

- certificate version: CER 4732

- owner's unique name allocated by the Community: NAD 3039 segment group 2

- owner's algorithm for signing messages: ALG Cxxx 4725 segment group 3

- owner's public key for signature verification: ALG C5xx 47x1, 47x2

- owner's name and address: NAD C058, C080

- expiry date of the certificate (not used for INCA pilots)

- certificate issuer unique name: NAD 3039 (there may be more than one).

The CA sends out a dedicated certificate message each time a new partner is accepted into the community. This message is sent to all existing members and contains segment groups 2 and 3, together with the public key of the new member signed with the secret key of the CA. The existing members validate the certificate message, by using the CA public key, and add the new information to their table of INCA community members.

Each message or enquiry sent by the INCA community to another member carries Security segments group 1 and 2 to identify themselves by their certificate number. This information is used to look up their public key and then to authenticate and validate the message.

The certificate number is carried in the body of the message, which is protected from unauthorised change by the digital signature.

A.7.11.1 Security Interfaces in the INCA Software

The principles of the interface between the translation module and the security module for the INCA implementation are described below. Many of these principles are generic to any implementation but some are specific to INCA.

In general terms, the following apply:

- the translator module is responsible for all manipulation of UN/EDIFACT message structures

- the translator passes all of the required data to the security module to enable it to perform its functions

- for outgoing messages, the security module passes back to the translator any calculated fields in a binary format

- for incoming messages, the security module passes

back to the translator an 'approval to process' once it has performed the required level of validation and authentication on a received message

- the security module is passed the data in the correct encoding format and the Result segment is passed in binary format.

A.7.11.2 Interface Implementation

Sending a message from an INCA gateway: The translator calls the security module and passes to it the message to be secured. The data passed starts at the SEC segment, the first segment following the UNH, and finishes just before the RST segment at the end of the message (to include the separator).

The message, as passed, must contain all the necessary parameters in the security segments already filled in. This data is fixed for a particular INCA message type.

The function call is:

MAKE-DS (file,RST)

The security module then performs the agreed functions on the data supplied. For INCA, this involves calculating a hash according to the GOC algorithm, specified in the security header, and then calculating the digital signature based on the secret key. For the INCA pilots, the secret key is held on a diskette which must be inserted into the diskette drive of the gateway PC. In the future a smart card could be used to hold the secret key instead of a diskette.

The security module passes back to the translator:

- The result (RST) segment value in binary

- A return value

    – 00 – correct execution

    – 01 – an internal error

    – 03 – a problem with the authorisation card in the card reader.

The translator applies the hexadecimal filter to the binary value and inserts the value into the RST segment before it continues to prepare the message for transmission by completing the UN/EDIFACT trailers and constructing the interchange.

Receiving a message into an INCA Gateway: The received interchange is broken into individual messages ready for calling the security module. The RST result segment is converted to binary using the hexadecimal filter. The message data is converted into the correct encoding according to the information in the header. For the INCA pilots this should always be 8-bit ASCII.

The public key of the sender is retrieved from the table using the certificate identifier (element 4718) from the CER segment as the key. If the public key identified does not exist on the data base then a message must be written to the error log and the rest of the translate process is stopped.

The translator calls the security module and passes to it:

- the message starting at the SER segment and finishing at the separator before the RST segment

- the RST segment data in binary

- the public key of the assumed sender.

The function call is:

   DECRYPT-DS(file,digital signature,public key)

The security module performs the pre-agreed functions, compares the result of the message hash with the result from the RST segment and determines the authenticity and validity of the message. It then passes back to the calling function one of the following return codes:

- 00 – correct execution and message is OK to process

- 01 – an internal problem has occurred

- 02 – the message does not pass the security checks

Annex A
Case Studies

– does not validate – does not authenticate etc.

- 03 – a problem with the authorisation card in the reader.

The translator either continues processing or writes an error to the log file and stores the message on an error file.

A.7.12 UN/EDIFACT security segments, example and usage for INCA

Only segment groups 1 and 2 are sent with each message. Segment group 3 is sent as part of a separate certification message, which is not shown here.

A.7.12.1 Segment group 1

This group of segments specifies the security functions that have been applied to the message. It specifies the references to the algorithms used for the hashing of the message, which are then digitally signed.

- SEC: Security segment

    4719 Security Function Qualifier, coded an..3

    value=NRO Non-repudiation of origin is the function

    4343 Response Type, coded an..3

    value=NAR No acknowledgement required

    4721 Filter Function, coded an..3

    value=HEX Hexadecimal filter applied to RST/binary

    4731 Coded Page, coded an..3

    value=AS8 Data for INCA in the standard gateway modules CCS is managed in 8-bit ASCII

    4730 Security Result Link

    not used. There is only one result segment in an INCA message.

- NAD: Name and address segment

    Not used for INCA since the information is carried in CER segments or in the body of the message.

EDI Implementation Guide

- RFF: Reference number segment

  Not used for INCA. The date and time are used as a check on duplicate messages if necessary.

- DTM: Date and time

  Not used for INCA. Date and time for the message are carried in the message or the UNB Header.

- ALG: Security algorithm

  This segment specifies the algorithm used for hashing when proving the 'validity' of the message.

  CXXX Security Algorithm composite segment

  YYYY Algorithm Qualifier, coded an..3

  value=OHA Owner hashing

  4725 Algorithm Identifier, coded an..3

  value=GOC Secure hashing algorithm

  3055 Code list responsible agency an..3

  value=INC INCA is the responsible agency

  C5XX Algorithm Parameters, composite element

  47X1 Algorithm Parameter Qualifier, coded an..3

  value=IVC The initialisation value follows in clear

  47X2 The Algorithm Parameter Value an..512

  value=INCAINCA The initialisation value of the algorithm is included here.

A.7.12.2 Segment group 2

This segment group contains the certificate information required by the receiver of the message to identify the public key of the sender. Only the certificate reference number is carried as a key to the table, which is maintained in the gateway.

Annex A
Case Studies

- CER: Certificate

    4718 Certificate Identifier an..35

    Contains the number of the sender's certificate as issued by the CA. This number is the key to the tables of public keys

    value=nnnn

    4731 Code Page, coded an..3

    This element is not used when sending an INCA message for which a certificate has already been exchanged.

    4732 Format Certificate Version n..3

    This element is not used when sending an INCA message for which a certificate has already been exchanged.

    C5RR Separator Character for Signature

    This element is not used when sending an INCA message for which a certificate has already been exchanged.

    4734 Certificate Issuer Public Key Name an..16

    This identifies the public key name related to the secret key used by the CA used to sign the certificate. It allows the CA to use more than one pair of public/private keys.

    This element is not used when sending an INCA message for which a certificate has already been exchanged.

    4736 User Authorisation Level an..35

    Specifies the authorisation level of the owner of the certificate. Initially for INCA this is the same for all users. There may be multiple levels in the future.

EDI Implementation Guide

This element is not used when sending an INCA message for which a certificate has already been exchanged.

- NAD: Name and address

    Used to identify the owner of the certificate and the name of the CA issuing the certificate.

    Only the certificate owner information is used in the security segments sent with each message.

    3035 Party Qualifier an..3

    value=OW Certificate Owner

    C082 Party Identification Details

    3039 Party ID identification an..17

    This carries a unique coded name for the identity of the certificate owner. The identity code is the same as for the AII segment in the messages (see Driver Licence message).

    C058 Name and Address

    3124 shows address line one an..35

    C080 Party Name

    3036 shows sender name in clear an..35

    3207 shows the coded country of sender an..3

- DTM Date/Time/Period

    This shows the validity period of the Certificate being referenced. This is not used in INCA. The time period is set, if necessary, as a fixed period from the certificate issue date.

A.8 MOD

The business imperative for EDI within MOD is based on three main factors:

- A number of areas within the MOD have EDI initiatives, all at different stages of development. The predicted benefits of these initiatives, combined with support for EDI from IS Strategies, illustrate both the desire for and potential of EDI within MOD. However, these initiatives are largely unco-ordinated in terms of standards and the sharing of infrastructure and experience.

- Organisations outside MOD have gained significant benefits from the use of EDI. These include both public and private sector organisations. The area in which the use of EDI is most advanced is electronic commerce, which encompasses the procurement process.

- The MOD procurement process has a number of strengths, including fast payment from receipt of invoice, reliability, integrity (the system is open and fair, and seen to be so), and adaptability to a large range of contract types. There are, however, a number of weaknesses, including lack of an overall sponsor, duplication of effort, and cost-effective procurement of lower-value items. It was envisaged that EDI can improve all of these, especially in reducing duplication and through the use of bulletin boards to improve cost-effectiveness of lower-value-item procurement. The lack of an overall sponsor can be addressed by moving responsibility for payment to the level of the EDI implementation, which would also lead to significant cost savings.

A.8.1 Costs benefits analysis

In summary, the MOD Corporate EDI Strategy is expected to cost around £15.5m, and realise £28.6m in savings, over a 5-year projection. These benefits and costs are made up as follows:

- Indicative benefits have been assessed, as follows:

    – Direct (tangible) benefits

- Staff savings

    It is estimated that implementation of the MOD Corporate EDI Strategy will lead to a reduction of staff involved in the procurement process, which could realise savings of around £32m over 5 years.

EDI Implementation Guide

- Price reductions

    Price reductions would be achieved by sharing the benefits of EDI with suppliers, as it should reduce their administration costs. This is expected to realise savings of around £3.3m over 5 years.

- Improved inventory control

    Faster and more reliable ordering would enable improvement of the turnover rates of stock in stores. Over 5 years this is expected to realise a saving of around £7.2m.

- Indirect (intangible) benefits

- Reduced error rates

    Reducing the level of manual intervention would result in lower error rates. The effect would not only be in terms of time savings, but also more accurate order status information.

- Reduction in lost/panic orders

    Savings would be realised in two main ways. First, a reduction in the error rate for orders, as a result of accurate advance shipping of notice/delivery notification messages. Second, improved order speed/efficiency resulting in a reduction in panic orders, thereby negating the need to pay higher prices for last-minute local purchases.

- Strategic benefits

- Common approach to industry

    Corporately defined use of standard EDI messages would allow the MOD to present a common face to industry.

- Speeds up ordering at time of crisis

    EDI will speed up ordering of vital equipment should the MOD have to react at time of crisis.

- The total cost of achieving this Corporate EDI Strategy is made up of the following elements:

    – Hardware

    – VAN use

    – Software

    – Staffing

    – Maintenance

    – Application

    – Change management programme

    – Education and training

    This amounts to £15.5m over 5 years.

A.8.2 Future Plans

The MOD is now about to embark on a major implementation programme to realise the above identified benefits. The concentration of effort will be in three areas:

- Improving Electronic Commerce

- Business process re-engineering of the procurement process

- Search for other business areas where EDI is applicable.

This effort will be managed corporately, but will include in its implementation all the key business owners within MOD. Although savings have been projected only over 5 years, it is anticipated they will increase as EDI becomes more prevalent and widely used.

EDI Implementation Guide

Annex B: Preparing an EDI Business Case

This annex is not a general guide to preparing a business case: it is concerned with what is different about the preparation of a business case for EDI. It looks at who benefits from EDI and for whom it is a cost, and provides some sample worksheets which might be used in the exercise.

IS Guide B4: Appraising Investment in Information Systems *should be used for guidance on how a business case should be built.*

B.1 Aim and scope of this annex

Page one of this Guide asks the question: 'Who should read this Guide?', and one of the answers given is 'business managers affected by EDI, especially those who need to produce cost-benefit cases'. The intent was not to imply that the Guide should be a comprehensive reference book on how to produce a cost-benefit analysis for EDI, but that it should explain those factors which are different in an EDI project compared to any other project. This annex summarises those factors which have been covered within the Guide, grouping them as a number of 'important considerations' that need to be taken into account when developing a justification for, or review of, an EDI implementation.

It is worth remembering that EDI is only a tool which can help improve processes, but that these processes are themselves simply a means to achieve a mission or objective as effectively as possible. It is all too easy to forget one or both of these facts and to focus on the process or the tool simply for its own sake. The objective of using EDI should be to help meet an organisation's mission or objective more efficiently or effectively. Therefore, the role of the cost-benefit analysis should be to measure by how much that aim can be met rather than simply to show that what is done today can be done more cheaply with EDI (as it may well be the wrong thing that is being done).

In the wider context, the cost-benefit analysis also forms an effective part of the management process when comparing available options – see the worked example at the end of this annex for confirmation of this point.

EDI Implementation Guide

This annex ends with a series of checklists and worksheets. These are intended for guidance only; they are not definitive and should not be used without first understanding the points covered in the preceding pages.

B.1.1 How to use this Annex

This annex should be read as a supplement to normal accounting processes or practices. Every organisation has its own rules or guidance on how business cases should be prepared, whether the basis for costing should be job, process, standard, uniform or differential, how depreciation, discounting and the cost of money should be addressed, how stock should be valued and budgeting should be approached. Whatever these practices in any department, agency or organisation (and in government these are particularly clearly defined – see Annex J, 'Bibliography'), then they apply equally well to an EDI project as they do to any other project.

What may be different is the scope and scale of the project and the difficulty of collecting some of the information which will be required to make a comprehensive case – indeed in some cases, the real difficulty is in foreseeing the total benefit that will accrue from implementing EDI.

It is for this reason that many practitioners restrict their cost-benefit analysis for EDI projects to the first phase only, based on savings in their existing process without consideration of subsequent benefits from process change or improvement. It is often true that this approach will provide sufficient justification to embark on the EDI project without the need to understand the total benefit of the endeavour.

B.2 Important Considerations

A business case or cost-benefit analysis should be prepared in the same form and manner as usual, but the information put into it will have additional elements peculiar to EDI. Options for re-organising the business need to be considered as well as the simple automation of existing processes. Also, it may be necessary to include the costs incurred in other organisations to get a true picture or to consider benefits in other departments outside of the managerial hierarchy. The following pages give examples of a range of these factors and give references to the main body of this Guide, where the topics are covered more fully.

Annex B
Preparing an EDI Business Case

B.2.1 Strategic or Tactical

In 4.6, 'The next steps', it is stated that:

> *EDI can be implemented in a piecemeal approach . . . but it is unlikely to yield the significant benefits that are available with a strategic implementation.*

This point can be more clearly explained if consideration is given to the potential benefits from EDI in the three stages outlined in Annex E, 'IS notice 31: Electronic Data Interchange'. These are:

- the use of EDI for existing processes

- changing and streamlining the existing processes to perform in a better and more cost-effective manner with the aid of EDI

- the development of business activities to take advantage of new opportunities which become available as a direct result of implementing EDI.

The first stage is relatively easy to understand. If the implementation of EDI brings the avoidance of postal delays and costs, but, otherwise, what is done is intrinsically the same as before EDI was implemented, then these are first-stage benefits of EDI.

Second-stage benefits require process change – for example, the decision to pay upon receipt of goods rather than in response to an invoice and thus the decision, in agreement with suppliers, not to receive invoices as they no longer serve a purpose. In this case, the saving is in the accounts payable department, as the whole reconciliation of invoice to 'Goods Received Note' or 'Delivery Ticket' is removed – perhaps the whole function or group is removed if the payment is fully automated upon successful receipt.

It is worth noting that first-stage benefits tend to be low-cost elements of the process, postage rather than stock, mail clerks rather than accounts payable clerks. This is not unusual and the comparison holds with the third stage, when brand-new activities become possible and the benefits are usually more significant than in the previous stages. The difficulty is always in predicting what the third stage will be and thus what benefits will be attainable. This is because, until a start is made on improving or changing the existing processes and seeing in practice what new alternatives become available, it is very difficult to perceive these alternatives.

One way to visualise the differences is to think of first-stage benefits as being due to automation-EDI; that is, EDI being used to automate what is done today (an EDI message directly replaces a business document).

Stage two is also a form of automation-EDI but it takes advantage of the information that EDI makes accessible. The reason invoices are no longer necessary in the example given earlier is because the information contained in the invoices is available in advance as a result of the details contained in the preceding EDI messages. Thus the second-stage benefits tend to be due to automation-EDI with an element of information-EDI.

Third-stage benefits are always due solely to information-EDI and reflect the new activities or practices that become possible because of the availability of information that was not previously accessible. In the INCA project (see A.7, 'INCA') the process that was automated was the transfer of information and the benefits perceived at the outset were of automation: faster response and less paperwork for the various driver and vehicle licensing authorities and police forces around Europe. At the end of the project, the real beneficiaries, not even considered at the outset, were customs personnel and traffic police who had the ability, previously unimaginable, to pro-actively check vehicles and to select which to check by reference to their licensing authority. The benefit here is not one of doing the job more efficiently, as in the first two stages, but in doing it more effectively. Suddenly they have the ability to know which vehicles have incorrect paperwork or whatever and can focus on them, rather than the many that were previously picked up in random checks in the hope of finding an offender.

There are many other examples of third-stage or information-EDI benefits and all have one thing in common – they could not have been foreseen at the outset. Also, they are normally improvements in effectiveness rather than efficiency and are thus more valuable.

Thus there is the piecemeal approach of taking each EDI project separately and evaluating the potential benefit of that particular implementation (for example, savings in goods inward if EDI dispatch advices are received), and there is the much wider or strategic approach of looking at the whole organisation and thus understanding the potential benefit in the accounts payable department, if the information in the dispatch advice can be used in place of an invoice with the resulting removal of need for reconciliation and all of the associated activities.

Additionally, there are three stages of costs which are associated with the three stages of benefits, yet which tend to decrease in magnitude from one stage to the next. So the overall case for a first stage implementation may be debatable for an EDI implementation while the second stage business case is much more appealing. However, each stage is not optional, the costs and benefits are cumulative and second stage process improvements will not be possible without first stage automation.

B2.2 Imbalance of Benefits Between Partners

As outlined in 2.5.1, 'Why are they different?' (p. 52), the imbalance of costs and benefits between trading partners can make cost justification difficult. For example, when someone sends a payment by cheque with a remittance advice attached, the sender pays the cost of the cheque and the postage and stationery and the recipient performs a reconciliation between the remittance and the previously received invoices. (It is worth noting that there is rarely a one-to-one correlation between invoice and remittance advice. A remittance advice will often cover items on several invoices and may well include part payments of others. Thus reconciliation is no small task and often, owing to the lack of invoice numbers or similar identifiers known to the recipient, the reconciliation becomes an act of guesswork rather than mathematics.) If the sender now decides to use EDI to send the payment, he will incur the higher bank charges associated with an EDI payment (compared to that of a cheque), with no obvious benefit. Indeed if the sender does not change his process, he will actually be worse off as the monies will leave his account more quickly. (Due to the removal of postal delays and hold-ups in the recipients accounts receivable function.)

However, the recipient of the payment may receive it sooner (as the postal and pre-banking delays have been

EDI Implementation Guide

removed) and will have much better control and information than the redundant reconciliation team could ever have given him.

Thus, we have an example where nearly all of the costs fall to one trading partner and nearly all of the benefits fall to the other. While extreme, this is not so unusual. When a University Examining Board asks schools to submit examination registrations using EDI, who benefits? The examining board obviously removes the need for all of the data entry that currently drives its process but what about the individual schools? Each has potentially to implement EDI for one transaction a year which they will probably manually key into the EDI package they buy. So, in effect, there is no saving, merely a transfer of cost in the form of data entry to another party in the chain. This is not necessarily bad. A school secretary entering details of known pupils is far more likely to be accurate than a data entry clerk who has a target of 5000 entrants a day to meet. However, in situations where costs are simply transferred, a cost-benefit analysis should recognise this and some attempt should be made to ensure that the benefits are spread at least enough to balance any costs incurred. It is for this reason that a number of the school implementations use either software and/or network access paid for by the examining board with which they are dealing.

B.2.3 Tangibles and Intangibles

In any cost-benefit analysis, the way in which intangible costs and benefits are handled is usually difficult and often imprecise. In an EDI project, the problems are the same as in any other and will need to be addressed in whatever manner is normally accepted within an organisation. However, intangible costs and benefits should not be ignored even though they are often significant and, unfortunately, often difficult to attribute directly to the project. As an example, a small manufacturer in the North of England produces goods and sells them locally. He would not normally consider providing supplies to a Korean manufacturer operating in a 'Just-in-Time' environment. However, as he has EDI, the Korean customer can be serviced as easily as the one just down the road. Is this additional business attributable to EDI (and should it, therefore, be included in the cost-benefit analysis) or is it solely due to the marketing and sales activities which have taken place overseas since EDI made it possible to operate there? The answer is that both are essential to winning and keeping this business and the cost-benefit analysis should reflect that. How? There is no simple answer unless the cost-benefit analysis grows to become a whole business model, which is unrealistic.

Perhaps the balance is between the strategic programme and the tactical project (alluded to in Chapter 3, 'Preparing for EDI') – that is to say, the business case for any individual project is only valid within the context of an overall EDI programme (or strategy). At the strategic level costs can be quantified within fairly broad limits and related to benefits on the basis of management judgement, partly on the basis of overall cost savings and efficiency improvements, and partly on the basis of an evaluation against the objectives of the organisation.

The strategic business case will identify the major implementation projects, and the outline costs and benefits associated with each. Within this framework, projects need to be defined and implemented, ideally in a sequence such that each delivers quantifiable and significant benefit either on a stand-alone basis or by building on the results of its predecessors.

Some items look very simple to measure and are obviously tangibles such as stock. If there is currently three weeks stock and EDI will take a week out of the order process, then it is logical to claim a third of the value of stock as the expected reduction and add this to the list of benefits. However, it is worth understanding what that three weeks constitutes. Is it simply to balance a three-week lead-time including ordering (two weeks lead-time plus one week ordering, using this example), or does it also include risk stock in case the supplier cannot meet the requested order quantity on the date specified? If this is true, what is the effect on the risk stock if the inability to supply is known a week earlier? Or, if EDI takes a week out of the process, is the discovery actually being made a week later, with a resultant need to increase the risk stock?

Money is another comparatively easy-to-measure resource, simply because there is no need to convert it before including it in the cost-benefit analysis. Ignoring whatever practice is used to evaluate the cost of money, there may still be problems in assessing the amount of this asset in an EDI project. For example, what will be the effect on float when EDI is implemented? It may be that banks (or international banking) are unaffected by the implementation, and, therefore the float which they control is unaffected. But don't forget the hidden float of the number of days a cheque currently takes to pass through in-house processes, the internal mail, the data entry group, etc. Conversely, once it is possible to provide better information and control and more reliable processing, will pricing change to reflect this? Will suppliers or customers expect or accept discounts when using EDI? All of these elements are very difficult to predict in advance but need to be considered if a complete and comprehensive cost-benefit analysis is to be developed.

It could be said that none of these examples give any benefits other than allowing a user to stay competitive – but this is perhaps the classic intangible benefit. If these benefits were not achieved and the organisation did not remain competitive as a result, what effect would that have on revenue and market share (to use private sector examples), should that effect be quantified and added into the overall case? It needs to be included at the strategic level and ideally, where calculable, also in those projects which directly improve competitiveness.

Better control and information has other effects. How much of an organisation's time and effort is expended resolving problems which arise owing to a lack of sufficient control or information? How much of its existing processes and business controls have been put in place to avoid or minimise this expenditure of effort? If EDI removes the root cause, how is the value to the organisation assessed? There can be no answers in this Guide as each organisation has to decide how to address these questions in the context of its own accounting practices. All the Guide can do is to empathise the need for these items to be given due consideration in building the EDI cost-benefit analysis.

Carry the list of questions a stage further and another layer of intangible items are uncovered: if there is better control and information and errors are reduced as a result, will this result in a better service to the customer and, if so, how can it be measured? If the service given is better, does this result in a competitive edge (and even in the most central of government organisations, competition always exists in some form)? Or instead of competitive edge, does it show in the form of enhanced relationships which result in more or better business for the organisation? (As elsewhere in this Guide, 'business' is used in its widest sense rather than being restricted purely to the practice of commerce for profit.)

All of these examples have one thing in common. They all show that it is not simple to measure the absolute effect of implementing EDI because, when it is done successfully, it changes the business in which it is used and, thus, it is a case of trying to separate cause from effect in order to attribute costs and benefits to any one element. It is for this reason that EDI cost-benefit analyses often concentrate on first- and second-stage benefits only (automation–EDI benefits) and ignore completely the impact of information–EDI, because the intangibility of the benefits is so great. However, the important thing to remember if this course is taken is that third-stage benefits rarely have associated costs. All of the costs have been borne in achieving first- and second-stage benefits and the third-stage benefits often come cost-free, based solely on having the managerial ability to identify them and then to attain them, the necessary infrastructure already being in place. This being the case, it is easy to argue that third-stage benefits are not, therefore, attributable to the implementation of EDI but are due to distinct management actions. This is also true, but could not be contemplated without the necessary EDI activity taking place first.

The recommendation must, therefore, be that certain assumptions are made and clearly specified in the cost-benefit analysis which justify the apportionment of benefits from the later stages between the initial EDI implementation and the subsequent management actions that will be required to achieve those benefits.

B.2.4 External Versus Internal EDI

When implementing EDI for intra-organisation communications, that is, in a situation where none of the participants or activities in the project involve anyone outside of the organisation implementing EDI, then the cost-benefit analysis suddenly becomes very like that of any other project.

As stated previously, the overhead of standards and translation in this environment needs to be seriously considered because if this implementation will always be a stand-alone, internal solution, then the additional cost can probably be avoided without loss of benefit. See Chapter 4, 'UN/EDIFACT', for a fuller discussion of the point.

B.2.5 Time

Don't underestimate how long it will take to achieve the benefits predicted. The commonest reason for failure or apparent failure of an EDI project is that plans are over-optimistic and expectations of take-up and/or roll-out speed are unrealistic.

In a normal project, it is possible to develop a plan, identify a critical path, specify checkpoints to ensure the appropriate amount of progress within each period and to instigate control procedures to identify when the plan starts to slip and to instigate actions to bring it back on schedule. In an EDI project, even with the correct level of sponsorship to avoid inter-departmental problems, success is wholly dependent upon the speed of take-up of EDI by trading partners. If they miss their plan dates, so does everyone else and there is very little that can be done about it.

Typically, the project will be vying with other projects for time and resources and their priorities and objectives will be different. So even if EDI is the number one item on the agenda, success is wholly dependent upon ensuring that EDI gets the same level of focus in the partner organisations. This is rarely achievable, so, instead, compensation has to be made by allowing them more time to meet their commitments and also by spending more time and resources working with them than with wholly internal projects. These problems can be minimised by following the advice in Chapter 10, 'Managing the implementation', but they cannot be avoided completely.

Add to this the time-lag once a decision has been taken to undertake EDI while they move up the same learning curve and the need, once EDI has been successfully implemented, to then roll it out across the business process and to a wider range of partners and it is not surprising that payback is typically 18–24 months, in spite of the comparatively low cost and small amount of effort required.

This is for stage 1 benefits. How long should be allowed for stage 3 benefits? How quickly does the culture of an organisation change? How long did it take for the last significant change to the operation of fundamental processes? In a fairly fluid organisation, where 2–3 years is a typical expectancy for any employee in any particular role (particularly managers), then full process change can be accommodated in this timeframe. In a fairly static organisation, similar change could literally take a generation or more, as the current incumbents are replaced by a management team not constricted by today's method of operation and the collection of experiences which have dictated that it should be this way.

B.2.6 Breadth of Process Covered

The point has been made many times already in this Guide, but is worth repeating, one more time, that the benefits from EDI will be greatest when it is used throughout a business process, say from order through to payment in a typical business cycle.

Many people realise this but forget it when planning an EDI implementation. They talk in terms of a critical mass of business partners being EDI-enabled in order to achieve break-even for a particular transaction (order, form, enquiry, etc) rather than a broad enough range of related transactions to benefit from the information that becomes available. This is typically because the focus of the cost-benefit analysis is at stage 1, the need to convert as much of the current volume to EDI in order to recoup the cost in postage and clerical effort saved, rather than the bigger picture of opportunity that a good cost-benefit analysis should endeavour to cover. Having made the point, it is as well to remember the objective of the cost-benefit analysis – if it is only to justify the cost of the project, and this can be achieved wholly with stage 1 benefits across a limited portion of the process, then this is sufficient and the cost-benefit analysis should be based on this. Indeed, as it is probably true that the *quick* benefits will come from getting a critical mass of trading partners and trading volumes, this should perhaps be the focus of the basic cost-benefit analysis. However, the project itself must not lose sight of the

EDI Implementation Guide

real potential and must be structured to achieve these much greater benefits.

B.3 **Financial EDI Peculiarities**

Chapter 9, 'EDI in Finance', has several pages that outline the benefits that can be obtained by each of the parties in a Financial EDI trading loop and, while these benefits provide a compelling justification for Financial EDI, when constructing the business case it is worth repeating the following points:

- the benefits obtained will be offset by the costs of changes to the business process. The total costs would include additional service prices, internal administration costs and bank transaction charges

- the recipient of Financial EDI payments will receive the greatest cost reductions. This imbalance can best be offset by both partners implementing Financial EDI at the same time

- the benefits are greatest where EDI is already used to enhance the supply chain and where Financial EDI is a natural extension

- the benefits to the supplier of Financial EDI will only be obtained if the accuracy of the reference information can be assured

- the benefits will be proportional to the amount and complexity of financial information to be processed, and greatest where the timing of the transaction must be assured.

While some of the banks encourage customers to start with Financial EDI, it is obvious that the earlier stages of the process need to be migrated to EDI if maximum benefit is to be obtained. The reasoning behind this is actually quite simple: unless the earlier stages use EDI, then the information for Information–EDI benefits (stage 3) will not be available and the only benefits achievable will be those of automation.

One point needs special emphasis before ending this section: business cases are expressed in terms of money and, when the commodity being measured is money, then the effect of improvements is to provide much greater financial benefits. As an example: a typical organisation in today's environment may have 30 days stock and 40 days debt. EDI could be used to reduce either or both of these. In a typical, large organisation, 30 days stock could be valued at several hundred thousand pounds, whereas 40 days debt will often be worth several million. A reduction in stock will free some working capital (cash). A reduction in debt has a positive impact on interest charges as well as cash. Thus, it is often very easy to show a much greater benefit from Financial EDI than for say, ordering. However, remember that to reduce debt a supplier needs customers to use EDI, whereas for stock, it is the suppliers that need to co-operate and it is always easier to move up the supply chain than down it. And to reiterate once more, there is a need to consider an overall strategy and trading partner relationship which will adjust terms and conditions to compensate those who bear more cost than is justified by individual benefit, in order to drive cost out of the whole supply chain.

B.4 Process Change Revisited

It should by now be very clear that the real opportunity with EDI is as part of a larger process-improvement initiative. Perhaps formally, as a process re-engineering exercise. Perhaps informally, as an act of normal management, monitoring the day-to-day operation, spotting opportunities for improvement and then managing their introduction to ensure that improvement is realised without undue impact.

Two final words of warning:

- Understand the bigger picture

    Many large corporates have implemented EDI-ordering with their suppliers and then, because many of the suppliers were small and lacked the sophisticated systems to give real benefit by returning EDI invoices, the corporates implemented self-billing (explained in detail in Chapter 9, 'EDI in Finance'). Self-billing is a process improvement – having automated ordering, the corporate moves on from receiving invoices and reconciling these against goods received notes to self-billing, where in response to goods received a statement is sent to the supplier detailing what has been received and will thus be paid for (and when). This gives the supplier the

EDI Implementation Guide

certainty of payment which is often craved but usually lacking and removes the need for reconciliation on the part of the corporate. But it does not remove it from the process – actually it just transfers it to the supplier who then has the onus of reconciliation and correction in order to ensure the correct payment.

This is not necessarily bad, but the overall effect on ALL parties does need to be understood when instigating a change of this nature.

- Understand the dependencies

There have been many examples throughout this Guide which show the interdependence between departments and organisations which need to be understood and accommodated or, better still, emphasised in order to maximise benefit. Whether a project succeeds or fails, it will be because this aspect of the overall picture received too little or not enough attention.

B.5 Checklists and Worksheets

B.5.1 Sample EDI Costs Worksheet

One-time Expenses	Labour hours	External expenses
Project planning	....	....
Project team education	....	....
Participating in standards groups	....	....
Electronic Commerce Association meetings	....	....
Users education	....	....
Modifications to procedures	....	....
Telecom design or selection	....	....
Telecom installation	....	....
Select and install additional hardware	....	....
EDI software design or selection	....	....
EDI soft development and test	....	....
Data translation definition and coding	....	....
Changes to existing applications	....	....
Design, develop and test new applications	....	....
Select, motivate and train partners	....	....
Conduct pilot test	....	....
Measure and evaluate	....	....
Per additional transaction	....	....
Per additional partner	....	....
TOTALS	....	....

Annex B
Preparing an EDI Business Case

B.5.2 Sample EDI operating costs worksheet

Operating Expenses	Labour hours	External expenses
Project management	....	....
Telecom hardware and software rentals	....	....
IS resources and support	....	....
EDI software rentals	....	....
VAN charges	....	....
PTT charges	....	....
Trading partners co-ordination	....	....
Helpdesk, hotline	....	....
Measure and evaluate	....	....
Per additional transaction	....	....
Per additional partner	....	....
TOTALS	....	....

B.5.3 Sample EDI maintenance costs worksheet

Operating Expenses	Labour hours	External expenses
Telecom hardware and software	....	....
EDI software and applications	....	....
New personnel training	....	....
Changes due to partners	....	....
Changes in standards	....	....
Problem isolation and solving	....	....
Per additional transaction	....	....
Per additional partner	....	....
TOTALS	....	....

B.5.4 Sample Benefit-by-department matrix

| Benefit | Department | | | | | |
	Treasury	Accounts	Transport	Manufacturing	Administration	Purchasing
Cash flow	....	....	....	....	....	....
Clerical effort	....	....	....	....	....	....
Document cycle time	....	....	....	....	....	....
Document storage	....	....	....	....	....	....
Improved T/C	....	....	....	....	....	....
Inventory cost	....	....	....	....	....	....
Paper, supplies	....	....	....	....	....	....
Postage, telephone	....	....	....	....	....	....
Company image	....	....	....	....	....	....
Competitiveness	....	....	....	....	....	....
Customer service	....	....	....	....	....	....
Productivity	....	....	....	....	....	....
Errors	....	....	....	....	....	....
Product Quality	....	....	....	....	....	....
Supplier Relationships	....	....	....	....	....	....

EDI Implementation Guide

This particular approach has the benefit of allowing department managers easy visibility of the cost and benefit to them of a particular project, which may help get more 'ownership' from functional managers.

B.5.5 The Financial Business Case – A Worked Example

This example is provided by Patrick Finch Associates, and is published with their permission.

B.6 Example of the Financial Business Case

Imagine two companies as follows:

	Company A	Company B
Employees	1,000	100
Annual Sales	150M	7.5M
Sales Force	75	5
Suppliers	2,000	220
Customers	20,000	150
Monthly:		
Invoices out	16,000	120
Invoices in	1,800	210
Orders out	3,000	330
Orders in	24,000	240

B.6.1 Stage 1 Savings and Costs

B.6.1.1 Administrative Savings

Mail Room Staff	8,196	225
Data Preparation Staff	38,700	810
Clerical Staff	78,400	1,620
Filing Staff	8,198	165
Supervisor	16,390	297
Total	149,884	3,117

Annex B
Preparing an EDI Business Case

B.6.1.2 Reduced Cost of Errors

Misdirected Orders	150,000	6,250
Lost Business (0.01%)	30,000	7,500
Inventory Shrinkage	6,000	300
Total	186,000	14,050

B.6.1.3 Improved Productivity

SOP Preparation	39,600	396
Errors on query handling	24,585	494
Easier Sales	13,333	120
Manufacturing Efficiency	18,000	1,980
Total	95,518	2,990

B.6.1.4 Improved Sales

Better Faster Service	150,000	7,500
Ability to respond	15,000	750
Locked in customers	15,000	750
Total	180,000	9,000

B.6.1.5 Reduced Inventory

12 days down to 9 days	60,000	3,000
Storage cost	30,000	1,500
Total	90,000	4,500

B.6.1.6 Time Value Benefits

Receivables down 3 days	123,288	6,164
Payables down 3 days	-73,973	-3,699
Total	49,315	2,465

B.6.1.7 Reduced Comms Costs

Reduced phone/fax	9,834	198
Reduced paper/postage	6,556	132
Total	16,390	330

EDI Implementation Guide

B.6.1.8 Summary of EDI Stage 1 Benefits

Administrative Cost Savings	149,884	3,117
Reduced cost of errors	186,000	14,050
Improved productivity	95,518	2,990
Improved sales	180,000	9,000
Reduced inventory	90,000	4,500
Time value benefits	49,315	2,465
Reduced communications	16,390	330
Total	767,107	36,452

B.6.2 Costs

B.6.2.1 One-time costs

Cost of hardware	30,000	3,000
Cost of start-up software	45,000	1,800
Internal professional	225,000	15,000
External software development	150,000	
Internal Management	225,000	7,500
Other one-time charges	10,500	1,200
Total one-time costs	685,500	28,500

B.6.2.2 Annual Costs

VAN Charges	23,520	945
Line Charges	5,040	203
Software Maintenance	63,000	4,020
Total annual costs	91,560	5,168

So EDI pays for itself at stage 1, but the DCF/NPV analysis shows that it is hardly irresistible for a company of this size, especially if the opportunity cost of management time is included. (All numbers in £000's)

Annex B
Preparing an EDI Business Case

Company A:	Year 1	Year 2	Year 3	Year 4	Year 5
Benefit %	33%	67%	78%	89%	100%
Benefit	253	514	598	683	767
Inflated benefit (at 5%)	253	540	660	790	932
One-time cost %	65%	25%	10%		
One-time cost	-446	-171	-69		
Annual cost	-92	-92	-92	-92	-92
Total Cost	-537	-263	-160	-92	-92
Inflated cost (at 5%)	-537	-276	-177	-106	-111
Net Cash	-284	264	483	684	821
Cumulative NPV at 10%	-284	-40	323	790	1,300
IRR	133%				

Company B:	Year 1	Year 2	Year 3	Year 4	Year 5
Benefit %	33%	67%	78%	89%	100%
Benefit	12	24	28	32	36
Inflated benefit (at 5%)	12	26	31	38	44
One-time cost %	65%	25%	10%		
One-time cost	-19	-7	-3		
Annual cost	-5	-5	-5	-5	-5
Total Cost	-24	-12	-8	-5	-5
Inflated cost (at 5%)	-24	-13	-9	-6	-6
Net Cash	-12	13	23	32	38
Cumulative NPV at 10%	-12	0	17	38	62
IRR	150%				

B.7 Stage 2 Savings and Costs

In stage 2 we can start 'performing better business processes'. An improved order-service system might mean we can now build-to-order more, rather than having to build-to-plan, so that inventory costs are greatly reduced. Through relieving the salesmen of the job of order-taking and giving them time to talk to (and listen to) the customers, we could target an improvement in sales. Through these examples and others, the example picture for stage 2 now looks as follows :

B.7.1 Annual Benefits

	Company A		Company B	
	Stage 1	Stage 2	Stage 1	Stage 2
		(Additional)		(Additional)
Administrative cost savings	149,884	74,942	3,117	1,559
Reduced cost of errors	186,000	279,000	14,050	21,075
Improved productivity	95,518	23,880	2,990	747
Improved sales, market share	180,000	1,440,000	9,000	108,000
Reduced cost of inventory	90,000	22,500	4,500	1,125
Time value benefits	49,315	24,658	2,466	1,233
Reduced communications costs	16,390		329	
Total Annual Benefit	767,107	1,864,979	36,452	133,739

B.7.2 Costs
B.7.2.1 One-time

Cost of hardware	30,000	300,000	3,000	3,000
Cost of start-up software	45,000		1,800	
Internal professional	225,000	300,000	15,000	18,000
External software development	150,000	75,000		3,750
Internal management	225,000	225,000	7,500	7,500
Other one-time charges	10,500		1,200	
Total one-time costs	685,500	900,000	28,500	32,250

B.7.2.2 Annual

VAN charges	23,520	11,525	630	463
Line charges	5040	756	135	30
Software maintenance	63,000	75,000	4,020	4,500
Total annual costs	91,560	87,281	4,785	4,993

Annex B
Preparing an EDI Business Case

And the corresponding DCF/NPV calculation (this time over six years):

Company A:	Year 1	Year 2	Year 3	Year 4	Year 5	Year 6
Stage 1 Benefit %	33%	67%	78%	89%	100%	100%
Stage 1 Benefit	253	514	598	683	767	767
Stage 2 Benefit %		20%	40%	60%	80%	100%
Stage 2 Benefit		373	746	1,119	1,492	1,865
Total benefit	253	887	1,344	1,802	2,259	2,632
Inflated benefit at 5%	253	931	1,482	2,086	2,746	3,359
Stage 1 one-time cost %	65%	25%	10%			
Stage 1 one-time cost %	-446	-171	-69			
Stage 1 annual cost	-92	-92	-92	-92	-92	-92
Stage 2 one-time cost %		65%	25%	10%		
Stage 2 one-time cost		-585	-225	-90		
Stage 2 annual cost	-87	-87	-87	-87	-87	-87
Total cost	-624	-935	-472	-269	-179	-179
Inflated cost at 5%	-624	-982	-521	-311	-217	-228
Net cash	-371	-51	961	1,774	2,529	3,131
Cumulative NPV at 10%	-371	-379	343	1,555	3,125	5,753
IRR	144%					

Company B:	Year 1	Year 2	Year 3	Year 4	Year 5	Year 6
Stage 1 Benefit %	33%	67%	78%	89%	100%	100%
Stage 1 Benefit	12	24	28	32	36	36
Stage 2 Benefit %		20%	40%	60%	80%	100%
Stage 2 Benefit		27	53	80	107	134
Total benefit	12	51	82	113	143	170
Inflated benefit at 5%	12	54	90	130	174	207
Stage 1 one-time cost %	65%	25%	10%			
Stage 1 one-time cost	-19	-7	-3			
Stage 1 annual cost	-5	-5	-5	-5	-5	-5
Stage 2 one-time cost %		65%	25%	10%		
Stage 2 one-time cost		-21	-8	-3		
Stage 2 annual cost	-5	-5	-5	-5	-5	-5
Total cost	-29	-38	-21	-13	-10	-10
Inflated cost at 5%	-29	-40	-23	-15	-12	-12
Net cash	-17	14	67	115	162	195
Cumulative NPV at 10%	-17	-4	46	125	226	386
IRR	212%					

EDI Implementation Guide

So the modest return at stage 1 has turned into a healthy return on investment growing at an impressive rate in stage 2.

But the real 'point' of EDI may lie in stage 3.

B.8 Stage 3

Stage 3 is concerned with using the potential of the new electronic infrastructure to change the nature of the business itself. It is not possible to present a 'generic' case-study for stage 3 since it is so specific to the particular circumstances.

An example is the emergence of 'follow the sun' trading in the world's money markets – using the same monetary asset on a non-stop basis without ever 'closing the books'. This is a whole new type of banking business – only made possible by the global electronic infrastructure. In the travel industry, the use of an efficient EDI operation enables tour operators to make last-minute assessments of their packaged holiday sales and to repackage the unused flights, hotels, etc or to sell them as unpackaged components. Again, this is a new kind of business not possible before the emergence of EDI.

So what's the point of EDI? The point is that there is a business case for EDI in the short term, and an overwhelming case for EDI in the medium term. Or perhaps the point is that EDI may mean survival in the long term – which may not be so very far away.

Annex C: Format of the Business Case

This annex describes the structure and content of the business case, with notes explaining how the information should be presented. The business case provides the necessary assurance to the approving authority that the project is a worthwhile investment and will be properly managed and controlled. It should provide the business, technical and financial arguments supporting the recommended solution and proposed expenditure. EDI is no different in this respect from any other change in working practices or implementation of an IS/IT solution necessary to meet a business need. Although this publication is concerned primarily with EDI projects, for the sake of completeness the more general details of the construction of a business case have been included here. The next annex highlights some areas for special attention when dealing with EDI projects and also includes examples of actual cost-benefit analyses.

C.1 Introduction

Where Private Financial Initiative (PFI) is an option under consideration, there may be a need to change the emphasis of some elements of the business case. In such a case, further advice should be sought from the departmental finance division or CCTA. HM Treasury will not approve any capital projects unless private finance options have been explored.

This section sets the scene, providing the approving authority with the background to the project, and summarising its aims and objectives. The details may be split between the *Introduction* and a separate *Management Summary*. An indication of the total costs and the benefits that are expected, if it is decided to proceed with the project, together with the resulting value of the project over its lifespan, the Net Present Value (NPV) and the project's place in the overall IS/IT plans for the Department (the IS strategy) should be included. It is recommended that every effort is made to examine the potential for Private Finance in the initial business case.

EDI Implementation Guide

This section should include brief coverage of the following:

- the overall aim or purpose of the project

- how and why the project originated

- senior management's view of the need for the proposed system

- the priority/importance placed on the proposed system

- the benefits that will accrue from the project

- reference to any significant changes to be made to existing practices

- the boundaries of the project

- the project's delivery timescale and the expected life of the proposed system

- consideration of PFI in relation to the project.

C.2   Strategic Issues

It is important to describe the position of the project in the Department's plans and objectives. Where there is an accepted IS strategy, it should be clear how the project fits in with those plans and the strategic business case, and it should also refer to the Department's intentions on the PFI initiative. In the absence of strategies/plans, the framework within which the project will exist and function should be highlighted.

The relationship of the project to other systems and services and any implications for the overall picture of IS/IT in the Department or projects under consideration must be explained. A more detailed reference should be made to those systems and services that may be affected by the project. There may be systems with which it has to interface and on which it will depend, or yet other systems which may rely on it – for example, if it is an infrastructure project.

C.3 Business Requirement

The definition of the business requirement is most important: it describes why the project exists and sets out its objectives. This section will relate closely with the user requirement, which has been produced during the Full Study stage. There is continual change in the operation of any Department, brought about by new methods for carrying out a specific task, new responsibilities, new technology and reorganisation.

Irrespective of the nature of the project, there needs to be a clear statement of what business objectives and requirements the project is aiming to satisfy, its scope and its boundaries. Examples of the nature of the project might be that it replaces a wholly manual system, replaces an existing information system, enhances an existing information system or is an infrastructure (or enabling) project. This section clarifies the objectives to be achieved and indicates the criteria against which it will be judged.

Reference can be made to how the operation is currently performed (the detail on existing systems comes in the next section) but, in general, descriptions should be given of the task that needs to be performed. This also applies in situations where:

- IS/IT provides a solution to a problem that has never been properly addressed before (in IS/IT terms)

- the requirement stems from a new responsibility placed on the Department

- there is an opportunity to extend the scope of an existing information system or to link it to other systems.

In this section explanations should be given of:

- the job that needs to be done and why

- the expectations of those who will use the proposed system(s)

- the assumptions made

- for how long the associated tasks will have to be carried out

EDI Implementation Guide

- the boundaries to the project
- the effect on existing information systems and services
- impact on staff and the need for consults.

In addition the following may be important issues:

- any external influences
- changes necessary or proposed to the organisational structure
- the constraints
- accommodation changes or requirements
- requirements for training.

The description of the business requirements should be followed by an explanation of how the project addresses the issues raised above, and the objectives by which the project can be judged should be set down (particularly with the user in mind).

A view should be included on the results that may be expected from introducing the new operation and an indication of the benefits accruing to the Department, but there is no need to discuss the business or technical options at this stage or to rule out specific options.

C.4 Existing Working Practices

The existing working practices should be described that perform the task or process in question. There can be no recommended approach to completing this section; much will depend on the reasons behind the project, its objectives, what is involved and the boundaries of the proposed system(s). For example, the current arrangements may cover more than one process (manual or IT system), which are to be combined in one information system. Perhaps two or more separate financial systems are to be replaced with a software package which will include additional functions that meets new business requirements. Or, in the case of an infrastructure project, a new data network may be proposed to replace two or more smaller local networks.

Annex C
Format of the Business Case

The aim is to convey a clear picture to the reader (the approving authority) of how the business is conducted currently. Where applicable, particulars should be provided of:

- the business or work of the Department that is to be addressed by the project

- the procedures, system or process now in place for processing that work. An account should be given of the numbers of staff and offices, the organisation structure and existing information systems

- a brief history of the current arrangements, particularly where an information system has been in place for some time and may have outlived its useful life

- the constraints of the current operation, disadvantages and other reasons for change

- where and why it does not meet the existing or future business requirements described in the section above.

C.5 User Requirement

This section should discuss and provide a brief description of the needs of those users involved in the business area(s) covered by the business case. This section should enable the reader to understand the individual functions which have been addressed (inputs, the processes carried out and outputs) in relation to the Business Requirements set out earlier in this document. This is particularly important where significant changes in the organisation structure are planned. While providing an explanation of the functions/facilities required by the users, this section also provides the opportunity to refer to the anticipated benefits and put them into context, thus providing a link to the particular section in the case which deals with the calculation and realisation of benefits.

C.6 Identifying Options

Once the objectives for the proposed system have been set, alternative ways of achieving them should be identified. The discussion of a wide range of options in the business case may illustrate the conclusions of any previous analysis but must eventually demonstrate that the chosen option represents the best value for money. In reality, options may represent assumptions (and eventually decisions) about the business and organisation of work, about the technology, and about purchasing and implementing a service.

Thinking about the options in each of these areas separately will assist in eliminating those which are impractical and will help to focus the subsequent financial evaluation more sharply. There are two basic categories of options that need to be considered – Business Options and Technical Options – however, a third set of options may be considered, namely, how the proposed system should be delivered.

C.7 Business Options

The examination of business options may relate to the scope of the IS system, to alternative ways in which the task(s) involved might be carried out, to change in the organisation and/or working practices of the people doing the job and to the level of service required to meet the business requirements.

C.8 Technical Options

Technical options may represent choices of technologies, such as Image Processing, EDI, Optical Character Recognition (OCR), or Geographic Information Systems (GIS):

- hardware, such as central processing, distributed processing, personal computers

- communication, such as wide area networks, local area networks, integrated service digital networks

- software, such as packaged versus bespoke software, database technology, programming language used.

It is useful to list the advantages and disadvantages pertaining to each option, clarifying the evidence that supports the preferred solution.

C.9 Identifying Variations

When identifying options, it is possible that by taking part of one and combining it with part of another, a new option presents itself. If a different outcome is arrived at as a result of varying an option which has already been identified, it should be included.

Annex C
Format of the Business Case

C.10 Delivery Options Various options relating to delivery of the system (eg in-house development, turnkey, outsourcing, different procurement paths and market testing) will have been considered at earlier stages in the project and the selected approach should be discussed in the business case. The argument in favour of the selected approach will be reflected in other sections of the case, such as Timetable and Risks.

It is government policy to use private finance in IS/IT to provide a means of harnessing private sector management, innovation, expertise and resources in the provision of capital assets and public services. The PFI requires a different approach and may be dealt with as an option within the business case or as an entirely separate issue.

C.10.1 Dismissing Options At this stage, options should not be dismissed. An attempt should be made to identify as wide a range of options as possible. Options considered should include:

The "do nothing" option

What will happen if nothing is changed? This is the base case for comparison.

The "do minimum" option

If 'do nothing' is not a viable option, what is the least that has to be done to the current system/operation to enable it to continue?

C.11 Analysing Options A full analysis of options should be carried out. The extent to which each option meets the objectives and is technically acceptable, and the associated risks, will help identify those which should be taken forward for financial evaluation. Where a large number of options have been identified it may be sensible to carry out a weighting and ranking exercise (sometimes described as a Multi Attribute Utility Analysis).

At the end of the analysis, there should be, say, half-a-dozen most likely options to take forward for appraisal in the business case. These should include a 'do nothing' and/or a 'do minimum' solution.

EDI Implementation Guide

These options should be discussed in the business case and assessed as to how they meet the agreed objectives, together with a discussion on any associated risks and sensitivities. The acceptable options and either the 'do nothing' or 'do-minimum' (the base case), or perhaps both, should be costed for comparative purposes. It should be stated clearly in the business case why options (those for which a Discounted Cash Flow (DCF) has been constructed and those for which the exercise has not been carried out) are being dismissed. Finally, this section of the business case will identify the preferred option and explain the reasoning behind that choice.

The risks associated with any option can be an important factor in the decision but the effort spent in analysing risk and uncertainty should relate to the scale and complexity of the project.

C.12 Financial Analysis of Options

The financial evaluation will form the keystone of the business case. The costs and the benefits must be explained together with the assumptions underlying the calculations. This is then supported by a DCF for each option in order that value for money judgements can be made. All costs and benefits should be expressed in cash terms as at the date of appraisal. Contingency costs should be made explicit and not hidden.

VAT alters price; it does not affect the basic value of goods or services. VAT needs to be taken into account for budgetary purposes, but for the purposes of financial evaluation is usually ignored. Care needs to be taken when comparing prices submitted by suppliers, which may or may not include VAT.

The effects of general price inflation are ignored in the appraisal unless there are items of significance that have such an affect on the appraisal that they must be included. In such a case a full explanation must be included in the case.

C.13 Costing Period

Costs (capital and all associated running costs) and benefits of the project need to be identified and profiled over the anticipated life of the system. This should be done for each option. The period of the DCF should commence with the year the costing is to be submitted to the approving authority.

Annex C
Format of the Business Case

Generally speaking, projects are appraised over their economic life (that is, to the next time that a significant investment or other change has to be made to allow the option to keep working) or will be based on the expected life of the associated hardware or software. Some projects will have clearly identified life spans; others will not be so obvious. So, advice should be sought from specialists as to what an appropriate life span is.

C.14 Whose Costs Should be Included?

The purpose of financial evaluation is to identify all costs that are associated with a project, no matter where they arise. This may mean that costs that other people have to bear may have to be included. Their agreement to meet those costs should be sought and recorded in the business case.

Some assumptions will have been made about costs and this section of the business case needs to set out those assumptions. In particular, it should be made clear how the figures that have been included in the DCF have been arrived at.

C.14.1 Staff Costs

All expenditure will incur staff costs in one form or another and the business case needs to record how they have been calculated. The most common method of calculation is to use the departmental Ready Reckoner. It is important to distinguish between development costs, system operating costs and the cost of using the system.

C.14.2 Sunk Costs

Costs incurred up to the time that the business case receives financial approval may be sunk costs – that is they do not form part of any decision and thus can be ignored in the DCF calculations, unless a cost previously incurred should properly be attributed to the project in the future, as an opportunity cost. However, assets may have been acquired or there may be outputs which have a further use and should be included in the appraisal. Sunk costs should be accounted for somewhere in the business case (perhaps in the narrative section explaining costs and benefits or in an appendix).

C.15 Implementation

The prime objective of this section is to describe the arrangements for managing and monitoring the project from conception through development to installation and acceptance by the users. It is concerned with how each component of the preferred approach/solution is to be

EDI Implementation Guide

funded, procured and developed. Project implementation consists of a number of interrelated elements which, when combined, provide the approving authority with proof that management is fully aware of its responsibilities towards the project.

When writing this section, the details of the management structure should be described first:

- overseeing the introduction of IS/IT throughout the Department

- the Project Board looking after the resources, development and welfare of the project and reporting to the IS Strategy/Steering Committee (ISSC)

- the Project Control organisation and the system or methodology to be used (such as PRINCE)

- a brief description of the lower levels of management, particularly important for large projects where there is likely to be more than one application system to be developed, together with perhaps networking or telecommunication requirements.

There follows a series of logical outputs that provide the details and plans that relate to a successful implementation, and which take account of the risks and uncertainties identified:

– the timetable

– resource plans

– training programme

– implementation plan

– change control procedures.

C.15.1 Timetable

This is a suitably detailed plan of the various activities, with dates of commencement and completion allocated to the task, such as Studies, Preparation of the Operational Requirement, Seeking Financial Approval, Procurement, Development and Training. This should be agreed with senior management, the project team, users and others

Annex C
Format of the Business Case

	who have an interest in the success of the project. In drawing up the project timetable, suitable milestones should be set when important decisions are to be taken; it should never be forgotten that sometimes it is necessary to 'pull the plug'.
C.15.2 Resource Plans	These set out details of the resources and skills (expertise) required to meet the project timetable and satisfy the user requirements and that will be available to the project. Resources may involve the use of staff from outside the Department, such as consultants. There should be sufficient detail to enable the reader to identify how long it is intended that they will be employed on the project. It should be remembered that reference will be made to this section in the costings.
C.15.3 Training Programme	This is an important element, particularly where there are a large number of staff to be trained in the use of the proposed system. In cases where an information system is being introduced for the first time, the costs are likely to be higher and care must be taken in planning the training programme to ensure staff are prepared before the actual installation of the system, and that ongoing training can be accommodated.
C.15.4 Installation Plans	The objective of this section is to provide the approving authority with a broad picture of the how the project will evolve within the timescale and with confirmation that there are sufficient resources of the right calibre to see the project through to a successful conclusion after acceptance testing the intended system.
C.15.5 Change Control Procedures	A brief description should be included of how changes to an element of the project, such as timescale or functionality, will be managed.
C.16 Risk	In post-mortems on IS/IT-related programmes and projects that have gone wrong, it has become apparent that many of the difficulties encountered could have been avoided if those responsible for managing the project had had the right information as well as sufficient time to deal with the situation – that is, to make an informed decision about the situation, or to exercise adequate control over it.

EDI Implementation Guide

Project risk analysis and management consists of:

- the identification of the risks attaching to the project, including dis-benefits

- the management of those risks.

Properly carried out, risk analysis is an aid to achieving the successful completion of the project to budget and on time, and in accordance with the User Requirement.

The effects of a risk should not be mistaken for its cause. For example, cost escalation on a project is an ever-present risk. Cost data should be used to determine the underlying causes of risk, ie why costs are escalating, before budgeted costs are exceeded.

If the causes of risk can be reduced to bring them within bounds, then the effects (in this case cost escalation) will not become a problem.

It is important to consider the interactions of risks. The effects of one risk may be the cause of another risk or one cause may give rise to several risks. The former case is especially pernicious, since diminishing one risk often causes another to increase – often in ways which are not obvious. For example, reducing the overall schedule time may increase the budgetary requirements.

The following are some of the main causes of risk to IS strategies and IT projects:

- the project may cost more to develop, implement or operate than expected

    – expected benefits are not realised

    – delay in project implementation

- poor system specification

- statistical errors, eg insufficient sampling when trialling or prototyping

- accommodation implications: costs and timescale for carrying out necessary work

- complexity
- novel technology
- changes to the Requirement
- underestimates of training
- required resources are not available
- volume risks – for example, much higher volumes of transaction than planned for
- failure to identify properly the effort required to tailor software packages etc.

The perceived risks associated with the preferred option should be set out and the intended action to be taken to minimise each risk discussed. Giving a value of high, medium or low, to a risk may assist in providing a clear presentation of the situation.

C.17 Sensitivity

One of the problems associated with IT projects, as with all projects, is that things may not turn out as anticipated. Things will occur that affect the anticipated costs and benefits. Some, but not all, will have been identified as a 'risk'. The objective is to try to quantify the effects of such uncertainty, or the likelihood, on the cash flow and net present value.

C.17.1 The Problem of Uncertainty

Uncertainties can arise both in estimating and valuing benefits. For example, it may be anticipated in the business case (and reflected in the project costings) that a proposed information system will perform at a lower cost and speed up the operation of a task previously done manually. There may be uncertainty surrounding the value applied to either or both of these benefits, which should be reflected in a sensitivity costing.

The technical risks involved in an information system project are a particularly important source of uncertainty. Decisions often have to be made about projects using unproven hardware and software. The possibility, therefore, arises that the expected benefits of a project may not materialise – at least to the extent envisaged – and that implementation costs may exceed original estimates.

Technical problems arise with both software and hardware. New applications may not come up to expectations, while hardware estimates may prove to be wrong.

When the installation of a computer system entails a significant reorganisation in the way an activity is carried out, the uncertainties increase.

The timing of the costs and benefits of a computer project is a further source of uncertainty. A delay, for example, in the acceptance of the system will defer the potential benefits.

C.17.2 Dealing with Uncertainty

How is uncertainty actually handled in an investment appraisal? How should the awareness that the actual value of a particular cost or benefit may fall somewhere within a wide range of figures be taken into account?

Sensitivity Analysis is a technique usually employed to determine the sensitivity of the results of an appraisal to changes in its assumptions. It identifies those assumptions which have a range of uncertainty such that their impact on the net present values is likely to be appreciable. Critical assumptions can often be readily identified, for example, by their size and variability; but sometimes they can only be identified in the process of carrying out the sensitivity analysis.

C.17.3 Accounting for Uncertainty in Investment Appraisals

For each assumption to be tested a decision has to be taken on the probable range within which it will fall. Assumptions not tested will be left constant. Staff savings for a project, for example, may be expected to fall within a range of £5m and £10m a year – that is, outcomes outside this range are considered improbable. Deciding ranges will be very much a matter of judgement for the appraiser. As a general rule, however, the greater the degree of uncertainty surrounding an estimate the wider the range should be.

Three variants should be constructed for each appraisal:

- the central variant – embodying the original estimates for each factor, before the ranges were constructed

- the optimistic variant – obtained by taking the

favourable end of the range for those assumptions provided with a range (ie for the costs of a project, the lower end of the range is taken; for the benefits, the higher end)

- the pessimistic variant – this goes to the opposite extreme and estimates an appraisal using all the unfavourable values.

This procedure will yield three net present value estimates for each appraisal. If, for example, in a cost-benefit type of case, all three are positive then the project can be recommended. Even if the pessimistic assumptions come to pass, the project will yield the necessary rate of return.

The conclusions of an appraisal become ambiguous when one or two of the variants yield negative net present values. In a number of cases only the optimistic variant may yield a positive net present value. One approach to this problem is to estimate the probability of each of the variants has of being the actual outcome.

C.18 Post Implementation Review

This section should contain a commitment to a post implementation review (PIR) at a specified date in the future. It should outline the way in which the PIR should be conducted. It will be necessary for baseline information for the PIR to be collected before implementation, and this section should also provide an account of how monitoring data will be collected in the course of project implementation.

C.19 Recommendation

This section contains a recommendation based on the previous analysis in the business case.

EDI Implementation Guide

Annex D: Other EDI Data Standards

This annex gives a general introduction to EDI standards other than UN/EDIFACT that are in current use.

The following standards are those that are most likely to be encountered other than UN/EDIFACT, which is the main focus of this book:

- United Nations Trade Data Interchange (UNTDI)

- American National Standards Institute X12 (ANSI X12)

- Uniform Communications Standard (UCS)

- Association Européen des Constructeurs de Materiel Aerospatial (AECMA)

- Verband der Deutschen Automobilindustrie (VDA).

D.1 UNTDI

This is one of the standards that was used as a starting point for UN/EDIFACT. The standard is no longer controlled by the UN but by the Article Number Association UK Ltd, better known simply as the ANA.

There are, or have been, a number of implementations of UNTDI whereby the syntax is followed although there are industry- or sector-specific messages. These include:

- TRADACOMS, which is widely used by the UK retail sector (eg supermarkets)

  The TRADACOMS messages are also controlled by the ANA.

EDI Implementation Guide

```
STX=ANA:1+ME-HERE+YOU-THERE+940622:092015+1++ORDERS'
MHD=1+ORDHDR:9'
TYP=0430+NEW-ORDERS'
SDT=1234567890123:ABCDEF+SUPERVALUE SUPPLIERS PLC+LI¦N INDUSTRIAL
ESTATE:LONDON:::NS57 2EW'
CDT=3210987654321:GHIJKL+CHEAP & NASTY PLC+HIGH STREET:NEWTOWN:::NE0 4XX'
FIL=1+1+940622+MSG001'
MTR=6'
MHD=2+ORDERS:9'
CLO=1000000000001+CHEAP & NASTY STORE+LOW STREET:NEWTOWN::::NE75 0YY'
ORD=ORD001/A:890921890922'
DIN=940624+940625+0000+0000+DELIVERY BAY AT BACK'
OLD=1+0000000000011++999999999991100+101+1++++BAKED BEANS'
OLD=2+0000000000012++999999999991200+102+2++++SLICED WHITE BREAD'
OLD=3+0000000000013++999999999991300+102+52++++CRISP (SMOKEY BACON)'
OTR=3+55'¦¦MTR=8'¦¦MHD=3+ORDTLR:9'¦¦OFT=3'¦¦MTR=3'¦¦END=3'
```

Figure 42:   Sample TRADACOMS message

- *ODETTE*, used by the European automotive industry (although much of this has now moved to a standard based on UN/EDIFACT syntax)

- *Brokernet*, used by the UK motor insurance market

- *Fleetnet*, used by the UK vehicle fleet market.

Recognition features: Look for the 'STX' and 'END' tags, which mark the beginning and end of an interchange.

Anybody familiar with UNTDI will immediately feel at home with UN/EDIFACT. The differences, although definite, are quite small.

D.2   ANSI X12

This is another of the standards that was used as a starting point for UN/EDIFACT. The standard is controlled by the American National Standards Institute (ANSI).

It is very widely used throughout North America and in any business contacts in that area it might be encountered.

ANSI has accepted that UN/EDIFACT is the standard of the future and all further development on X12 messages will cease in 1997.

Annex D
Other EDI Data Standards

```
ISA*00**00**ZZ*CCPP.CCP077*ZZ*CCPP.CCP049*940609*233 ¦ *U*00200*000000222*0*P*:!
GS*PO*CCP850*ELF850*910409*2330*259*X*002001!
ST*850*0558!
BEG*01*SA*YYYWFJ***940609!
REF*FI*YYYWFJ 811935XXXXCRPECV21!
TAX*DP000030-NY-7228345*SP*NY*********3!
N1*BY*IBM CORPORATION*92*CCPP CCPHOST!
N3*P.O. BOX 800!
N4*HOPEWELL JUNCTION*NY*12533!
PER*BD*SCOFIELD!
N1*SE*XXXX CORP OF AMERICA-CP DIV!
N2*10833 VALLEY VIEW STREET!
N4*CYPRESS*CA*90630!
PER*OC*H. KUBOTA!
N1*BT*IBM CORPORATION*92*990!
N2*ACCOUNTS PAYABLE!
N3*ROUTE 52!
N4*HOPEWELL JUNCTION*NY*12533!
ITD*ZZ*5**********PER-VPA!
PO1*1*1000*PC***BP*68X6281*EC*A97093*CG*DP!
SLN*1**I*1000*PC*3.75*CT*I*CR*A01933!
PID*F****8KX8 29NS SRAM!
REF*IL*052200!
N1*ST*IBM LOCATION (114)*92*114!
N2*WANGARATTA, AUSTRALIA*C/O ARNOFF MOVING AND STORAGE!
N3*682 DUTCHESS TURNPIKE*ATTN: T.A.G. PRODUCT!
N4*POUGHKEEPSIE*NY*12603!
SCH*1000*PC****010*910621!
CTT*1!
SE*28*0558!
GE*1*259!
IEA*1*000000222!
```

Figure 43: Sample ANSI X12 message

One feature of ANSI X12 which may be appropriate for UN/EDIFACT is that for every message there is a response – an invoice is sent from party A to party B; party B sends party A a notification of receipt.

Recognition features: Look for the 'ISA' and 'IEA' tags, which mark the beginning and end of an interchange.

D.3 UCS

This is another US EDI standard, used by the retail sector. It is controlled by the Uniform Code Council, Inc. (UCC), but all its messages have now been incorporated into the ANSI X12 transaction set. The UCC is also interested in bar-coding standards within the US.

EDI Implementation Guide

```
BG*00**123456789012*210987654321*940609*2330*00222'
GS*PO*CCP850*ELF850*910409*2330*259*X*002001'
ST*850*0558' ¦ ¦ BEG*01*SA*YYYWFJ***940609'
REF*FI*YYYWFJ 811935XXXXCRPECV21'
TAX*DP000030-NY-7228345*SP*NY*********3'
N1*BY*IBM CORPORATION*92*CCPP CCPHOST'
N3*P.O. BOX 800'
N4*NO HOPE JUNCTION*NY*12533'
PER*BD*SCOFIELD'
N1*SE*XXXX CORP OF AMERICA-CP DIV'
N2*10833 VALLEY FLOOR STREET'
N4*CEDAR*CA*90930'
PER*OC*H. KUBOTA'
N1*BT*IBM CORPORATION*92*990'
N2*ACCOUNTS PAYABLE'
N3*ROUTE 52'
N4*STILL NO HOPE JUNCTION*NY*12533'
ITD*ZZ*5**********PER-VPA'
PO1*1*1000*PC***BP*68X6281*EC*A97093*CG*DP'
SLN*1**I*1000*PC*3.75*CT*I*CR*A01933'
PID*F****8KX8 29NS SRAM'
REF*IL*052200'
N1*ST*IBM LOCATION (114)*92*114'
N2*WANGARATTA, AUSTRALIA*C/O ARNOFF MOVING AND STORAGE'
N3*682 DUTCHESS TURNPIKE*ATTN: T.A.G. PRODUCT'
N4*POUGHKEEPSIE*NY*12603'
SCH*1000*PC****010*910621'
CTT*1'
SE*28*0558'
GE*1*259'
EG*00222*1*1*32'
```

Figure 44: Sample UCS message

Recognition features: Look for the 'BG' and 'EG' tags, which mark the beginning and end of an interchange.

D.4 AECMA

This is primarily a standard for the aerospace and defence industries. It follows the UN/EDIFACT standard, where possible, but there are features used which make it incompatible with the published standard. These include variable, repeating data elements.

Annex D
Other EDI Data Standards

```
UNB+ACEA:1+GBABC ABC1:ZZ+GBXYZ
XYZ001:ZZ+941201:1152┆188++AECMA++++1'UNH+340+CSN
IPD:1:0:0'IPH+IPP:0581BTEST+ADD:K0378+DRD:2U4900+DRS:021+FID:E+IPS:URBINE,
H.P.+ ISS:M1+LGE:KT+MOI:20+MTP:CSNIPD+TOD:0581B'VAS+CHG:N+┆ID:K0378NN12326
2+SNS:0000000008401'CAS+CHG:N+CSN:7251001 000 +IND:1+ISN:00A+MFC:K0
378+NSN:0000000028401+PNR:NN12326+QNA: 1+RFS:8+TQL 1'CBS+DFL:RFS 8 BECAUSE
ASSY CAN BE POTENTIAL SPARE FOR ITS LOWER LOCATION+NIL:-
'CDS+ESC:1'CES+CHG:N+SM
R:PAOLDX+SRV:GYL'CJS+CHG:N+MOV:A1'CES+CHG:N+SMR:PAOL┆X+SRV:ITA'CJS+CHG:N+MOV:A1'
CES+CHG:N+SMR:PAOLDX+SRV:SPA'CJS+CHG:N+MOV:A1'CES+CH┆:N+SMR:PAOLDX+SRV:UK1'CJS+C
HG:N+MOV:A1'CAS+CHG:N+CSN:72510001 001
+IND:2+ISN:00┆+MFC:K0378+NSN:000000002840
1+PNR:NN11881G01+QNA: 1+RFS:6+TQL: 1'CBS+NIL:-'DS+ESC:2'CES+CHG:N+SMR:PAOL
DX+SRV:GYL'CJS+CHG:N+MOV:B1'CES+CHG:N+SMR:PAOLDX+SRVITA'CJS+CHG:N+MOV:B1'CES+CH
G:N+SMR:PAOLDX+SRV:SPA'CJS+CHG:N+MOV:B1'CES+CHG:N+SM:PAOLDX+SRV:UK1'CJS+CHG:N+M
OV:B1'CAS+CHG:N+CSN:72510001 002
+IND:2+ISN:00A+MFC:┆0378+NSN:0000000053301+PNR: ┆ 1013670+QNA: 2+RFS:1+TQL:
2'CBS+NIL:-'CDS+CSR:1┆5+ESC:2'CES+CHG:N+SMR:PAOZZ ┆
X+SRV:GYL'CJS+CHG:N+MOV:C2'CES+CHG:N+SMR:PAOZZX+SRV:┆TA'CJS+CHG:N+MOV:C2'CES+CHG
┆
:N+SMR:PAOZZX+SRV:SPA'CJS+CHG:N+MOV:C2'CES+CHG:N+SMR┆PAOZZX+SRV:UK1'CJS+CHG:N+MO
┆V:C2'CAS+CHG:N+CSN:72510001 003
+IND:2+ISN:00A+MFC:K┆378+NSN:0000000053651+PNR:1 ┆ 013667+QNA: 1+RFS:1+TQL:
1'CBS+NIL:-'CDS+CSR:10┆+ESC:2'CES+CHG:N+SMR:PAOZZX ┆
+SRV:GYL'CJS+CHG:N+MOV:C2'CES+CHG:N+SMR:PAOZZX+SRV:I┆A'CJS+CHG:N+MOV:C2'CES+CHG:
┆
N+SMR:PAOZZX+SRV:SPA'CJS+CHG:N+MOV:C2'CES+CHG:N+SMR:┆AOZZX+SRV:UK1'CJS+CHG:N+MOV
┆:C2'CAS+CHG:N+CSN:72510001 004
+IND:2+ISN:00A+MFC:I9┆05+NSN:0000000053061+PNR:EN ┆ 2929-050020+QNA:
15+RFS:2+TQL: 15'CBS+ASP:1+NIL:-┆CDS+CSR:105+ESC:1'CES+CHG:N ┆
+SMR:PAOZZX+SRV:GYA'CJS+CHG:N+MOV:C1'CES+CHG:N+SMR:P┆OZZX+SRV:ITA'CJS+CHG:N+MOV:
C1'CES+CHG:N+SMR:PAOZZX+SRV:SPA'CJS+CHG:N+MOV:C1'CES┆CHG:N+SMR:PAOZZX+SRV:UK1'CJ
┆S+CHG:N+MOV:C1'CAS+CHG:N+CSN:72510001 005
+IND:2+ISN┆00A+MFC:K0378+NSN:000000005 ┆ 3101+PNR:UP71195+QNA: AR+RFS:2+TQL:
AR'CBS+ASP:1+┆IL:-+SMF:F'CDS+CSR:10+ESC:1 ┆
'CES+CHG:N+SMR:PAOZZX+SRV:GYL'CJS+CHG:N+MOV:C5'CES+C┆G:N+SMR:PAOZZX+SRV:ITA'CJS+
┆CHG:N+MOV:C5'CES+CHG:N+SMR:PAOZZX+SRVSPA'CJS+CHG:N+┆OV:C5'CES+CHG:N+SMR:PAOZZX+
┆SRV:UK1'CJS+CHG:N+MOV:C5'PAS+CHG:N+DFP:RING,LOCKING+┆NC:77777+MFC:K0378+NSN:0000
┆000053651+PNR:1013667'PBS+UOI:EA+COM:0+PLC:2+PLT:7+S┆C:0+SPC:1+SPQ:0+STR:0+TOP:0
┆5'PDS+UPR:1000+CUR:LIT+PCD:R'PFS+PSC:I'PAS+CHG:N+DFP┆RING,SEALING+INC:77777+MFC:
┆K0378+NSN:0000000053301+PNR:1013670'PBS+UOI:EA+COM:1┆PLC:2+PLT:8+SLC:0+SPC:1+SPQ
┆:0+STR:0+TOP:05'PDS+UPR:1000+CUR:LIT+PCD:R'PFS+PSC:I┆PAS+CHG:N+DFP:PIN,LOCKING+I
┆NC:77777+MFC:K2963+NSN:0000000053151+PNR:APS102'PBS+┆OI:EA+COM:1+PLC:2+PLT:7+SLC
┆:0+SPC:1+SPQ:0+STR:0+TOP:05'PDS+UPR:1000+CUR:LIT+PCD┆R'PFS+PSC:I'UNT+82+340'UNZ+
┆1+188'
```

Figure 45: Sample AECMA message

Closely related to this standard is AECMA-2000M, also used in the aerospace and defence industries.

Recognition features: At first glance it may be indistinguishable from a standard UN/EDIFACT message, but it allows for data items to be sent not in any pre-determined order, making automatic processing more difficult. It perhaps gives too much flexibility.

D.5 VDA

This is primarily a standard for the automotive industry in Germany. It is a very simple standard that looks like an 'in-house' format with a short record identifier on the front. However, it satisfies the business requirements of its user community.

361

EDI Implementation Guide

```
5110122890    50156    0016800169920203
5120111 02C            920205000                 000000 EUB 6H0 609  0           244692    105601141KGL  S
513019201210000800192012100002668000000000576205555 5      922731000002380000000
51801
5120111 02C            92020502B                 920129 EBM 2R6 700  0           244728    105601142KGL  S
5130100000000000000000000000000000000000000009202 2000054000000000
51801
5120111 02C            92020502A                 920124 EBP 2Y7 800  0           000001    105601142KGL  S
513019201280000801392012800002324000000009660509202 60000560009203040000560009203090000560009203120000560009203200000056000
51401555555          9214180001680009219220001120009 232600005600092273100002762600000
51801
5120111 02C            92020502A                 920124 EBP 2Y9 000  0           000001    105601142KGL  S
513019201310000803292013100002404000000018175109202 40001740009202210001740009202280001740009203050001740009203120000174000
514019203180001740009203240001740005555555      9 1418001044000921922000870000922326001044000922731000423269000000
51801
5120111 02C            92020502A                 920124 EBS 2A8 790  0           000001    105601145KGL  S
5130192012900008021920129000016920000000008482055555 5      9214180001268000000
51801
5120112 02C            92020502A                 920124 ECA IF0 816  5           000001    205541253KGL  S
513019201300007029592013000002844100000001527143333 30000315594444440000284419203160000600005555555            921418000060000
514019219220000600009223260000443555000000
51801
5120112 02C            92020502A                 920124 ECA IF0 816  5           000001    205541253KGL  S
513019112090001027191120900002962100000001090849202 9000060000555555       9214180001200009219220000600009227310000255544
51401000000
51801
5120112 02C            92020502A                 920124 ECA IF1 016  0           000001    205541253KGL  S
513019201200004028992012000002530000000007312073333 300028693544444400004306592021300011000092022500011000092030600011000
514019203170001100009203270001100005555555      9 1418002200009219220003300009223260002200009227310001076360000000
51801
5120121 02C            92020502A                 920124 EVB 6F1 004  2           000006     60573214DKGL  S
513019201270000712920127000023055000000019237533333 30001769459202190000030559202250000200009203020000200009203090000020000
5140192031300002000092031900002000092032500002000005 5555      9214180001000009219220001000009223260000800009227310001000083
51401000000
51801
51901000000100000090000009000000700000000000000090000 01
```

Figure 46: Sample VDA message

Recognition features: Without prior knowledge, a VDA message is not easily distinguishable from a simple file of data. However, each record is identified by a three-character tag (eg 511) and a version control number (eg 01) on the front, followed by data. As with other EDI standards, it includes its own integrity checking – appropriate headers and trailers with control totals in them.

Annex E: IS Notice 31: Electronic Data Interchange

E.1 Introduction

This Notice examines a number of major issues concerning Electronic Data Interchange (EDI) and offers outline guidance on the use of EDI within government departments and Agencies.

E.2 Background and Purpose

There has been a considerable increase in the level of interest in the wider application of EDI within the public sector in recent months. This interest has not been confined to departments, Agencies and local authorities only, but has also been expressed strongly by the private sector. A number of articles in various technical journals and national newspapers have particularly focused on the desirability and opportunity for the use of EDI within UK government departments and Agencies. The significant developments and widespread acceptance of EDI in other European public administrations have also been highlighted.

This Notice is an overview of EDI. It is being issued as part of a central initiative to encourage and assist departments and Agencies to undertake a thorough examination of all aspects of their business practices, in order to identify those areas which would benefit most from the use of EDI. The result of the exercise should yield a comprehensive plan for action for EDI. It is essential that this activity is commissioned and managed at a high level within a department or Agency as, ultimately, the successful use of EDI might require internal reorganisation and restructuring of work practices.

E.3 EDI in Action

It is generally acknowledged that the UK private sector leads the rest of Europe in the commercial and financial application of EDI. Some 3000 companies covering a wide spectrum of trade and commerce have already implemented EDI. Its usage has been well established and proven in many multinational organisations. Indeed, a number of industry sectors are now entirely dependent on EDI for their day-to-day activities and regard it as part and parcel of their business.

EDI Implementation Guide

The adoption and growth of EDI as a business tool for administrative applications by the UK public sector has been much less than in the private sector. Although a small number of departments have been exploiting EDI successfully, the take-up of EDI for discharging government business functions has been low. Even where EDI has been applied, such transactions only account for a small fraction of the total when compared with the number of paper-based exchanges being handled by the departments concerned.

Private sector experience, and the limited public sector application of EDI, clearly point to a broader scope for departments and Agencies to benefit from reduced costs, improvement in efficiency and the provision of better quality of service to its customers by maximising the use of EDI. The latter is particularly relevant in the context of the recent development of the Citizen's Charter, which among other things requires all government administrations to deliver high quality public services.

E.4   What is EDI?

Electronic Data Interchange (EDI) can be defined as a process of direct business-to-business transfer of transactions from one computer system to another in electronic form. The transactions are structured in pre-defined formats and obey certain rules which allow the computer systems to interpret the data correctly. EDI differs from electronic mail as the latter involves exchange of largely unformatted data at a personal level.

EDI itself does not require any new hardware technologies; it is a business application using conventional techniques. Indeed, the use of punched cards and paper tape in the early 1960s to transfer highly structured information from one computer to another maps closely to the concept of EDI. The subsequent use of magnetic tapes, diskettes and communication networks as transfer media have all added to the ease and speed of transfer, without altering the principles involved.

E.5   EDI Action Plan

There are likely to be many applications within government which would benefit from the use of EDI. To achieve these benefits it is essential that government users identify the opportunity within their IS Strategies and develop EDI Action Plans to manage the process

Annex E
IS Notice 31: Electronic Data Interchange

effectively. The elements of such a plan should include:

- investigation of candidate business processes which could be redesigned to exploit information interchange using EDI

- assessment of potential benefits and full appraisal of investment

- consideration of Standards, use of networks and security issues related to the use of EDI.

Some of these issues are discussed in outline in the following sections.

E.6 Candidate Business Processes

The task requires a careful analysis of all the existing processes in order to select those most suited for the application of EDI. To begin with processes which involve a high volume of re-keyed data and paper-based transactions may prove to be the most suitable candidates for conversion to EDI. However, once initial investment has been made and sufficient experience gained in the use of EDI, other areas of work for conversion to EDI can be considered.

In addition to a detailed EDI introduction plan, it will also be necessary to identify the new working procedures and information interchange agreements which would need to be implemented to support each selected EDI application. The exercise should also provide a useful opportunity to review the existing work practices, with a view to simplifying the processes and optimising the use of available resources.

E.7 Costs and Benefits

It is essential that full cost-benefit analysis of all the identified applications is undertaken to justify and prioritise the introduction of EDI.

Clearly, the cost of implementing EDI will vary according to the scope and complexity of the projects undertaken by departments. However, the use of existing computer systems and other IT resources should allow costs to be kept at a low level. In most cases, based on EDI experience within the private sector, users can expect full cost recovery of the initial investment within 18–24 months of live EDI usage.

EDI Implementation Guide

The potential benefits of EDI usage to departments and Agencies can be classified into three distinct areas of application:

i. the use of EDI for existing business processes

ii. changing and streamlining the existing processes to perform in a better and more cost effective approach to business applications with the aid of EDI

iii. the development of business activities to take advantage of new opportunities which become available as a direct result of implementing EDI.

In the context of central government applications, the potential cost savings as a result of using EDI purely for existing processes could be high. Such usage of EDI may also yield other business benefits in the form of:

- better understanding and increased awareness of business functions and processes

- tighter control, improved accuracy, increased discipline and accountability in the work areas converted to EDI

- reduced stockholding and better inventory management

- reduction in order cycle and order processing time leading to a better quality of service to customers.

However, significantly greater benefits can be expected from the redesign and optimisation of the scope of business processes which are made possible by the introduction of EDI. The realisation of such benefits in the public sector is very much dependent on the nature of an organisation's activities and the ability, willingness and determination of its managers to positively exploit the use of EDI to their advantage.

E.8 EDI Standards

EDI standards provide message design guidelines and other building blocks which allow users to construct specific messages for exchanging information. In addition, different standards provide a varying number of ready made messages for most common business exchanges, such as placing an order, acknowledgement and invoicing.

The three most widely known EDI Standards are:

- EDIFACT

- TRADACOMS

- ANSI X12

Electronic Data Interchange for Administration, Commerce and Transport (EDIFACT) is the only EDI standard which has been formally recognised by European and International standards organisations. The use of EDIFACT (ISO 9735) would also enable departments to comply with the EC IT Standards Decision (EC 87/95) and EC Directive 88/295, which require public procurements over a certain value to specify relevant European or International standards. CCTA's Government Open Systems Interconnection Profile (GOSIP) Version 4, provides up-to-date guidance on the use of EDIFACT.

Although TRADACOMS is by far the most widely used EDI standard in the UK, it is only a 'de facto' standard and departments should refrain from its use. It is not recognised at a European or international level and many of its users accept the need to migrate to the international standard, EDIFACT, in the near future.

The ANSI X12 standard was developed in the USA and its use is mostly confined to North American countries. The construction of EDI messages using ANSI X12 is generally considered to be more complex and it has no international recognition.

There are a number of other industry-specific organisations and standards which cater for EDI in particular business sectors, such as the motor industry, banking, aerospace, transport etc. Various software packages are also available which allow conversion and interworking between users of different standards. The general availability of the conversion software, combined with the almost universal acceptance of EDIFACT as the only long term EDI solution, tends to consolidate the

EDI Implementation Guide

widely held view that there are no standards issues which should deter users from implementing EDI now.

However, the use of conversion software does have a number of drawbacks and overheads. Its usage needs to be carefully evaluated by departments and, if it is required, it should be only adopted as a temporary measure with clear migration plans to use EDIFACT by all parties involved in EDI exchanges.

E.9 The Network Options

One of the important areas for consideration by any new EDI user concerns the type of network necessary for EDI connections between itself and each of its partners. The most commonly used approaches to EDI networking are:

- use of dial-up public networks

- provision of leased lines

- use of a suitable network owned and managed by a third party. This is often referred to as VANS (Value Added Network Services) or VADS (Value Added Data Services).

Most EDI users in this country use third party networks. This option offers a low-cost entry to EDI and provides a rich source of access to many other potential partners who are already connected to the same network. Also, the use of VANS relieves the user of the problem of resolving communications issues related to the use of private networks. The most widely known suppliers of such network services are BT, GEIS-INS, IBM and AT&T ISTEL. INS claims over 60% share of the total UK VANS market.

Another benefit of using a third party network comes from the added security facility offered by the 'Store-&-Forward' principle, commonly used by VANS to forward messages from one party to another. This method involves the transfer of data from its origin to its final destination in two stages. The first stage copies the message from the sender's system to the VANS system for temporary storage. In the second stage the addressee of the message is notified, which allows the information to be retrieved by the receiver from the VANS system. The process enables the sender's and receiver's computer systems, and the data stored on them, to be isolated from each other, as all direct interactions take place with the VANS system.

It should also be noted that the introduction of EDI generally provides a better level of control over applications, compared to what was available previously under paper-based systems. It is likely that the use of EDI for government applications will yield similar benefits. Although the use of 'Store-&-Forward' and other in-built security features of EDI systems does offer a certain level of protection, it is still essential for government users to formally examine and evaluate all aspects of their security requirements for the proposed EDI applications.

The use of public and privately leased lines can be considered where the volume of EDI information is high and the number of partners involved in exchanges is low. Any spare capacity on existing leased lines may also be considered for the exchange of EDI information.

E.10 Action

Departments and Agencies are invited to note the contents of this Notice and consider the use of EDI to assist them in carrying out their day to day business functions. In addition they may wish to adopt the following guidelines when examining and implementing EDI:

- formulate an EDI plan for action within their overall business plan to cover all aspects of exchange of information, with particular emphasis on processes involving re-keying of data and paper-based transactions.

- adopt EDIFACT as the EDI standard

- consider the formation of common interest user communities, with members from both inside and outside government, to promote and establish a critical mass necessary to cost-justify the introduction of EDI

- ensure that the implementation of the EDI Action Plan is controlled at the highest management level in order to carry out the reorganisation of staff and work practices in a post-EDI environment

EDI Implementation Guide

- consider the development of business activities to offer improved and better quality of service to its customers by taking full advantage of the enhanced speed and accuracy of operations which should result from the use of EDI.

E.11 Enquiries

Requests for further information about this Notice, and any enquiries concerning the use of EDI, should be addressed to Ian Baker at the address below, telephone GTN 3040 4561 or 01603-704561.

CCTA
Information Interchange Branch
Rosebery Court
St Andrews Business Park
Norwich
NR7 0HS

Annex F: Standard Interchange Agreement

The following document is an example of a widely used EDI Interchange Agreement. It is published by the Electronic Commerce Association, 148 Buckingham Palace Road, London, SW1W 9TR, and is reprinted with their permission.

STANDARD ELECTRONIC DATA INTERCHANGE AGREEMENT

The Terms of this Agreement shall govern the conduct and methods of operation between the Parties in relation to the interchange of data by teletransmission for the purposes of or associated with the supply of goods and/or services. They take account of the Uniform Rules of Conduct for Interchange of Trade Data by Teletransmission as adopted by the International Chamber of Commerce.

PARTIES:

1. Signature _____
   Name _____
   Position _____

   On behalf of _____

   Address _____
   _____
   _____

   Date _____

2. Signature _____
   Name _____
   Position _____

   On behalf of _____

   Address _____
   _____
   _____

   Date _____

3. Signature _____
   Name _____
   Position _____

   On behalf of _____

   Address _____
   _____
   _____

   Date _____

4. Signature _____
   Name _____
   Position _____

   On behalf of _____

   Address _____
   _____
   _____

   Date _____

THE EDI ASSOCIATION TERMS OF THE STANDARD ELECTRONIC DATA INTERCHANGE AGREEMENT

1. **Definitions**

    'Adopted Protocol':
    the accepted method for the interchange of Messages based on the UN/EDIFACT standard for the presentation and structuring of the transmission of Messages, or such other protocol as may be agreed in writing by the parties.

    'Message':
    data structured in accordance with the Adopted Protocol and transmitted electronically between the parties, including where the context admits any part of such data.

    'Data Log':
    the complete record of data interchanged representing the Messages between the parties.

    'User Manual':
    the commercial and technical procedures and rules and legal requirements which, by agreement between the parties, are applicable to the transmission of Messages using the Adopted Protocol.

2. **Scope**

    2.1 This agreement shall apply to all Messages between the parties using the Adopted Protocol and the parties agree that all such Messages shall be transmitted in accordance with the provisions of any applicable User Manual.

    2.2 Notwithstanding the existence of a User Manual the parties may agree terms to reflect additional or different requirements which they may have for the interchange of Messages, which terms shall be included in an Appendix which shall form part of this Agreement.

3. Security of Data

3.1 Each of the parties shall:

    3.1.1 take all such appropriate steps and establish and maintain all appropriate procedures so as to ensure that as far as reasonably practicable Messages are properly stored, are not accessible to unauthorised persons, are not altered, lost or destroyed and are capable of being retrieved only by properly authorised persons.

    3.1.2 ensure that any Message containing confidential information as designated by the sender of the Message is maintained by the recipient in confidence and is not disclosed to any unauthorised person or used by the recipient other than for the purposes of the business transaction to which it relates. Messages shall not be regarded as containing confidential information to the extent that such information is in the public domain, or the recipient is already in receipt of it prior to transmission by the sender or receives the information from a third party entitled to disclose it. Any authorised disclosure to another person shall be on the same terms as to confidentiality as required by the sender or as contained in this clause.

    3.1.3 upon becoming aware of any breach of security in relation to any Message, or in relation to the procedures implemented under this clause, immediately inform the other parties to this agreement and shall use all reasonable endeavours to rectify the cause of such a breach as soon as possible.

    3.2 Where permitted by law, the parties may apply special protection to Messages by encryption or by other agreed means including those set out in any applicable User Manual. Unless the parties otherwise agree, the recipient of a Message so protected shall use at least the same level of protection for any further transmission of the Message.

4. **Authenticity of Messages**

    4.1   Every Message must identify the sender and recipient(s) and must include a means of verifying the authenticity of the Message either through a technique used in the Message itself or by some other means provided for in the Adopted Protocol.

    4.2   Parties may by agreement also use higher levels of authentication to verify the Message.

5. **Integrity of Messages**

    5.1   Each party being a sender shall ensure that all Messages are complete, accurate and secure against being altered in the course of transmission by the sender and, subject to clauses 5.2 and 5.4, shall be liable to any other person for the direct consequences of any failure to perform his obligations under this clause.

    5.2   Each party accepts the integrity of all Messages and agrees to accord these the same status as would be applicable to a document or to information sent other than by electronic means, unless such Messages can be shown to have been corrupted as a result of technical failure on the part of machine, system or transmission line.

    5.3   Where there is evidence that a Message has been corrupted or if any Message is identified or capable of being identified as incorrect it shall be re-transmitted by the sender as soon as practicable with a clear indication that it is a corrected Message. Any liability of the sender which would otherwise accrue from the sender's failure to comply with the provisions of this clause 5.3 shall not accrue if clause 5.4 applies.

    5.4   Notwithstanding clauses 5.1 and 5.3, the sender will not be liable for the consequences of an incomplete or incorrect transmission if the error

Annex F
Standard Interchange Agreement

is or should in all the circumstances be reasonably obvious to the recipient. In such event the recipient must immediately notify the sender thereof.

5.5 If the recipient has reason to believe that a Message is not intended for him he should notify the sender and should delete from his system the information contained in such Message but not the record of its receipt.

6. Confirmation of Receipt of Messages

6.1 Except where receipt of a Message is automatically confirmed the sender of a Message may request the recipient to confirm receipt of that Message.

6.2 When the recipient has received such a request for confirmation of receipt or where any applicable User Manual requires a confirmation of receipt the recipient must send it without unreasonable delay.

6.3 Each party shall process or deal with received Messages in accordance with any response times specified in any applicable User Manual, or as the parties may agree or, in the absence of specification or agreement, as soon as possible.

6.4 Confirmation of receipt in accordance with this clause 6 is intended merely to denote that a Message has been received and shall be deemed not to give rise to any legal obligation, or confer any right on any person, or constitute acceptance of any offer contained in any such Message.

7. Storage of Data

7.1 Each party shall maintain a Data Log without modification.

7.2 Subject to any requirements of the national law in the country of the party maintaining a Data Log or any requirements contained in any applicable User Manual, the parties may agree a period during which the Data Log must be stored unchanged but, in the absence of such agreement, a party shall have the right to maintain its Data Log for such period as it thinks fit.

7.3 The Data Log may be maintained on computer media or by other suitable means provided that the data can be readily retrieved and presented in readable form.

7.4 Each party shall designate a person to be responsible for its obligations under this clause 7.

8. Intermediaries

8.1 If a party to this Agreement uses the services of an intermediary in order to transmit, log or process Messages, that party shall be responsible towards another party or other parties to this Agreement for any acts, failures or omissions by that intermediary in its provision of the said services as though they were his own acts, failures or omissions, and for the purposes of this Agreement the intermediary shall be deemed to be an agent of that party.

8.2 If a party instructs any other party to use the services of such intermediary for transmitting a Message, then that party shall be responsible towards the other party for such intermediary's acts and omissions.

8.3 Any party giving such instructions shall ensure that it is a contractual responsibility of the intermediary that no change in the substantive data content of the Messages to be re-transmitted is made and that such Messages are not disclosed to any unauthorised person.

9. Term and Termination

9.1 This Agreement shall take effect from the date of this Agreement. A party may terminate its participation in this Agreement at any time by giving to the other party or parties not less than four weeks notice.

9.2 Notwithstanding termination for any reason, Clauses 3, 7, 8 and 15 shall survive termination of this Agreement.

9.3 Termination of this Agreement shall not affect any action required to complete or implement Messages which are sent prior to such termination.

10. Interpretation of The User Manual

10.1 Any question relating to the interpretation of an applicable User Manual may be referred by the parties to the body responsible for the publication of that User Manual or the Council of the EDI Association as may be applicable acting as experts and not arbitrators, whose decision shall be final and binding on the parties making the reference.

11. Force Majeure

11.1 A party shall not be deemed to be in breach of this Agreement or otherwise be liable to any other party by reason of any delay in performance, or non-performance, of any of its obligations hereunder to the extent that such delay or non-performance is due to any Force Majeure of which he has notified such other party; and the time for performance of that obligation shall be extended accordingly.

11.2 For the purposes of this clause 'Force Majeure' means, in relation to any party, any circumstances beyond the reasonable control of that party (including, without limitation, any strike, lock-out or other form of industrial action).

12. Invalidity and Severability

12.1 In the event of a conflict between any provision of this Agreement and any law regulation or decree affecting this Agreement, the provision of this Agreement so affected shall be regarded as null and void or shall, where practicable, be curtailed and limited to the extent necessary to bring it within the requirements of such law regulation or decree but otherwise it shall not render null and void other provisions of this Agreement.

13. Notices

13.1 All notices or other forms of notification, request or instruction required to be given by a party to any other party under this Agreement shall be delivered by hand or sent by first-class post to the address of the addressee as set out in this Agreement or to such other address as the addressee may from time to time have notified for the purpose of this clause or sent by electronic means of message transmission producing hard copy read-out including telex and facsimile, and shall be deemed to have been received:

13.1.1 if sent by first-class post: 3 business days after posting exclusive of the day of posting;

13.1.2 if delivered by hand: on the day of delivery;

13.1.3 if sent by electronic means: at the time when any such notice enters the information system controlled by the recipient in such a way that it can be retrieved by the recipient during the recipient's business hours or, if not during the recipient's business hours, one hour after the commencement of the recipient's next working day.

14. Amendments in Writing

14.1 Any terms agreed between the parties as additions or amendments to this Agreement shall only be valid if they are set out in the Appendix referred to in clause 2.2 or are otherwise in writing and signed by the parties.

15. Disputes and Law

15.1 Unless the parties agree to submit the matter to arbitration or other procedure for the resolution of disputes, or to select a different jurisdiction, any matter or dispute arising from, out of or in connection with this Agreement, as to its validity, interpretation, construction or performance shall be subject to the sole and exclusive jurisdiction of the English Courts.

15.2 Unless the parties otherwise agree this Agreement shall be construed and have effect according to English Law.

STANDARD ELECTRONIC DATA INTERCHANGE AGREEMENT EXPLANATORY COMMENTARY

PART I

The purpose of an Interchange Agreement

Any method of communication requires discipline in order to be effective. The discipline is achieved by applying rules of conduct which by their use have become customary or by law have been imposed. Electronic Data Interchange (EDI) has not yet been in existence long enough to have acquired in these ways a collection of standard rules of conduct. An Interchange Agreement provides them.

The Standard Electronic Data Interchange Agreement (SIA) can be used in bilateral or multilateral EDI relationships. Its terms govern the conduct of the parties and set out those rules which are applicable to the general use of EDI. If they use the SIA, the parties are confirming their intention, when communicating by EDI, to be committed to each other and they cannot claim ignorance of the rules of behaviour or that they do not accept them and are not bound by them.

The distinction between an Interchange Agrement and other contract or agreements

A fundamental principle is that the SIA relates to the interchange of data, not to the various underlying commercial or contractual obligations of the parties. The SIA is not itself a substitute for any individual contracts, express or implied, between trading partners, such as those for the supply and purchase of goods or services. Such underlying contracts and contractual relationships are assumed to exist, or to be brought into existence, just as they would if the exchange of information between the parties had been by means other than electronic. The SIA should not disturb or interfere with these normal commercial and contractual relationships. In this respect, as in others, the SIA follows the precepts of UNCID, developed in 1987 by the International Chamber of Commerce.

General Rules

The SIA addresses in a conveniently uniform manner those issues which are present in all EDI relationships and some which are present in most. Its rules can, therefore, be used by any EDI pair or group. A detailed commentary on the SIA clauses is in Part II.

Special Rules, User Manuals and Appendices

In individual trade sectors there will be additional rules concerning communication between the parties; rules which are specific to the requirements of that trade and not to all others. Such rules need to be set down somewhere and to be embraced by the same commitment evidenced by the SIA.

In most EDI operations there are User Manuals ('UMs') or Message Implementation Guidelines ('MIGs'). These contain the procedures and rules for the technical aspects of transmission and may contain the commercial meanings of the messages used in that trade. A UM/MIG can be a suitable place in which to set down the legal requirements associated with the specialist, trade-specific messages.

Annex F
Standard Interchange Agreement

Not all trade sectors, however, will have developed and published formal UMs/MIGs or it may be that these are for some reason not the most suitable place for some trade-specific additions or modifications. The SIA therefore provides, as an alternative, for the additional or different trade-specific requirements to be included in an Appendix forming part of the Agreement.

Liability

If a party to an agreement fails to ensure that his obligations under it are met, it is possible that damage will be caused. The liability for that damage then falls upon the party whose breach caused it to occur. Unless this principle needs special emphasis or must be modified for some special reason, there is no need for an agreement to elaborate on the attribution of liability. The SIA makes little reference to attribution of liability; and then only for emphasis.

Agreements might also contain references to liability in order to place limits on it. In the SIA there is no general limitation of one party's potential liability to another because that would be to the detriment of the latter.

The SIA deals only with the conduct of the parties' communications, not with their obligations to act in accordance with the terms of their underlying commercial contract. A breach of the terms of the SIA is not of itself likely to be the direct cause of damage. If damage is caused it is more likely to have arisen out of the negligence of one party or from a breach of the underlying commercial contract which will have, if necessary, its own terms for attributing or limiting liability.

It is for these reasons that the SIA contains no special clauses about attribution or limitation of liability. If any liability were to occur it would lie where it falls.

Insurance

For reasons similar to those used in considering liability, one party or another does not acquire a significant additional burden of risk just because of the use of EDI. There is, therefore, no obligation on the parties to make special insurance arrangements. It is nevertheless recommended that individual users should check their existing insurance arrangements, advising their brokers or underwriters that they are intending to use EDI.

PART II

The implications of many of the Clauses are self-evident but the following is an explanation of the reasoning behind some of them, where this might be helpful.

Clause 1

The importance of the EDIFACT standards is reflected in the definition of the 'Adopted Protocol'.

Clause 2.2

The use of a UM or a MIG or an Appendix has been referred to in Part I of this commentary.

Clause 3.1.1

An important clause dealing with the security of messages.

Clause 3.1.2

'Confidentiality' is an obvious requirement in certain cases but it needs some qualification in order to avoid one party unreasonably using it to describe information which is not really confidential.

Clause 3.2

It is inappropriate for the SIA to compel encryption or any other particular methods of message protection; they must be selected by those engaged in the trades concerned. It is, however, a sound principle that the same level of protection should be required for further transmissions. It should be noted that encryption, or some methods of it, may not be permitted in some jurisdictions.

Clause 4 & 5

There could be some confusion as to the terminology frequently used; 'integrity', 'verification', 'authenticity', 'identity', 'completeness' etc.

Clause 4 requires a sender of a message to state his 'identity' (and, obviously, that of his addressee). There must be a means of checking that his statement is true ('verification') so that the other parties know that his message and his identity are genuine.

Clause 5 deals with the 'integrity' of messages; meaning that messages must be complete and have no inaccuracies and that they stay that way. With this integrity, together with the authentication resulting from Clause 4, there is no reason for parties to the SIA to regard an EDI message as inferior in reliability to other means of communication. They can, therefore, agree that they will regard an EDI message as having as good a status as is possessed by a document or other form of communication. Moreover, provided the level of authentication and the technique used are good enough, they can even be confident that the message has the same essential and characteristic attributes which are present in a written communication which has ben signed.

Clause 5 also deals with the procedural discipline necessary if there is obvious message corruption or misdirection.

Clause 6

There has been debate about whether every message should be acknowledged by the recipient. It is felt that to insist on this would result in an unnecessarily and unacceptably large and costly volume of transmissions. With some messages it is not important for the sender to know that his message has been received. With some messages the sender will be made aware of the receipt because of some subsequent action by the recipient which he would not have taken if the message had not been received. Many EDI systems in any case automatically provide an acknowledgement signal.

Nevertheless, it is important that some messages have their receipt acknowledged. The particular trade-specific rules, which may be contained in a UM, MIG or Appendix, will specify what is to be done; alternatively the sender will request the acknowledgement. The recipient must then comply.

Clause 7

This clause deals with the maintaining of a Data Log. Its text is such that it should result in the parties retaining essential records to satisfy commercial, administrative and fiscal requirements. Such records should also satisfy most evidential requirements, both as to admissibility and as to probative value.

Clause 8

It is not a purpose of the SIA to lay down the terms and conditions of network service providers' contracts with their clients. That must be dealt with by the clients negotiating with their network operators. However, the use of a network should not be an excuse for a sender to escape his responsibilities under the SIA. This clause, therefore, makes the sender's obligations clear. He is responsible for the network's acts, failures or omissions. The exception is when his use of the network is on the instructions of another party, in which case the latter party is responsible.

Clause 10

This clause refers to questions of interpretation of the contents of the User Manual. This is not to be confused with the actual settlement of disputes arising from the Agreement, which is referred to in clause 15.

Clause 12

It is possible, though not probable, that under some jurisdictions some provisions of the SIA might not be permissible. This clause enables the SIA to be widely adopted but without partial exclusions invalidating the whole agreement.

Clause 14

Additions or amendments should only be considered if they are absolutely necessary. This clause sets out the disciplined manner in which they should be made.

Clause 15

Some trades prefer Arbitration for dispute settlement. Furthermore, some parties may require that their dispute settlements are made in particular jurisdictions or that particular laws should apply. This clause provides for these alternatives to be arranged by the parties if they wish. In the event, however, of the parties making no such special arrangements, rather than having no applicable law or jurisdiction, this clause provides for English law and the English courts to be used.

3rd Edition December 1993

Annex G: Sample Operational Attachment

This annex gives an example of a document additional to the Interchange Agreement as discussed in Chapter 7, 'Legal Issues', and Chapter 11, 'Operational Management'.

Electronic Data Interchange Agreement – Operational Attachment

EDI Agreement No. EDI Operational Attachment No.

TRADING PARTNER PROFILES AND CONTACTS
The Organisation   Trading partner
Name **Address** **Contact** **Department** **Title** **Telephone** **E-mail id** **Fax** **Telex**

1. **TRANSMISSION TYPE**

    - The messages to be exchanged are:

      List the message names/versions/releases here.

    - The direction(s) of each message will be:

      From your organisation to your trading partner or the other way.

    - The maximum volumes for each message will be:

      An estimate perhaps, at first, to be revised in the light of experience.

2. INTERCHANGE STANDARDS

- The standards to be used will be ISO 9735, Application Syntax Rules for Electronic Data Interchange for Administration, Commerce and Transport (EDIFACT).

- The subset to be used will be:

    The name or responsible organisation if subsets are

    used.

- The version of each subset to be used will be:

- The only general exceptions to this will be that some segments/elements will only be used in certain circumstances. Full details are included in the following:

    Explanatory text, if needed.

- Except where specified to the contrary in this Attachment, the meanings of data elements and codes used in EDI Transmissions are defined by the United Nations Trade Data Elements Directory (UNTDED) ISO 7372.

    Explanatory text, if needed.

- ISO 9735 Character Set A will be used.

    Some trading partners use a looser interpretation of this character set to include lower case 'a' to 'z', so you may want to note this here.

3. NETWORK SERVICE

- **The Organisation**

    - The Network Services Provider will be *your network provider.*

    - The time period during which EDI Transmissions will take place, subject to network availability will be:

Annex G
Sample Operational Attachment

Specify as appropriate.

– The frequency of

- EDI Transmissions via the network will be:

Specify as appropriate.

- opening the EDI Mailbox(es), subject to network availability, will be:

Specify as appropriate.

- **The Trading Partner**

  – The Network Services Provider will be *your network provider.*

  – The time period during which EDI Transmissions will take place, subject to network availability will be:

  Specify as appropriate.

  – The frequency of

  - EDI Transmissions via the network will be:

  Specify as appropriate.

  - opening the EDI Mailbox(es), subject to network availability, will be:

  Specify as appropriate.

4. **USER-IDS**

The authorised user-ids for transmissions between the parties are:

	The Organisation	Trading partner
User-id (Test)		
User-id (Production)		

5. AUTOMATIC CONFIRMATION OF RECEIPT

- **The Organisataion**

    - The method of requesting confirmation of receipt will be:

        Specify as appropriate.

    - The method of confirmation of receipt will be:

        For example, telephone, E-mail, post

- **The Trading Partner**

    - The method of requesting confirmation of receipt will be:

        Specify as appropriate.

    - The method of confirmation of receipt will be:

        For example, telephone, E-mail, post

6. STIPULATED TIME FOR ACKNOWLEDGEMENT

If needed, specify a time.

7. BUSINESS DAY DEFINITION

Within the scope of this Agreement, the term 'Business Day' is defined as follows for The Organisation and the trading partner:

- **The Organisation**

    Potentially a key definition . . .

- **The Trading Partner**

    Potentially a key definition . . .

8. **DISASTER RECOVERY CONTINGENCY PROCEDURE**

- This will be:

    This may well be a pointer to yet further documentation.

- The timescale within which day-to-day operational recovery, to repair, or replace, any failing component (hardware or software) and/or to recover 'lost' data is:

    Appropriate text . . .

Signed for and on behalf of:

	The Organisation	The Trading partner
Authorised Signatory Name Title Date		

Annex H: HM Customs & Excise Guidance on EDI Usage

The following is the text of a document issued by HM Customs & Excise to all those intending to send or receive UN/EDIFACT INVOIC messages (including both invoices and credit notes) which are subject to VAT. It is applicable to EDI invoicing within the United Kingdom only. If you are sending more thn one INVOIC message per EDI interchange then the recommended method of VAT reconciliation is to use the **TAXCON** *(TAX CONtrol) message. This message has been defined as part of the* UK EDIFACT Trade Message Convention, *a joint initiative between the Article Numbering Association (ANA) and Simpler Trade Procedures Board (SITPRO).*

Guidelines for users exchanging accounting information issued by the Computer Audit Branch of HM Customs & Excise.

1. **Introduction**

The use of an electronic data interchange system does not, in principle, change the obligations of VAT registered bodies to fulfil the normal requirements of VAT law as enacted under the Value Added Tax Act 1994. There are, however, certain additional requirements imposed under Schedule 11, paragraph 3, of this Act upon organisations who exchange VAT invoice information between computer systems.

2. **General Requirements**

All taxable persons are required to keep and preserve certain records and accounts. A detailed explanation is given in Public Notice 700 (The VAT Guide), Section VIII, obtainable from local VAT offices. Computerised accounting systems designed to exchange accounting information by electronic means such as orders, delivery notes, invoices, credit notes, statements, correspondence and so on, must be able to meet these requirements, eg the need to preserve the data for the necessary statutory period (or such shorter period as may have been agreed with Customs and Excise) must be taken fully into consideration.

Records need not be maintained in any set way but they must be maintained in a manner which is acceptable to Customs and Excise for audit purposes (special requirements apply to invoices). Records may be retained on computer media, provided they can be readily converted into a satisfactory legible format and made available to Customs and Excise on request. Records may also be retained on micro film or microfiche, again provided copies can be easily produced and there are adequate facilities for allowing a Customs and Excise officer to view them when required.

3. Invoices

The exchange of tax invoice data is subject to special requirements and these are advised to each organisation concerned by letter before the commencement of any system.

The requirements vary slightly depending on whether invoices are being transmitted or received, and there are slightly differing requirements for exchanges on computer media and direct transmission. An explanation of the requirements is annexed.

Unless the law and all the conditions are met in full, the documents issued will not be acceptable as tax invoices for VAT purposes.

Appendix 1

The requirements regarding computer data interchange of invoice for Value Added Tax purposes.

A guidance note as supplied to trade organisations.

A. The law requires:

1. Notice of intention

Before any system for transmitting tax invoices can be accepted as operational, each organisation involved must give the Commissioners of Customs and Excise at least one month's notice in writing. This should be sent to your local VAT office. It should be borne in mind that the longer the period of notice, then the

Annex H
HM Customs & Excise Guidance on EDI Usage

greater the time that will be available to sort out any problems.

2. **Compliance with requirements**

The organisations involved must comply with the Requirements imposed by the Commissioners of Customs and Excise. Please note that these requirements may be amended or supplemented from time to time.

B. **The requirements** — a summary of the conditions imposed by the department.

1. **System trials**

The parties concerned must first trial the system and provide Customs and Excise with the opportunity of attending one or more of these trials to observe the trial and inspect the results.

2. **System changes**

Any significant change in the system, such as a change from exchange on magnetic tape to exchange via electronic transmission, or a major change in the computerised accounting system which produces the invoice information, must be advised to Customs and Excise at least one month before implementation. Again, the earlier, the better.

3. **Control information and reports**

   3.1 **The sender**

   For each invoice file created for transmission purposes, the sender must produce a control document on paper for retention in his records. This must show, among other things:

   (a) the full name and address of the recipient of the invoice file and the sender's name, address and VAT registration number;

   (b) the unique transmission reference (see paragraph 4), or other unique reference allocated to the invoice file, and the transmission date;

(c) the total numbers and types of invoices (or other documents) on the file;

(d) for each tax rate, the total tax exclusive value of supplies mentioned in the file;

(e) the total tax charged at each rate on the above; and

(f) the total value of any exempt supplies in the file.

All of the above information must also be included as control data within the transmitted invoice file and provided that the receiver can fulfil certain other requirements, a copy of the control document need not be sent to the recipient.

3.2 The Receiver

On receipt of a transmission, the file will be deformatted from the transmission message standard to the installation's own transaction file format.

The data values at (a)-(f) in paragraph 3.1 must be printed out on a control report. The values at paragraph 3.1 (c)-(f) must now be re-calculated by totalling the relevant values from the invoice file at transaction level, again the calculated totals must be printed out. Providing the two sets of values agree exactly, then the file may be processed normally as purchase invoices received. If, however, a discrepancy is identified at this stage, then the file must be rejected (either partly or wholly) and a copy of the control/discrepancy report(s) must be forwarded to the sender to take corrective action. Copies of all control and discrepancy reports must be retained as part of the business records.

If, for technical reasons, it is not possible to receive or read a transmission, then the transmission may be treated as not received and a control document need not be raised. The sender should, of course, be advised to re-transmit.

If, for any other reason, it is not possible to read and print the control information at para 3.1 (a)-(f) but the file is accepted for processing, a copy of the sender's control document must be obtained and the control totals thereon verified by totalling the requisite values at invoice transaction level.

4. Unique identification of invoice files

Each invoice file must be uniquely identified by data within the transmission. This identification is usually the generation and version number of the file related to the customer and supplier details. The sender will normally maintain a discrete generation number series for each customer, the generation number being incremented by one for each file transmitted. Installations are, of course, free to agree on some other suitably unique identification if they so choose.

5. Monitoring to ensure no duplication

The recipient of an invoice file must set up a system which will detect and report the receipt of a duplicated transmission. The monitoring of the generation number and version number series would seem to be a suitable method for most systems, but, an additional control on the value of transmission files received could also be used. This should provide:

(a) a control to ensure that all invoice files transmitted have been received; and

(b) an appropriate means of identifying a duplicate invoice file.

6. Provision of evidence

(in accordance with Section 5(4) of Civil Evidence Act 1968/ Law Reform (Miscellaneous Provisions) (Scotland) Act 1948/ The Civil Evidence Act (NI) 1971, Section 2(4)

You must provide, or arrange for the provision of a certificate in accordance with Section 5(4) of the Civil Evidence Act 1968(2) should this be requested by Customs and Excise.

7. Computer bureau services

If you are using a computer bureau or similar organisation for any part of the procedure, then you must obtain an undertaking that the company involved:

(a) is aware that the provisions of Section 10 of the Finance Act 1985 apply in respect of any computer used for transmissions of invoice data, either on magnetic tape or electronically; and

(b) will provide a certificate in accordance with Section 5(4) of the Civil Evidence Act 1968(2) if so required by the Commissioners.

8. Names and addresses on invoices

The full name and address and VAT registration number of the supplier and the full name and address of the receiver may be recorded once per invoice file, eg in the trailer record, provided all the conditions are met in full.

9. Alternatively to 8 – shortened names and addresses may be shown on each invoice record

Providing Customs and Excise have been given prior notice, the name and address records may be reduced to a shortened version of the name and full post code, or other shortened form, on condition that:

(a) the file control report shows the full names and addresses; and

(b) the same short name and postcode, or other shortened form, must not be used by two or more companies separately registered for VAT or reallocated to another user.

10. Preservation of documents and audit trail

You must retain copies of all documents related to a particular transmitted file for the statutory period required by VAT legislation unless a shorter period has been approved by your local VAT office.

The historic record of the invoice data must contain all the invoice details and may be stored on paper magnetic media or similar or in microform. It is desirable from an audit viewpoint that where possible a record of the constitution of the file at transaction level be maintained.

For instance the constitution of the transmitted file may be recorded within summary reports, eg a listing of invoice numbers, values, etc associated with the unique file reference or the invoice records are retained in such a way that the transmitted file content can be reproduced either manually or on magnetic media for audit purposes.

11. Changes in requirements

In order to meet changes in legislation, or in order to make changes found to be necessary in the light of experience, the Commissioners of Customs and Excise reserve the right to amend or change these requirements as they see fit.

EDI Implementation Guide

Annex I: Useful Contacts and Addresses

CCTA
Information Interchange Branch
Rosebery Court
St Andrews Business Park
Norwich
NR7 0HS
Tel: 01603 704704   Fax: 01603 704817

Article Number Association
11 Kingsway
London
WC2B 6AR
Tel: 0171 240 2874   Fax: 0171 240 8149

Central Unit on Procurement
HM Treasury
Allington Towers
19 Allington Street
London
SW1E 5EB
Tel: 0171 270 1628   Fax: 0171 270 1639

Electronic Commerce Association
Ramillies House
1–9 Hills Place
London
W1R 1AG
Tel: 0171 432 2500   Fax: 0171 432 2501

HM Customs & Excise
ITD Branch 37
3rd Floor NE
Queen's Dock
Queen's Wharf
Liverpool
L74 4AAB
Tel: 0151 703 8302   Fax: 0151 703 8303

ODETTE UK
SMMT
Forbes House
Halkin Street
London SW1X 7DS
Tel: 0171 235 7000

SITPRO
Venture House
29 Glasshouse Street
London
W1R 5RG
Tel: 0171 287 3525   Fax: 0171 287-5751

TEDIS
Commission of the European Communities
DGXIII-D5
Rue de la Loi 200
B-1049 Bruxelles
Belgium
Tel: +32 2 299 0285

UN/ECE
Trade Division
Palais des Nations
CH-1211 Geneva – 10
Switzerland
Tel: +41 22 917 27 45

Western European EDIFACT Board Secretariat
Commission of the European Communities
DGXIII-D5 B-24 01/06
Rue de la Loi 200
B-1049 Bruxelles
Belgium
Tel: +32 2 299 0250

Annex J: Bibliography

- J Berge, *The EDIFACT Standards*, NCC/Blackwell, 1994

- M Cannon, *EDI Guide, a Step-by-step Approach*, International Thompson Publishing, 1993

- Charles Chang and David Hitchcock, *The Vans Handbook*, Blenheim Online, 1989

- Margaret Emmelhainz, *EDI: A Total Managmeent Guide*, Van Nostrand Rhineholt, 1993

- Mike Gifkins, *EDI Technology*, Blenheim Online, 1989

- Mike Gifkins and David Hitchcock (eds), *The EDI Handbook: Trading in the 1990s*, Blenheim Online, 1988

- M Hendry, *Implementing EDI*, Artech House, 1993

- Richard Hill, *EDI and X.400 using P_{edi}*, Technology Appraisals, 1990

- Peter G W Keen, *Competing in Time*, Ballinger Publishing, 1988

- Peter Jones and David Marsh, *Essentials of EDI Law – UK Edition*, EDIA, 1993

- A Marcella and S Chan, *EDI Security, Control and Audit*, Artech House, 1993

- M Parfett, *What is EDI?*, EDIA, 1992

- M Parfett (ed.), *The EDI Implementors' Handbook*, NCC/Blackwell, 1992

- Phyllis Sokol, *EDI: The Competitive Edge*, McGraw Hill, 1994

- Anne Troye, 'Liability and Legal Issues: The European Dimension', *Proceedings of the EDI90 Conference*, CEC, 1990

- Anne Troye, 'Legal and Audit Considerations: European Issues', *Proceedings of the EDI90 Conference*, CEC, 1990

- Ian Walden (ed.), *EDI and the Law*, Blenheim Online, 1989

- Ian Walden and Ashley Braganza (eds), *EDI, Audit and Control*, NCC Blackwell, 1993

- *BPR in the Public Sector*, HMSO, 1994

- *The EDIA Information Service*, ECA, 1994

- *EDI Electronic Payments – A framework for Financial EDI*, Electronic Commerce Association in association with the Article Numbering Association, 1993

- *EDIFACT Security Information Guidelines*, UN/EDIFACT SJWG, 1993

- *The EDIFACT Service*, SITPRO, 1994

- *The Legal Implications of Trans-border Messaging in Europe*, European Electronic Messaging Association, 1994

- *Electronic Data Interchange in Government: The Business Opportunities*, CCTA, 1994

- *Payment Systems in The Group of Ten Countries*, Bank for International Settlements, 1993

- *Security Framework for Electronic Data Interchange for Administration, Commerce and Transport*, UN/EDIFACT SWJG, 1994

- *The EDI Association Casebook*, ECA, 1994

- *The EDI Yearbook 1994*, Blenheim/NCC, 1994

- CCTA Information Management Library

    – *Data Management* – ISBN 0 11 330634 2

    – *Data Management Standards* – ISBN 0 11 330670 9

Annex J
Bibliography

- CCTA IS Guides

    - *A5: A Project Manager's Guide* – ISBN 0 471 92525 X

    - *B4: Appraising Investment in Information Systems* – ISBN 0 471 92529 2

    - *C4: Security and Privacy* – ISBN 0 471 92537 3

- CCTA IT Infrastructure Library

    - *Capacity Management*, 1991 – ISBN 0 11 330544 3

    - *Change Management*, 1990 – ISBN 0 11 330525 7

    - *Computer Installation and Acceptance*, 1993 – ISBN 0 11 330556 7

    - *Help Desk*, 1990 – ISBN 0 11 330522 2

    - *Service Level Management*, 1990 – ISBN 0 11 330521 4

    - *Software Control and Distribution*, 1989 – ISBN 0 11 330537 0

    - *Testing an IT Service for Operational Use*, 1993 – ISBN 0 11 330560 5

- CCTA Management of Risk Library

    - *Management of Programme Risk* – ISBN 0 11 330672 5

- CCTA Programme and Project Management Library

    - *A Guide to Programme Management* – ISBN 0 11 330600 8

    - *An Introduction to Programme Management* – ISBN 0 11 330611 3

    - *PRINCE – An Outline* – ISBN 0 11 330599 0

    - *Using SSADM with PRINCE* – ISBN 0 11 330598 2

Annex K: Glossary of Terms and Acronyms

AECMA	Association Européen des Constructeurs de Materiel Aerospatial (European Association of Aerospace Equipment Manufacturers)
AFNOR	Association Francaise de Normalisation (French Standards Association)
ANA	Article Numbering Association
ANSI	American National Standards Institute
API	Application Programming Interface
APPC	Advanced Program-to-Program Communication
APPN	Advanced Peer-to-Peer Networking
ASC	Accredited Standards Committee
ASCII	American National Standard Code for Information Interchange
ATM	Asynchronous Transfer Mode
BACS	Banks Automated Clearing Systems
BPR	Business Process Re-engineering
BSC	Binary Synchronous Communications
CA	Certification Authority
CADDIA	Co-operation in Automation of Data and Documentation for Imports/Exports and Agriculture
CAD/CAM	Computer Aided Design/Computer Assisted Manufacturing
CALS	Continuous Acquisition and Lifecycle Support
CCCJS	Co-ordination of Computerisation in the Criminal Justice System
CCITT	Comite Consultatif International de Telephonie et de Telegraphie (International Consultative Committee for Telephony and Telegraphy)
CCS	Country Control System
CEFIC	Conseil Européen des Federations de l'Industrie Chimique (European Council of Chemical Industry Federations)
CEN	Comité Européen de Normalisation (European Committee for Standardisation)
CHAPS	Clearing House Automated Payments System
CIA	Confidentiality, Integrity and Availability
CJN	Criminal Justice Network
CJO	Criminal Justice Organisations
CJS	Criminal Justice System
CMDS	Contract Minimum Data Set
CMPB	Clinical Messages Programme Board
CPS	Crown Prosecution Service
CRAMM	CCTA's Risk Analysis and Management Methodology
CRS	Computerised Reservation System
CSDN	Circuit Switched Data Network

EDI Implementation Guide

DCF	Discounted Cash Flow
DEDIG	Deutsche EDI Gesellschaft (German EDI Association)
DES	Data Encryption Standard
DIN	Deutsches Institut fuer Normung (German Standards Institute)
DSA	Digital Signature Authentication
DSS	Digital Signature Standard
DTE	Data Terminal Equipment
DVLA	Driver and Vehicle Licensing Agency
EAN	International (originally 'European') Article Number association
EBCDIG	Extended Binary Coded Decimal Interchange Group
EC	European Commission
ECODEX	Electronic COmmercial Data EXchange
EDCD	UN/EDIFACT Composite Data Element Directory
EDCL	UN/EDIFACT Code List
EDCS	Electronic Data Capture Service
EDED	UN/EDIFACT Data Element Directory
EDI	Electronic Data Interchange
EDIA	EDI Association (now Electronic Commerce Association)
EDIFACT	Electronic Data Interchange for Administration, Commerce and Transport
EDIFICE	EDI For companies with Interests in Computing and Electronics
EDMD	UN/EDIFACT United Nations Standard Messages Directory
EDSD	UN/EDIFACT Segment Directory EEC European Economic Community
EEMA	European Electronic Messaging Association
EFTA	European Free Trade Association
EFTPOS	Electronic Funds Transfer at Point of Sale
ENS	European Nervous System
EU	European Union
FHSA	Family Health Service Authority
FHSCU	Family Health Services Computer Unit
GDN	Government Data Network
GIS	Geographic Information Systems
GOC	Generateur des Octets Chiffrants (Ciphering Bytes Generator)
GP	General Practitioner
GPFH	GP Fund Holder
GTN	Government Telecommunications Network
HDLC	High-level Data Link Control
HMC&E	HM Customs & Excise
IDA	Interchange of Data between Administrations

Annex K
Glossary of Terms and Acronyms

I-EDI	Interactive EDI
INCA	Information Net and Card for the Adapted Management of European Road Transport and Traffic
INSIS	Inter-institutional Integrated Services Information System
ISDN	Integrated Services Digital Network
ISO	International Organization for Standardization
ITU-T	International Telecommunications Union – Telecommunication
KB	Kilobits
LAN	Local Area Network
LCMG	Local Communications Management Group
LURG	Local User Representative Group
LIMNET	London Insurance Market EDI NETwork (UK)
LU	Logical Unit
MDG	Message Development Group
MHS	Message Handling Service
MIG	Message Implementation Guideline
MOD	Ministry of Defence
MTA	Message Transfer Agent
NCP	Network Control Program
NHS	National Health Service
NPSI	NCP Packet Switching Interface
NWCS	NHS-wide Clearing Service
NWN	NHS-wide Networking Management
OCR	Optical Character Recognition
ODETTE	Organisation for Data Exchange by Teletransmission in Europe
OFTP	ODETTE File Transfer Protocol
ONP	Open Network Provision
OSI	Open System Interconnection
PAD	Packet Assembler Disassembler
PC	Personal Computer
PCSDN	Public Circuit Switched Data Network
PDN	Public Data Network
PIR	Post Implementation Review
PNP	*Patients Not Paper*
PPSDN	Public Packet Switched Data Network
PRINCE	PRojects IN Controlled Environments
PSDN	Packet Switched Data Network
PTT	Public Telephone and Telegraph
PU	Physical Unit
PURSUIT	PURchasing and Supply: Unified Information Technology

RFT	Request for Transfer
RHA	Regional Health Authority
RINET	Re-insurance and Insurance NETwork
RSA	Rivest Shamir and Adleman
SDLC	Synchronous Data Link Control
SIA	Standard Interchange Agreement
SITPRO	SImpler Trade PROcedures Board
SJWG	Security Joint Working Group
SME	Small and Medium-sized Enterprises
SMTP	Simple Mail Transfer Protocol
SNA	Systems Network Architecture
SSADM	Structured Systems Analysis and Design Method
SSCP	System Services Control Point
SWIFT	Society for Worldwide International Financial Telecommunications
TCP/IP	Transmission Control Protocol/Internet Protocol
TDCC	Transportation Data Co-ordinating Committee
TP	Transaction Processing
TEDIS	Trade Electronic Data Interchange Systems
TRADACOMS	TRAde DAta COMmunications Standard
UA	User Agent
UCC	Uniform Code Council
UCS	Uniform Communications Standard
UM	User Manual
UNCID	UNiform Rules of Conduct for the Interchange of Trade Data by Teletransmission
UN/ECE	United Nations Economic Commission for Europe
UN/JEDI	United Nations Joint EDI Group
UNSM	United Nations Standard Messages
UNTDED	United Nations Trade Data Element Dictionary
UNTDI	United Nations Trade Data Interchange
VADS	Value Added Data Services
VANS	Value Added Network Services
VAT	Value Added Tax
VDA	Verband der Deutschen Automobilindustrie (Association for German Automotive Industry)
WAN	Wide-area Network
WE/EB	Western European EDIFACT Board